Studies in Economic Ethics and Philosophy

Springer
Berlin
Heidelberg
New York
Barcelona
Budapest
Hong Kong
London
Milan
Paris
Tokyo

Studies in Economic Ethics and Philosophy

P. Koslowski (Ed.)
Ethics in Economics, Business, and Economic Policy
(out of print)
192 pages. 1992

P. Koslowski · Y. Shionoya (Eds.)
The Good and the Economical
Ethical Choices in Economics and Management
212 pages. 1993

H. De Geer (Ed.)
Business Ethics in Progress?
124 pages. 1994

P. Koslowski (Ed.)
The Theory of Ethical Economy
in the Historical School
345 pages. 1995

Antonio Argandoña (Ed.)

The Ethical Dimension of Financial Institutions and Markets

With 4 Figures

Springer

Professor Dr. Antonio Argandoña
IESE International Graduate School of Management
University of Navarra
Avenida Pearson 21
08034 Barcelona, Spain

ISBN-13: 978-3-642-79725-5 e-ISBN-13: 978-3-642-79723-1
DOI: 10.1007/978-3-642-79723-1

Softcover reprint of the hardcover 1st edition 1995

SPIN 10498776 42/2202 – 5 4 3 2 1 0 – Printed on acid-free paper

Foreword

Amongst the varied phenomena making up Western Society of the latter years of our century, the growing interest, both theoretical and practical, in ethics applied to the economy and the world of business, is yet significant.

There are many reasons for this renaissance. Firstly, in the theoretical plane, as the conventional economy has been fine-tuning and carrying to extremes its starting-point assumptions, criticism based on the insufficiency of their anthropological and ethical assumptions has also been multiplying.

Secondly, studies on economy and management nowadays echo approaches which place emphasis on the initiative, freedom and dignity of economic agents, which underline the need for a change in the way things are done in business, and which stimulate review of the formulation of strategy to make room in it for an ethical dimension.

However, it is above all in the world of practice, in the daily lives of companies and in their reflection in public opinion, that the urgent need to recover the talent of ethics is most patent. In view of the victims of the leak of toxic gases in the Union Carbide factory in Bhopal (India), of the long-lasting risk of pollution as a result of the accident at the nuclear power plant in Chernobyl, or the deterioration of the environment as a result of the Exxon-Valdez accident in Alaska, society is wondering how the executives set at the head of these companies are exercising their social responsibility.

And then we return our gaze to daily life, and we are astounded by the creation and exploitation of opportunities for unfair profits by the employment of insider dealing in the financial markets, or by the corruption of civil servants by company directors to buy favours, or by the corruption of company directors by politicians to finance their parties illegally, or the destruction of viable businesses by hostile takeovers, or the captious use of advertising, or the disregard with which the health or lives of people is played with in the production of no mean number of foods, and a long etcetera.

And we conclude, rightly, that it is necessary for ethics to return to the world of economy and business. Or rather, since ethical behaviour has never ceased to be present in the markets and in companies, we ask for it to be invested with more power and to be generalized, not just for reasons of personal conscience, but also for reasons of social welfare, for us to live together in peace and prosperity, and for economic efficiency. Because the alternative - the intervention of governmental powers - strikes us as a poor remedy short-term, and counterproductive long-term.

FOREWORD

In this renaissance of ethics in the world of business, finances have been paid special attention. On the one hand, because the deregulation of the markets and financial innovation have also multiplied opportunities for profit, the morality of which is not always patent. On the other hand because, if finances are the lubricant - or rather the fuel - of economic activity, the ethical running of the institutions and financial markets seems to be a necessary - although insufficient - condition for the successful operation of the other sectors. Thirdly, because governmental powers have a very close participation in the activities of the financial markets, with the consequent risk of corruption. And, lastly, because in the mind of the man on the street and of no small number of intellectuals, there continues to niggle the prejudice - a throwback to old conceptions which are nowadays abandoned - that managing money, lending and charging interest, is always a less than upright activity, which of needs stains the hands of the one doing it. And, even though this may be a mistaken idea, it needs to be analyzed afresh, to correct injustices and to clear up confusion.

This book is a response to this interest. It sets out a selection of the texts presented at the meeting on „The Ethical Dimension of the Institutions and Financial Markets“, which was organized in Madrid by the BBV Foundation, and the management of which was entrusted to me. From an initial distribution of subject matters, a range of experts in ethics applied to the economy and finances was commissioned the task of drafting a paper setting out the main points of the debate and the criteria for the angle on it and its solution. Subsequently, two people, experts in the theoretical or practical aspects of the economy, the institutions and the financial markets, were asked to provide a commentary on each paper. And all the authors, panel-members and commentators were given a very free rein when choosing the approach, scope and details of their contributions.

The papers thus prepared were widely debated, with the other authors and with the varied audience - economists, professors of management and finances, directors and figures from the markets and the institutions, philosophers, theologists, sociologists, journalists, etc. - which filled the Auditorium of the Banco Bilbao Vizcaya at Madrid, Spain, from June 15th to 17th, 1994. Part of this material - that part which seemed most relevant for readers less interested in the peculiarities of Spanish institutions and financial markets - is now being presented in this book, duly corrected by the authors.

In it, the reader will find theoretical studies - of economy, ethics and finances - passionate defence or attack on academic and practical stances, ideas for reflection, pointers for future research and suggestions for drawing up strategies or for daily activities.

As Director of the meeting and editor of the book, my task has been very rewarding, in view of the quality and the standard of the pieces presented, the excellent disposition of the authors and the dedication and professionalism of the Management and the staff of the BBV Foundation, to whom I would like to offer my thanks. When it came to preparing the final version, I left the authors the same free rein I gave them in their first draft. Thus, the merit lies with each of them.

Barcelona, 6th December 1994.

Antonio Argandoña
Professor, IESE,
International Graduate School of Management, University of Navarra.

Contents

CONTENTS

Chapter 1

The Treatment of Ethical Problems in Financial Institutions and Markets

ANTONIO ARGANDOÑA

I. Introduction

Ethics is in vogue in the world of business, probably because there is an alarming lack of ethics in the business world - although probably no more than there is in personal, family, political or social life.

Ethics is in vogue in the world of finance, probably because the business opportunities which derive from unethical behaviour are more patent in financial institutions and markets. Here large quantities of money are handled, often with no other purpose than that of obtaining quick easy short-term profits, by taking advantage of the speculative bubble; or money from immoral businesses is laundered, or companies are purchased in order to split them up and sell their assets, with no regard for any other considerations.

Society is concerned about the lack of ethics in the business world, and, above all, in the financial arena. Perhaps it suspects that there are greater incentives to unethical conduct in this field; or that this arena serves as a mirror, an indicator, or even an inducement, that could have a contagious effect on other spheres; or perhaps it is concerned that the lack of ethics in financial businesses may have pernicious effects on economic activity as a whole, if, for example, a large financial institution ends up in a compromising situation, dragging others along with it and endangering the stability of the system; or perhaps it fears that the proliferation of immoral conduct may lead regulation to be tightened up; or because a dangerous symbiosis may be formed between financial and political immorality, ...

Whatever the reason, financial institutions and markets are at present good candidates for ethical analysis. *The object of this paper is to provide a frame for the ethical analysis of financial markets and institutions.* But ethical problems do not exist as separate entities - problems are always complex: they have economic, political, human, sociological,... and also ethical aspects. Thus, then, it is a question of examining the ethical side of financial activity, and explaining why it is important and why any analysis which omits it is necessarily incomplete.

II. Why Ethics in Business and in Financial Institutions

The need to study ethics in business does not arise as an additional extra to financial and economic analysis, but appears at a more profound level, which is manifested in three areas:

1) *People.* Ethics is the science that teaches each person to reach his goal as a person (his perfection, development, plenitude, holiness, happiness, ...). Everyone who takes part in economic activity -workers, managers, entrepreneurs, owners, customers, suppliers, etc., have the right (and the duty) to behave ethically, because they have the right (and the duty) to provide the means (ethics) to achieve their own goals.

2) *The company.* As a human organization, the company has an aim of its own, which is different from - but not in opposition to - the goals of the people who take part in it. Its organization, its working rules, its hierarchy of ends and means, its culture, etc., must be aimed, first of all, at achieving the corporate goal, which also has an ethical side to it. But, what is more, these should, at least, not prevent, and, as far as possible should facilitate and foster ethical conduct in the people in the company and its environment. The company does not exist to make people ethical, but it is not something it can overlook, since the achievement of its goal is at stake.

3) *The system.* The whole of the social, political and economic system should be governed by ethical rules, so that the different societies - in-

cluding companies - can harmoniously reach their goals, while helping people to reach theirs.

This conception of ethics implies that ethics is, in economic terminology, like the state of equilibrium of the different systems[1]. Thus, a person who normally behaves in an unethical fashion will be able to achieve some personal goals over a shorter or longer period, but will inevitably trigger a process that will set him back as regards achieving his personal goal - he will not reach long-term (stable optimum) „equilibrium". Similarly, a company which does not respect and develop ethical criteria will produce internal and external conducts and reactions which will break up its cohesion and unity and, in short, its capacity to reach its goal - even if the indications of economic success are brilliant, over what could be quite a long period of time. Lastly, a society that turns its back on ethics will set off processes that upset the equilibrium; these will probably be slow, but they will be inexorable, and will eventually destroy its capacity to reach its goal as a society - and thus will make it more difficult for smaller societies, including companies and people, to achieve their goals.

The key to this conception of ethical processes is *apprenticeship* - a dimension which is not generally present in economic models[2]. Man learns through his actions: he acquires knowledge (like economic theorems), aptitudes or skills (like using a computer) and attitudes, values and virtues (like service, loyalty, sincerity or prudence). And this apprenticeship alters his conduct[3]- and that of others, since man grows and develops in society („social apprenticeship").

---

1 Equilibrium concept of this is a situation where the economic agents has two additional implications: it should be an optimum - at least relative -equilibrium for the agent or agents, and should be a stable equilibrium (in the sense that its continuity maintains the equilibrium). On ethics as an equilibrium condition, cf. ARGANDOÑA (1989), POLO (1991).

2 In ARGANDOÑA (1994b) I developed a simple explanation of the whys and wherefores of ethics in business, and extended the idea mentioned here.

3 Some of these apprenticeships change the constraints on the conduct of economic agents - for example, discovery of a new technology moves the frontier of production possibilities - while others alter their very objectives and the way in which they are reached. STIGLER and BECKER (1977) discussed some of the facets of this human apprenticeship, but economists have yet to analyze the implications of ethical apprenticeship - of values, attitudes and virtues.

The theory behind this paper is that *people, organization and society as a whole must be ethical, if they wish to achieve their goals*: ethics is not „the icing on the cake", an additional extra for altruistic people and businesses, but part and parcel of the behaviour processes of human beings and their organizations.

Each person, organization and society must practise ethics according to their nature and their situation in life. We should all be sincere, loyal and prudent, because that is what our condition as social creatures demands. But each one of us should practise these virtues according to our social roles[4]: as a father or mother, a citizen, an employee, a member of a sports club, a trade union or a shooting club, etc. This does not mean that ethics is different in every circumstance - *ethics is unique*, because every person is unique. But ethics has to be practised in accordance with the circumstances: no less loyalty is required of a bank teller than of a Member of Parliament, but these loyalties will be manifested in different ways.

III. The Ethical Dimension in Economic Activity

There are always three dimensions to every corporate or market problem:

1) An *economic* dimension, which refers to the allocation of scant resources, and takes shape in prices, costs, interest rates, profits, sales volumes, etc. It is what economics and financial science study.
2) A *socio-political* dimension, which is to do with the relationships between people: conflict, cooperation, authority, command, etc. This is the field of sociology, social psychology and political science.
3) *Ethics*, when referring to the achievement of people's goals (and the corporate goal, insofar as this is oriented towards them). This belongs logically enough, to the field of ethics.

These three facets are to be found in each and every decision, although, in some cases, one of them may be more dominant, while the other, or others, virtually disappear. If, for example, one is analysing whether it is better to request a mortgage at a fixed interest rate or at a variable rate, the economic

4 Cf. SOLOMON (1992).

consideration will clearly predominate[5] (without the other two disappearing completely). But if one is studying the possibility of launching a take-over bid for a rival bank, none of the three dimensions should be overlooked - if they are, the analysis will be incomplete.

If the different dimensions are present in every act, *ethics cannot be an imposition from outside*, from some ideological, philosophical or religious system, but must arise from the very nature of the action - in other words, of the person and his social dimension. Indeed, whether he likes it or not, every time a person performs an action, he will be moving closer to or further from his goal, which thus gives this decision a moral dimension. Similarly, every norm, rule or custom can be an obstacle to or a springboard for people's development (people within the organization or those related with it), which also gives these norms, rules and customs an ethical meaning.

Ethics, then, is not something to be considered *at the end* of the decision-making process, but, within it, at the same time, *as part of the process*. If, for instance, the management of an institution encourages employees to place a financial asset which is overpriced or of dubious solvency, they may obtain profits in the short term, but they are starting a process which has unforeseeable consequences. In the first place, they are obliging their staff to degrade themselves morally, since they will probably have to lie in order to place this asset[6]. But, what is more, they are sending them a dangerous message: „in this institution, in order to make money it is acceptable to lie to the customer and betray the confidence he has deposited in us“. The employees may understand this as: „if profitability makes it advisable, they will

---

5 In the example of the mortgage, the decision will include an estimate of future interest rates, which will be compared with the fixed rate proposed. This estimate is an exercise in the virtue of prudence - in a word, an act with moral content, although it may only seem to refer to financial and economic criteria. It is important to underline that there are not two acts, one economic and the other ethical, but only one, which is at once economic and ethical.

6 The argument that business ethics has different rules from personal ethics, and that a business can - and should - do what one would never do in one's personal or family life does not hold water. This is an attack on a person's moral unity and his dignity, in the name of the superiority of unjustifiable business interests, and it forgets that a person acts according to what he is: thus, employees' conduct in the future will be affected by the actions imposed on them today.

also lie to me, or wrong me in some other way"- and they will also lose confidence in the institution. Or „if it suits me, I can also lie to the company, or take advantage of it in some other way" - and loyalty is betrayed. Or they may interpret it in some other way, given the wide variety of possible reactions.

Ethics does not change the economic content of decisions: a business with a high economic return does not stop obtaining this (if the calculations were correct) because its product is immoral. *Ethics makes us aware of other dimensions*: the direct effects on other people and, principally, on the agent himself; the apprenticeships that will be generated, the deterioration (difficult to envisage in the short term) in the way the agent and his environment work („acting comes after being", as the classics said), etc. The moralist cannot tell the drug-trafficker that he is going to lose money on an operation, because it is not true (if he did his calculations right); but he can tell him that, even though he may make large profits, he is going to hurt other people and himself, he will be a worse person and will also hurt his family, those who are close to him, and society. And it is obvious that this non-economic dimension is very important - and is also important if profits are to continue to be obtained in the future.

IV. The Social Function of Financial Institutions and Markets

What I said above is as valid for a manufacturer of household appliances or a magazine distributor as for a bank or a factoring company, since the ethics of financial institutions and markets is no different from the ethics of business or of the markets in general. But it has one or two peculiarities deriving from what is specific to these institutions and markets: *their social function*, the singular service they lend society[7]. We should all be loyal and prudent, but the loyalty of a fund manager or the prudence of the manager of

7 The manuals on the financial system generally include these functions in greater or lesser detail. For example, cf. CUERVO, PAREJO and RODRÍGUEZ (1987), PÉREZ and QUESADA (1991), TRUJILLO, CUERVO-ARANGO and VARGAS (1988). TIROLE (1993) also mentions these functions in the context of financial regulation.

a savings bank has certain peculiarities deriving from the specific nature of their business.

Financial institutions and markets perform the function of *intermediation*, facilitating the flow of savings towards investment. The savers (or divestors) want to place their surplus in financial assets which combine certain conditions regarding maturity, liquidity, the return, currency, risk (interest rate, exchange rate, inflation, default of payment, etc.), fiscal treatment, etc. At the other side of the market, the investors (or non-savers) are looking for resources with certain conditions regarding cost, maturity, etc.[8]. And as it very difficult and expensive for every saver and investor to seek and find an opposite number that corresponds to their desires, there is a place for this task of intermediation.

Financial intermediaries are institutions which, generally speaking, issue liabilities (secondaries) which they place with savers (or divestors), according to their preferences and needs, and buy assets (primaries) issued by investors (or non-savers), also according to their needs or preferences. The list of financial institutions is long and varied, and includes the central bank, banks, savings banks and credit cooperatives, stockbroker agencies and companies, funds (mutual, pensions, etc.), insurance companies, finance institutions, financial leasing firms, mortgage firms, etc.

The financial markets are approached by investors, who require funds (loans) and offer financial liabilities, and by savers, who want to place their funds (they offer credit and demand financial assets). The relationship between the two may be direct or through one of the intermediaries mentioned above.

The *financial system* is like a big market where the flow between the supply of funds (saving) and demand for funds (investment) occurs, and where some transactions are carried out with the assistance of intermediaries (or even simply between them). Within this big market there is a wide variety of specific markets, where certain assets or liabilities (which are greater or lesser substitutes for the other assets) are exchanged, either directly between final suppliers and demanders, or between the latter and intermediaries. This accounts for the appearance of the money and capital markets, the short and long-term markets, the primary and secondary markets, the fixed income and equities markets, the national or foreign currency markets, the deriva-

8 In this paper the word „investment" is used in the macroeconomic sense (demand for capital goods, machinery, installations, homes, etc.: physical capital,) not in the financial sense (placing savings.)

tives markets, etc. The social function of financial institutions and markets includes:

1) *Offering savers (or divestors) a wide range of financial assets with different characteristics* as regards maturity, liquidity, return, currency, risk (interest rate, exchange rate, inflation, default of payment, etc.), fiscal treatment, etc., *where they can place their wealth.*
2) *Placing resources at the disposal of investors (or non-savers) with different conditions* as regards cost, maturity, currency, guarantees, risk (interest rate, exchange rate,...), fiscal treatment, etc., *to finance their operations.*
3) Carrying out this intermediation *efficiently*, i.e. with minimum use of resources (which generally means a small spread between interest rates on assets and on liabilities.)[9]

These main functions can be presented in other ways, which are related to the above and with each other:

a) *Changing maturities*, so that, for instance, those demanding funds may receive long-term funds, while suppliers place them in the short term.
b) *Supplying the liquidity necessary for converting one type of financial asset into* another, at low cost. This is a function of great systemic importance: the financial institutions are a mechanism for supplying liquidity when there are economic hiccups[10].
c) *Low transaction costs when changing the composition of portfolios (assets and liabilities)*, taking advantage of economies of scale and specialization.

---

9 Sometimes a distinction is made between distributive or allocational efficiency (in the transfer of funds from saving to investment,) economic or operational efficiency (which will be shown in the maximization of the volume of funds which can be lent at the minimum cost) and functional efficiency (the financial system's reponse to the requirements of the economy and its agents). Cf. FUERTES and MARTÍNEZ (1992).

10 But they cannot guarantee this function globally, unless there is an agent (which is generally the central bank) that takes the cost of supplying liquidity outside the system (e.g. to the citizens, through the tax system, inflation included.)

d) *Spreading the savers' risk*, by allowing them to have a portfolio of assets with different conditions as regards maturities, risk, fiscal treatment, etc. This is possible because the intermediaries, in turn, have diversified portfolios, or have the means with which to control the risk on their assets, or have an external insurance mechanism (the central bank as lender in the last instance, an institution which insures deposits, etc.).
e) *Spreading the risk of investors in general*, and of each of them in particular. This is possible thanks to the study, monitoring and control of investment projects and of the borrower's history, thanks to the intermediary's shareholders' equity, the control and regulation requirements, etc.
f) *Encouraging saving*, insofar as a high yield, low risk and low transaction costs can be offered. This is not a natural function of the financial system, but rather an effect of it functioning efficiently.
g) *Encouraging investment*, by means of a moderate capital cost and by adapting the availability of funds to the needs of each investor. Neither is this a natural function of the financial system; it depends on variables outside its control, such as the existence of profitable projects, the evolution of aggregated demand, expectations, psychological and political factors, etc.
h) Some intermediaries offer *collection and payment mechanisms* (clearing houses, collection services and debt settlement, etc.) with low transaction costs.
i) The knowledge acquired and the specialization developed also put them in a position to carry out *advisory and financial management functions*, for and on behalf of their customers[11].

Note that these functions are no more than what the literature on social responsibility presents as the social function of the company[12] transferred to the world of finance: *producing and distributing goods and services to satisfy needs, efficiently* (i.e. with high added value, which is the difference between revenues and expenses) *and with a vocation for self-continuity* (which we

11 Financial institutions and markets are also the means of transmitting monetary policy, although this is not, strictly speaking, a component of their social function. The derivative markets perform some specific functions, although these are related to the above functions: separating the different types of risk, deciding the prices of the different components and redistributing the risks between the intermediaries which are in the best conditions to cope with them.

12 Cf. GALLO (1987).

have taken for granted here). Moreover, like all companies, financial institutions *should allow and encourage its members to achieve their goals*, at the same time as it is realizing its own goal. This is a function common to all human organizations - and also to the organizations supplying economic goods and services. Indeed, when the economic manuals explain the birth of the company they present, for example, a group of hunters who join forces to make the most of the division of work and specialisation, not only through exchange (market), but also through recourse to common management[13]. Thus, it is obvious that the company is, above all, *a means by which its members may best satisfy their needs and achieve their development as people, through their contribution to the corporate goal* - the efficient production and distribution of goods and services.

V. Profit

And what about profit? Did we not say that *the object of the company is to maximize profit*, and even that this is its (only) social function?[14]. In order to resolve this question, we should consider three possible functions of profit (and several other meanings of its eventual maximization): as a measure of efficiency, as a corporate goal or objective and as motivation for its managers or owners.

1) Profit is the residual income (the difference between the income from the company's economic activity and the expenses incurred by it), which is attributed to the owner as the ultimate holder of the rights and obligations deriving from the contracts for acquiring production factors and for selling products[15]. *Profit*, then, *is the measure of corporate efficiency.* The owner's (or manager's) efforts to obtain maximum efficiency in the production process will be seen in the minimization of costs and the maximization of income, i.e. in the maximization of added value -and, in competitive conditions on the factors market, where prices are already

13 On the function of the company, see COASE (1937); also see ARGANDOÑA (1992a).

14 The traditional reference is FRIEDMAN (1970).

15 Cf. ARGANDOÑA (1990b), TERMES (1989).

fixed for the company, this maximum added value will become maximum profit.

However, two things should be pointed out with regard to this affirmation. First, there is a set of conditions which are necessary for *the maximization of profit to guarantee economic efficiency*; these are expressed as the absence of market failures, the lack of competition on the goods and factors markets, the existence of external effects (contamination, congestion, etc.), public goods, etc.

The second point is related to the question about *what efficiency is*[16]. We have defined it as a quotient (or a subtraction) between results and expenses. But what do we include in the numerator and in the denominator? The answer depends on what we want to measure, because *the concept of efficiency is not unambiguous*, not even in economics. Do I only take short-term revenues and expenses into account, or do I include long-term? Then, should I include the effects of the decisions that I am taking as regards the company as a whole, its staff's capacity to continue to act as one in the future, the training processes which take place in the company? And what about the effects corporate actions have on its environment? Should Y, in a word, consider the socio-political and ethical consequences of actions?

As we economists measure it, efficiency is limited; it only refers to certain results and certain costs - those which are reflected in economic terms[17]. The fact that it is a limited authorize criterion does not us to abandon it. But we cannot make it an absolute either.

2) If the brief reference we made above to the origin of the company has any meaning, *we cannot say that the goal of the company is profit*, but rather, as we explained, it is to satisfy the needs and contribute to the development of the people who form part of the company, through the efficient production and distribution of useful goods and services.

This statement may sound like celestial music to those of us who have been educated in the positivist economic tradition. And yet it is not incompatible with this. According to this scientific view, a theory should not be valued because of its assumptions, but because of the explanatory

16 Cf. ILLANES (1992).

17 The efficiency we are referring to originates from PARETO's optimum, which is founded on ethical, and not strictly economic, grounds. Cf. HAMLIN (1986).

force of its conclusions[18]. There is no point, then, in discussing whether the aim of a company is this or that: what is worthwhile is to have a theory which provides us with useful explanations and predictions. And this theory is said to be based on the assumption that companies maximize profits - or rather that they act as *if* they were maximizing profits. It does not exclude, then, other formulations of the corporate goal, but, for practical purposes, it means that the company acts as *if* it were maximizing profits, since useful theories can be arrived at using this assumption alone. It does not state - it cannot state - that this is the company's aim because, according to the positivist paradigm, considering the goal is outside the sphere of economic science.

However, do we not often say that the company *should* maximize profits to achieve economic efficiency? We do, but then we are getting out of the positive and into the normative sphere. The most an economist can say is that, *if* one wishes to maximize economic efficiency, *if* this is defined according to exclusively economic variables, *if* the conditions are right for the economic optimum (that is to say, perfect competition, absence of external effects and public goods, etc.) and *if* there are no effects deriving from other dimensions of economic activity (socio-political and ethical), then, in order to act efficiently companies *should* maximize profits, defined according to purely economic variables. But, all the same, this cannot be defined *as the corporate goal*.

3) Lastly, is maximizing profit *the motivation for the owners or managers* of the company? The answer would logically seem to be that it is: what the owners of the shares in a company should want is the maximization of the value of their property, i.e. of the present value of expected future profits. However, this statement also has to be qualified. Human motives are many, rich and complex, and all of them are generally present in every action[19]. The shareholder, who we assume is motivated by maximum profit, also has preferences as regards risks, prestige, power, influence, convenience, etc.[20] - and the fact that we do not pay at-

18 Cf. FRIEDMAN (1953).

19 For human motives and how they apply to business, cf. PÉREZ LÓPEZ (1991, 1993).

20 That is why maximization of profits is sometimes replaced by maximization of the utility deriving from wealth; but this means including considerations on aversion to risk, the value of leisure, etc., and implies recognizing the multi-dimensional nature of motives. Cf. DOBSON (1993).

tention to these other motives in economics does not mean that they are unimportant[21].

As far as the manager who is not a shareholder is concerned, the modern agency theory[22] emphasizes the fact that there is no reason why his motives should coincide with the owner's. And although there are reasons to believe that it is advisable for him to maximize profits, there are many other reasons to believe that he will have other motives, which are not always compatible with this maximization.

To summarize what has been said in this section, *profit is a measure of the company's economic efficiency* - a partial and incomplete measure, but important all the same. *It is not the goal of the company*, although it is part of it, because it includes efficiency in production. And *it should be an important motive - although not the only one - for the owner*, and a less important one for the manager.

But all of this does not mean that the principles of economic efficiency and, by extension, profits, should be abandoned in corporate decisions. Quite the contrary: what distinguishes the company from other human societies is, above all, its vocation for efficiency. But this cannot be a definitive criterion.

VI. Ethical Contents of the Social Function of the Financial System

After arguing that ethics is necessary in a company, does the fact that we are referring specifically to financial institutions and markets make any substantial difference? No substantial difference, but there are a few important nuances, since the way of being ethical in the world of finance adapts to the peculiarities of its social function. The men and women who manage or work in banks, stockbroker companies or leasing institutions should practise

21 The theory that the company owner does not maximize profits, but is only concerned that they reach a „sufficient" or „satisfactory" level (SIMON 1976) may be consistent with this plurimotivational idea - although the approach is unsatisfactory.

22 Cf. JENSEN and MECKLING (1976).

the same virtues and be guided by the same values as other managers and employees, but in accordance with the specific features of their businesses. That is why there are some ethical features specific to the financial system, like the ones mentioned in the list below, which does not pretend to be exhaustive:

* *Professional competence*. This is the first duty arising from the requirement of economic efficiency, since the goal of a financial institution is hardly likely to be achieved unless the means are provided to reach the efficiency which characterizes it, and neither will the people in the institution achieve personal perfection if they do not look after the professional side of their lives. It is worth pointing out that professional training does not only include knowledge and aptitudes or skills, but also moral attitudes, values and virtues which need to be developed[23].
* *Service to the customer*, including the preeminence of the customer's interests over those of the institution, loyalty, etc.[24]. But not service as an economic value - which it is - but as a moral principle. A purely economic strategy based on service to the customer uses him as means to an economic end; thus, if profits so dictate, the service will be abandoned. However, service as a value does not subordinate itself to profits. This has important long-term consequences: the type of culture generated in the company, ethical apprenticeships (and personal development), the constraints implicit in the conduct of managers and employees, the credibility of the institution, etc., will be different in each case. Ethics is „something else".
* *Confidence*. The intermediation function of financial institutions implies a set of moral values which revolve around confidence, and which include the confidentiality of information about customers, veracity, the fulfilment of commitments (including those which are merely implicit in business relations), transparency, etc.
* *Justice*, giving each customer what he deserves, and treating different customers equally.

---

23 Professional competence has numerous economic repercussions, which are also ethical repercussions: foreseeing and anticipating changes in the environment which may affect the financial business; introducing opportune innovations; fomenting the growth and competitiveness of the institution; keeping costs down, etc.

24 Service is based on a moral value which is superior to the mercantile sphere: recognition of and respect for people's dignity.

* *Moral responsibility*. The financial phenomenon veils real activities. Thus, customers' responsibility projects itself onto the responsibility of financial institutions. That is why a bank should provide reasonable means so as not to intermediate in money-laundering operations, or grant loans for immoral or illicit operations.
* *Prudence*, perhaps to a greater extent than in other economic activities, because financial institutions have to offer opportunities of placing funds with the appropriate risk, which the customer cannot always value adequately for himself. That is why they must always guarantee their solvency, liquidity (because they supply liquidity to third parties), etc.[25]. Prudence is a virtue essential to a financial manager and should form part of his stock-in-trade[26].
* *Legality*. Abiding by laws and regulations is also an ethical duty, which has to be observed for moral reasons, and not only because of the coercive nature of the law[27], especially in the financial arena, where regulation plays an important role as a stabilizer. But being ethical is more than simply observing the law: thus, the moral duty of looking after the solvency of the institution is not only restricted to respecting the legislation on shareholders' equity, concentration of risk, etc.[28].

---

25 „Taking a gamble," taking risky decisions to get out of difficult situations, is a common example of imprudent conduct, although it is attractive to shareholders and managers, since, with luck, it can get them out of a spot, or may force the authorities to relax capital adequacy requirements, precisely when these are most necessary (cf. TIROLE 1993).

26 Cf. PIEPER (1969).

27 This point is important. If a financial institution obeys the law for fear of punishment and because of its consequences on the income statement, then it is not dismissing the possibility of disobeying it on some occasion if it could obtain some advantage in this way. But if the law is respected because of an ethical commitment, this alternative will disappear -and, if it decides not to obey the law on some occasion, then this will be because it is applying some superior moral principle. In any case, moral apprenticeships, the corporate culture developed and personal growth will be very different in each case.

28 Legality and morality do not coincide: not all that is legal is moral, nor is what is moral reduced to what is legal; cf. ARGANDOÑA (1994a). This also shows that ethics does not concern the Government or the central bank, nor is it achieved through regulations (although these may be necessary in an immoral society).

* *Excellence*. Ethics is not a science of minimums but of optimums, as it is concerned with the achievement of the goals of men and organizations[29]. As regards staff training and developing the corporate culture, minimum ethics - observing the law, not committing fraud - is insufficient, because ethics aims at personal perfection.

These are not all the ethical contents of the financial business. All the virtues - strength, magnanimity, patience, constancy, sobriety, veracity, honesty, ... - must be exercised. Because, in the end, a person is a whole and there can be no separate compartments where ethics has no place.

When it comes to analyzing and judging financial decisions from the ethical point of view, two stances can be taken. One is to examine each action or decision separately. It is interesting as an intellectual exercise, but exhausting and unviable in practice. The other is the one suggested above: fomenting the practice of virtues amongst the men and women who work in the sector, because *if the agents are ethical, their actions will also be ethical.* Instead of imposing restrictions on unethical conduct, it is preferable to encourage ethical motivations. That is why there is a need for the institutions to clearly define the „rules of the game" - and the main responsibility for this falls on management's shoulders.

VII. Some Specific Questions

As we pointed out at the beginning, the financial system is often criticized for a supposed lack of ethics in its behaviour. We will now identify some of the possible unethical types of behaviour or attitudes, which may be behind these criticisms[30].

29 Once again this can be considered on the economic plane (for profits), on the socio-political plane or on the ethical plane. But these three planes must not be confused; they may or may not be simultaneously present in any programme to foment excellence, but they will lead to different long-term results. „What for" is very important in ethics.

30 Cf. SALINS and VILLEROY (1994) for a more detailed look at some points.

* *The uselessness of financial operations*

Are financial operations really useful? Do they finance economic activity or do they simply finance themselves? Have they grown too much? Have they eventually created a fictitious world, detached from productive activities?

There is no answer to these questions, which have a clear ethical meaning, unless one can explain what the ideal financial system is, or what framework can be used as a reference for judging it, since simply comparing it with the past or with other financial systems is not sufficient. But, as we mentioned, the system has a social function, so that the criticism should be levelled at concrete aspects or specific episodes.

It is true that *many financial transactions take place between intermediaries*, and do not refer directly to the placement of saving or financing investment. But these two tasks do not constitute the whole of their social function, but are complemented by others, such as converting maturities, spreading risk, providing liquidity or operating payment mechanisms, which to a large extent justify intra-system transactions. Moreover, it is not easy to explain how those who are concerned with the return on their operations allow themselves to get involved in mechanisms which, on average, cause expenses, but not profits. This does not mean that unnecessary operations are never carried out, but probably no more than in the world of commerce and in the production of other goods and services.

It is also true that *non-financial institutions are carrying out more and more financial transactions* - placing surpluses, risk coverage, etc. But this does not mean that they are unproductive activities.

A variation of the problem mentioned above is the supposedly *unproductive nature of certain financial placements*. For example, it is claimed that putting funds into shares helps to finance production, but does not do so if they are put into Treasury Bills or bank deposits. This criticism may be justified in the case of public debt, but not, generally speaking, in the case of financial intermediaries: there is no reason why the proliferation of financial opportunities should work to the detriment of real investment[31]. If this falls,

31 Financial assets are always the liabilities of someone who had previously created these liabilities in exchange for other assets, etc. At the end of the chain, the net value of financial instruments is equal to net financial saving (saving less investment), as the financial statements for the economy show (cf. Bank of Spain, 1993).

the causes are not to be found in the higher return on financial assets, but in the phenomena behind this: the public deficit, an anti-inflationary monetary policy, the exchange rate policy, etc.

* *Excessive indebtedness*

In the eighties there was *a large increase in the level of indebtedness of households, companies and public administrations.* Can the financial system be blamed for this? Does it generate excessive demand for loans, which could be harmful for the economy as a whole?

Leaving public sector performance to one side, the debt levels of companies and households do not appear to have been exceptional, according to historical criteria. Moreover, the reasons for this higher indebtedness seem to be independent of the functioning of the financial system (e.g. the sharp growth of consumption in Spain in the second half of the eighties seems to be the cause, rather than the effect, of the increase in consumer credit).

It is also likely that certain changes which took placed in the financial system (deregulation, extending loans at variable interest rates, securitization, possibilities of risk cover, etc.) affected the nature of financial restrictions for the private sector, and accentuated elasticities and reactions. If this is so, the financial institutions must bear this in mind when it comes to controlling risks and providing services. It is also probable that the higher debt level was due to changes in fiscal incentives.

When *valuing indebtedness from the ethical point of view*, traditional criteria have to be taken into account: the exercise of the responsibilities of lender and borrower[32], and the purpose and efficiency of the loan[33].

32 On occasion, the risks are made to fall on third parties; e.g. through deposit insurance, or the legislation on bankruptcy and suspension of payments.

33 Classical theory assumed that it is acceptable to become indebted in order to invest, because the necessary income is generated to return the debt, while, in the case of consumption, debt must be handled with particular prudence. Cf. BUCHANAN (1987).

* *The instability of the financial system*

Is the financial system unstable? Does its instability have a negative effect on the real economy? These questions are not easy to answer either. The majority of modern theories do not tend to attribute instability to monetary causes[34], although there are those who do[35], or those who suggest that financial instability is a mechanism that propagates and extends the cycle[36].

In principle, the functioning of the financial system seems stable, especially when control and regulation mechanisms[37] operate - these are not foreign to the system itself, in the same way that the economic system contains a legal and institutional framework which is necessary for it to function[38].

However, from time to time, we witness *disorders that shake the stability of the system*. Some originate from the real economy - such as, for example, the increase in bad debts in periods of recession, or the decrease in the value of financial assets when the stock market falls - and they seem to indicate that the financial system is unable to correct the disorders on its own, which should not surprise us. But there may be some responsibility - perhaps systemic - for these disorders when banks do not pay sufficient attention to the quality of their assets during an economic boom, or if they take a gamble when difficulties arise.

Other disorders appear to have a *purely financial origin*, such as the bursting of speculative bubbles, stock market crashes, or speculative attacks on currencies. In any case, it is still not clear why these phenomena occur, nor whether their causes are purely financial, nor whether they have important effects on the real economy or not: the stock market crash of 1929 did, but this was, above all, the result of the mistakes in the economic policy that accompanied it; however, the 1987 crash hardly affected the productive economy, probably because the emergency measures worked[39]. And the speculative attacks affecting some European currencies in the summer of 1992 can be explained by the correction of erroneous expectations.

---

34 See a recent development in BLANCHARD and FISHER (1989).

35 Cf. MINSKY (1982, 1986).

36 Cf., for example, KINDLEBERGER (1978).

37 Such as capital adequacy ratios, the central bank's role as lender in the last instance, the deposit insurance, etc. See TOPOROWSKI for the theory that the diminishing of these mechanisms caused the crash in October 1987.

38 Cf. ARGANDOÑA (1991).

39 See ARGANDOÑA (1988, 1990a) on the causes and effects of the 1987 crash.

From the ethical point of view, all of this leads us to the conclusion - at least a provisional conclusion - that the system can fulfil its social function, and fulfil it quite well, even in emergencies, thanks perhaps to the existence of correction mechanisms. In any case, it is more of a technical problem than a moral problem, unless the system encourages unethical conduct and this causes the problems (which we will be dealing with now) or if it neglects the norms of prudence and foresight when the economy is booming.

* *The system encourages unethical conduct*

Public opinion often claims that *the financial system makes it possible to „get rich quick"*. And it is true: the return on buying shares at 100 and selling them at 105 a month later is gross 71% a year, much more than can be obtained on ordinary businesses, and with much less effort. But this is only partly true: this type of operation is not ordinary; the return that can be obtained on managing a portfolio is considerably lower (and corresponds to a social function). Moreover, it has to be compared with the risk assumed.

However, *the popular image of „getting rich quick"* can effectively be an inducement to conduct of debatable morality. The person who withdraws his resources from a mutual fund, where he was obtaining a normal yield, to move directly onto a booming stock market (as happened before the 1987 crash) does so with the explicit desire to make a lot in a short time and with little effort (although he is running a high risk, but perhaps this was not made explicit). And the same can be said of some of those who started certain financial businesses during the economic boom of the eighties, without a genuine vocation for service[40].

But, *is it immoral to want to take advantage of an opportunity*, such as a sudden rise on the stock market or expectations of currency devaluation, to make large gains in a short time? In itself, it is not. But the morality of an action includes two main elements: the action itself and the intention[41]. *It is the intention that might make the desire to make money fast subjectively immoral.*

Obviously, the financial system (alone) is not to blame. But it may help to encourage this type of conduct by *creating unethical cultural models* - the „making a quick killing" culture -, by confusing goals, etc. What is more, *it*

40 ARGANDOÑA (1994c).

41 Cf. ARGANDOÑA (1994b).

may serve as an incentive to behaviour which is directly illegal and/or immoral, such as manipulating prices, seeking privileged information[42], fraud, corruption, etc., or taking on excessive risks[43].

* *The market behaves impersonally*

On many markets for goods and services, the customer is a person is with a face, but on the commodities and financial assets markets the personal relationship is missing. Often an intangible asset is bought from or sold to an unknown customer, who is no more than an entry in a computer. And this, it is claimed, can also serve as encouragement for unethical conduct. *Responsibility is not made explicit* - „those are the market rules“-, there are no victims - there are, but they cannot be identified -loyalty to the customer is betrayed.

That is true, but it can happen on other markets too: the person who buys a pair of shoes may be a person of flesh and blood to the salesman, or he may simply be a customer who is only of interest because of his money. Dealing with somebody personally may help to develop ethical attitudes, but it is not necessary if everyone -from the bank's general manager to the trader on the bond market - always behave according to moral rules.

* *The social function of ownership and „short-termism“*

The owners of a company are those who exercise what has been called *the „social function“ of ownership* - which is no more than monitoring and checking that the company is managed in accordance with their goals and with the common good of the society in which it operates[44]. Some financial intermediaries (pension funds, mutual funds, insurance companies, banks,

---

42 Cf. ARGANDOÑA (1992b).

43 The argument that excessive risk is reflected in the corresponding premium and included in the interest rate is not valid, if the information is not perfect. Moreover, imprudently taking on a high risk can be immoral; perhaps the lender has already made up for it with the risk premium (at least on average), but other people will be hurt by the default of payment or the bankruptcy of the business risked.

44 In ARGANDOÑA (1994d) I have developed this concept, its economic grounds and its ethical implications.

etc.) play an important role as *institutional investors* who are the owners of large blocks of company shares. However, it is difficult for them to develop this responsibility, because they do not usually own majority stakes and these stakes change over time, since it is expensive to exercise careful control of each of the companies in which they have stakes, and it is usually more profitable to dispose of the shares of a company in difficulties than to try to influence management.

In any case, *institutional investors do not feel that they are co-proprietors of a company*, but of an „index" or balanced set of assets, from which they only expect to obtain a yield in the short-term (since they themselves are valued in the short term, at least in comparative terms) together with risk coverage (which is usually carried out through operations on the derivatives markets: futures, options, etc.)

The fact that *institutional investors see themselves as being judged in the short term*, in accordance with the quarterly rankings, suggests that they will also demand a *short-term return (short-termism)*[45] from the companies in which they have stakes, and this may not be the most suitable conduct for the company, if this means that decisions on growth, long-term investors, expenditure on research and development, etc., are neglected, or that high levels of risk are taken on (through high weight of debt against shareholders' equity). The ethical consequences of all of this are important, because they suggest that control (and the exercise of the social function of ownership) is effectively neglected[46]. In any case, even if financial institutions act according to these short-term criteria, this probably does not affect the management of the companies in which they have stakes.

VIII. Conclusion

We started this paper by stressing that the interest in ethics in the world of finance seemed to be related to the proliferation of unethical conduct,

45 There are other reasons for short-termism, such as fiscal incentives or the assymetry of information between small owners and managers. Cf. MILES (1993) for empirical evidence.

46 Cf. BALL (1990), CADBURY (1992), Institutional Shareholders' Committee (1991), PRENTICE and HOLLAND (1992).

which had alarmed society because of its possible role as a de-stabilizer and a propagator of moral disorder. This does occur, but probably no more than in other spheres of economic life, or in other fields.

In any case, extreme judgements should be avoided. If everything were rotten, financial activity would have already disappeared, devoured by the law of the jungle. However, we cannot say that the financial system in Spain, or in the countries in our environment, is a model of ethical conduct. It would also be a mistake to expect moral problems to be resolved through regulation: the remedy would be worse than the disease, as financial immorality would eventually fuel political immorality.

Neither can we expect to find a list of precepts which, once duly learnt, would guarantee the correct moral functioning of the financial markets[47]. There are no clear ethical guidelines, not because there are no sound principles - there are - but because human actions are complex, and always require prudential judgements which consider all their dimensions (economic, socio-political and ethical) and lead to decisions which will necessarily be uncertain.

However, the person who behaves in this way, even if he makes a mistake, will be acting correctly in moral terms, will be a better person, and will be capable of creating the appropriate climate in the financial institutions and markets for making decisions which are economically efficient, socially constructive and morally positive. The key lies precisely in educating people, helping them to behave ethically and creating motivations, rules of behaviour and valuation criteria which help and encourage them to always act efficiently and morally, while, of course, looking after profit, which is the basis of efficiency, but without endangering the unity and coherence of the company, its future growth and the development of the people in it. And this is possible, although it is not easy.

It is not certain whether ethics is profitable for an institution in the short term: its benefits are of a different ilk. But, in the long term, if the system behaves according to moral rules, everyone will reap the advantages of this. Like in the „prisoner's dilemma“, there is an optimum social equilibrium,

47 Some of these may be useful at least to draw attention to the moral content of some decisions. For example: do not do anything you would be ashamed of if your children found out; do not do anything that you cannot totally justify to your superiors or the customer; never trade stocks on behalf of the institution without first having looked after the customer; never generate fictitious transactions, etc.

superior to private equilibrium, which improves everyone's condition. But our economic system lacks instruments to make this always operational: the „sponger", the „free-wheeler" who acts against other people's interests, comes out winning. But only in the short term. In the long term, everybody stands to gain if everybody is ethical. For this reason, ethics is the equilibrium condition for the social optimum.

References

ARGANDOÑA, A. (1988): *Crisis y reforma del mercado de valores en España*, Barcelona: Bolsa de Barcelona.

ARGANDOÑA, A. (1989): „Relaciones entre economía y ética", *Documento de investigación IESE*, no. 166, April.

ARGANDOÑA, A. (1990a): „Sobre las causas de la crisis bursátil de octubre de 1987", *Información Comercial Española*, 679, March.

ARGANDOÑA, A. (1990b): „Sentido y funciones del beneficio empresarial", in: ACCIÓN SOCIAL EMPRESARIAL: *Etica empresarial*, Madrid: ASE.

ARGANDOÑA, A. (1991): „La economía de mercado a la luz de la Doctrina Social Católica", in: *Doctrina Social de la Iglesia y realidad socio-económica en el centenario de la Rerum Novarum. XII Simposio Internacional de Teología de la Universidad de Navarra*, Pamplona: EUNSA.

ARGANDOÑA, A. (1992a): „La estructura interna de la empresa en la visión de Coase", presented on the course „La empresa, entre el taylorismo y el humanismo ético", El Escorial summer courses, Universidad Complutense, 6-10 July.

ARGANDOÑA, A. (1992b): „Los problemas éticos de la información privilegiada", presented at the *II Coloquio Interdisciplinar de Etica Económica y Empresarial*, IESE, October.

ARGANDOÑA, A. (1994a): „Business, law and regulation: Ethical issues", in B. HARVEY (Ed.): *Business Ethics: A European Perspective*, New York: Prentice Hall.

ARGANDOÑA, A. (1994b): *La ética en la empresa*, Madrid: Instituto de Estudios Económicos.

ARGANDOÑA, A. (1994c): „Ibercorp: an economic and political scandal", *mimeo*.

ARGANDOÑA, A. (1994d): „La economía y la función social de la propiedad", presented at the *II Conferencia Española de Ética*, Economía y Direccion, Madrid, May.

BALL, Sir J. (1990): „Financial institutions and their role as shareholders", in: NATIONAL ASSOCIATION OF PENSION FUNDS: *Creative Tension?*, London.

BANCO DE ESPAÑA (1993): *Cuentas financieras de la economía española (1983-1992)*, Madrid: Banco de España.

BLANCHARD, O. J. and S. FISCHER (1989): *Lectures on Macroeconomics*, Cambridge: MIT Press.

BUCHANAN, J. M. (1987): „Public debt", in J. EATWELL, M. MILGATE and P. NEWMAN (Eds.): *The New Palgrave Dictionary of Economics*, London: Macmillan, vol. 3.

CADBURY, Sir A. (dir.) (1992): *Report of the Committee on the Financial Aspects of Corporate Governance*, London.

COASE, R. H. (1937): „The nature of the firm", *Economica*, IV, November.

CUERVO, A., J. A. PAREJO and L. RODRÍGUEZ (1987): *Manual del Sistema Financiero: Instituciones, mercados y medios en España*, Barcelona: Ariel.

DOBSON, J. (1993): „Ethics in financial contracting", *Business & Professional Ethics Journal*, 11, 3/4.

FRIEDMAN, M. (1953): „The methodology of positive economics", in: *Essays in Positive Economics*, Chicago: University of Chicago Press.

FRIEDMAN, M. (1970): „The social responsibility of business is to increase its profits", *The New York Time Magazine*, 13 September.

FUERTES, A. M. and A. MARTINEZ ESTEVE (1992): „Eficiencia y sistema financiero español", in J. L. GARCÍA DELGADO (Ed.): *Economía Española, Cultura y Sociedad.* Homenaje a Juan Velarde Fuertes, Madrid: Eudema, volume II.

GALLO, M. A. (1987): „Responsabilidades sociales de la empresa", IESE, DGN 313.

HAMLIN, A. P. (1986): *Ethics, Economics and the State*, Brighton: Wheatsheaf Books.

ILLANES, J. L. (1992): „El mercado: Ética y eficiencia", presented at the *II Coloquio Interdisciplinar de Ética, Económica y Empresarial*, IESE, October.

INSTITUTIONAL SHAREHOLDERS' COMMITTEE (1991): *The Responsibilities of Institutional Shareholders in the United Kingdom*, London: ISC.

KINDLEBERGER, C. P. (1978): *Manias, Panics and Crashes*, New York: Basic Books.

MILES, D. (1993): „Testing for short-termism in the UK Stock Market", *Economic Journal*, 103, November.

MINSKY, H. P. (1982): *Can It Happen Again? Essays on Instability and Finance*, New York: M. E. Sharpe.

MINSKY, H. P. (1986): *Stabilising an Unstable Economy*, New Haven: Yale University Press.

PÉREZ, F. and J. QUESADA (1991): *Dinero y sistema bancario. Teoría y análisis del caso español*, Madrid: Espasa-Calpe.

PÉREZ LÓPEZ, J. A. (1991): *Teoría de la acción humana en las organizaciones. La acción personal*, Madrid: Rialp.

PÉREZ LÓPEZ, J. A. (1993): *Fundamentos de la dirección de empresas*, Madrid: Rialp.

PIEPER, J. (1969): *Prudencia y templanza*, Madrid: Rialp.

POLO, L (1991): *Quién es el hombre. Un espíritu en el mundo*, Madrid: Rialp.

PRENTICE, D. D. and P. R. J. HOLLAND (Eds.) (1992): *Contemporary Issues in Corporate Governance*, Oxford: Clarendon Press.

SALINS, A. DE and F. VILLEROY DE GALHAU (1994): *Le developpement modern des activités financières au regard des exigences étiques du christianisme*, Vatican City: Libreria Editrice Vaticana.

SIMON, H. (1976): *Administrative Behaviour*, New York: The Free Press, 3rd ed.

SOLOMON, R. C. (1992): „Corporate roles, personal virtues: An Aristotelean approach to business ethics", *Business Ethics Quarterly*, 2.

STIGLER, G. J. and G. BECKER (1977): „De gustibus no est disputandum", *American Economic Review*, 67, March.

TERMES, R. (1989): „Elogio del beneficio", Lecture at the Cámara de Comercio, Industria y Navegación in La Coruña, January.

TIROLE, J. (1993): „On banking intermediation", *Cuadernos de Trabajo, Fundación BBV*, Madrid.

TOPOROWSKI, J. (1993): *The Economics of Financial Markets and the 1987 Crash*, Aldershot: Edward Elgar.

TRUJILLO, J. A. C. CUERVO-ARANGO and F. VARGAS (1988): *El sistema financiero español*, Barcelona: Ariel, 3rd. ed.

Chapter 2

Ethics and Regulation in Financial Institutions and Markets*

FEDERICO BASÁÑEZ and LUÍS CORTÉS

This paper proposes to show the opportuneness and importance of ethical considerations and of efficiency, and to conclude that there is a need for some regulation in the financial sector (particularly as regards the evaluation and management of risk and information.)

The approach we will be following tries to understand the relationship between ethics and regulation, an understanding that is, in principle, easier

* The authors would like to thank J. L. MALO DE MOLINA (Bank of Spain) and the others attending the Seminar on „The Ethical Dimension of Financial Institutions and Markets" (Madrid, 15-17 June 1994), for their very helpful comments, the chairman of the seminar, *Antonio Argandoña* (IESE-Barcelona) for his observations, and the Fundación BBV (Bilbao) and the Instituto de Filosofía de la Economía (Seville University) for their support.

to share than that of the Ricardo or Friedman's more controversial proposals of *narrow banking* or Hayek or Fama's proposal of *free-banking*. However relevant these may be as a theoretical exercise, to blame nearly every ethical problem on the existence of regulation, deposit guarantees or state monopolies on legal currency issues undoubtedly means adopting unrealistic courses of action.

The paper is organized as follows: section 1 contains the introduction and a description of the state of the question; section 2 aims to characterize ethics in relation to the financial system, and mentions some of the ethical implications of economic decisions and the time horizon in financial systems; section 3 does the same from the point of view of regulation, and considers its theoretical justification and the relations between financial intermediaries and regulating agents; section 4 explains the relationship between the ethical approach and the regulative approach; section 5 analyses some forms of regulation in the financial markets and their ethical implications; section 6 deals with the relationship between regulation and risks, and our conclusions are summarized in section 7.

I. Introduction

1. Presentation of the Subject

Even in the most liberal economies, the stability and efficient functioning of the financial system tends to be regarded as a good which is in the public interest, largely owing to the strategic role of intermediation played by financial institutions in the economic system. For this reason, legislators have always paid special attention to it, whatever their interventionist or liberal preferences.

In recent times, the world of finance has witnessed some notable banking and stock market scandals, and the publicity given to these has created an increasingly sensitive climate as regards the regulation of financial markets and institutions, and the need to promote „ethical conduct“ in economic life (and financial life in particular.)

The truth is that regulation and cases of corruption have always existed side by side, ever since financial intermediation first saw the light of day. While corruption can be said to have been constant, the regulation of the financial markets has not followed a steady course. It is not an easy matter, as is illustrated by the contradictory legal axioms „the best regulation is that which does not exist“ and „a bad regulation is better than no regulation at all“. One author (Becker 1994) even claims that the more regulation and intervention, the greater the corruption.

In fact, regulation increased in the past for reasons connected with the inadequate institutional structure of the market and as a result of the appearance of market failures. However, excessive regulation led to „regulatory fatigue“ and to the intolerable inflation and dispersion of norms.

The pressure to deregulate grew stronger when the economic costs of certain regulations, the loss of efficiency deriving from inadequate regulations, or the danger of the excessive interference of political authorities in areas which belong to free initiative and the action of private individuals were particularly notable. Deregulation, which enabled institutions to participate on the markets, had very noticeable effects, especially as far as banking was concerned (Cooper and Fraser 1986).

Moves to deregulate have generally been accompanied by greater insistence on alternative prudential means of prevention and control (supervision, self-regulation), and on encouraging a more ethical disposition at financial intermediaries (through norms of behaviour and codes of conduct). The initial enthusiasm for deregulation recently appears to have waned and is being replaced by complementary ideas on re-regulation (especially as regards technical details).

In this sense, it is important to stress from the beginning that deregulation does not mean or necessarily imply less regulation, but rather „a different sort of regulation“ (i.e. efficient agile regulation which foments free enterprise and operations as far as security permits, and avoids unnecessary constraints).

2. The State of the „Ethics-Regulation“ Question

Today's world of finance is undoubtedly difficult for the regulator. Not so much because of its supposed likeness to a casino, as because financial regulation has become an important instrument in competition between nations, which compete with each other in regulation or deregulation in order to maintain their international positions.

The difficulties mainly reside in how to harmonize the objectives of freedom and security. Although the principle of freedom is the basic criterion behind financial behaviour, it can never be equivalent to anarchy or to relinquishing responsibilities. For this reason, security and risk control are also important, insofar as stability and transparency are the essential conditions for the functioning and growth of these markets.

The stability of the financial system depends specifically on maintaining the externalities related to any individual's confidence that his liquidity needs (withdrawing deposits from a bank or selling assets on the stock market) will be satisfied at the appropriate time and at a suitable cost. This right to dispose of or withdraw funds makes financial institutions essentially unstable enterprises, which means that guaranteeing the conditions associated with stability is the primary objective of the different regulations of the sector (Zunzunegui 1992). In the case of the financial system, it also seems to be particularly valid to uphold that security is, to a large extent, the best guarantee of freedom („confidence is good, but control is better" is an opinion shared by many regulators).

It is sometimes said that what is really important and decisive is for these principles to be firmly implemented, and for an „ethical financial culture" to be created, which would mean that technical regulations and their details could take second place[1]. General ethical principles are certainly fundamental, but they are also open to a wide variety of interpretations, especially if we consider how much individual perceptions of „what is just" and what is allowed" differ. And if any market is to function well, then we need to have some idea of what to expect of other people's behaviour (because, if not, amongst other things, transaction costs would become infinite). As Sánchez Asiaín (1992, p. 134) states, it is impossible to deny the strict „need to create a new culture of money, a new ethical concept of finance and bank engineering". But this intrinsically implies the implementation of a regulation which is not only fair, but also efficient and operational, and which combines general ethical principles with regulations and more technical specifications.

An excellent regulation on paper, however, only produces optimum results if it is applied by people who are professionally competent and ethically prudent, who understand the technical specifications and share the spirit of the regulation.

1 In 1990 when the *Securities and Investment Board* (SIB) adopted ten general principles for behaviour and reference, the majority of which were clearly ethical (called „Ten Commandments",) the evolution of the British regulatory system was misinterpreted by some people in this way.

Consequently, the importance of regulators' professional competence and of a better ethical education and a greater financial culture, both on the part of the public and the intermediaries, cannot be sufficiently emphasized. As financial markets develop rapidly, the risks of inefficiency or corruption deriving from obsolete regulations, „traditional" practices or mechanisms which generate „perverse incentives" increase operating costs and public distrust. „Getting the regulation right" is not, then, a question of regulators' good intentions, but of thorough professional know-how.

3. The Evolution of Regulation

Following an inveterate interventionist tradition, the financial sector has always been particularly subject to extensive regulation in Spain, even at the times of greatest „liberalisation". The historical inadequacy of our financial system in terms of market laws was precisely due to excessive political protection against foreign competition (regarded as „excessive competition"), aided and abetted by regulations that were economically and ethically unsuitable.

Since 1977 the general approach to reform in the Spanish financial system has been moving more towards the market economy. The profound changes and upheavals in the national financial arena and in the rules of its game were due to „internal" reasons, like changes in institutional and private behaviour, as a result of the public's greater economic and financial „literacy": and to „external" reasons such as the change in the reference framework, as our financial system joined the most highly liberalized European and international markets (Steinherr 1990).

Generally speaking, we could say that the Spanish financial sector is in the process of innovation, deregulation and disintermediation, and has move from a rigid interventionist framework (on the domestic front) to a framework of free functioning and increasing integration (in a competitive international environment).

In the leading international financial centres, common regulation formulae are becoming more and more highly valued; these are particularly necessary insofar as new instruments and products have brought new risks, have increased the opacity of balance sheets and income statements, and have made it more difficult for national authorities to supervise institutions involved in intermediation. The emphasis is, in fact, placed on achieving minimalist regulatory harmonization (minimum standards for capital adequacy ratios, limitations to shares owned in the non-financial sector, deposit guarantee, etc.) and on the creation of a common legal framework which facilitates international supervision (Muller 1984).

The greatest importance is perhaps given to the adoption of common general principles which can serve as a reference for every regulatory authority when it is drawing up its own rules. In the case of the bank market, these principles often come from the Agreements adopted by the Committee on Banking Regulations and Supervisory Practices (Basle Committee). In the European Union specifically, the process of harmonizing regulation has been carried out through the recommendations of the Bank Advisory Committee and the Directives of the European Commission; as these rules have no direct effect, national legislators have to adapt their own rules and regulations. Stock market harmonization has similar characteristics[2].

II. Ethics in the Financial System

Ethics contributes to the financial system by instilling confidence, thus reducing uncertainty and transaction costs. If economic agents follow ethical principles, their behaviour is more predictable (if someone is known to be ethical, then one can foresee that they will fulfil contracts, keep their word, will not seek to cheat, will be loyal and will not deceive, etc.). But, obviously, a person is ethical if he wants to be, and if he has no desire to be ethical, then he is not. Indeed, the incentives to dishonesty are particularly strong in financial businesses and in trading securities.

That is why an operational institutional framework needs to be promoted, to facilitate ethical and socially beneficial behaviour, whatever the subject's intentions may be. This operational institutional framework is identified as being (albeit partially) generic to the legal framework and covers the set of principles, traditions, customs and other formalized patterns which aspire to regulate the conduct of the agents operating on the market. This framework or „public economic order“ is complementary to, and occasionally a substitute for, an ethical disposition (which is illustrated by the fact

2 Harmonization does not mean uniformity. Now, the absence of strict fiscal or accounting uniformity should not lead to discrimination between the different market players.

that the classical principle of „*caveat emptor*," for example, is today complemented by that of „*neminem laedere*")[3]. On other occasions, the ethical disposition cannot be replaced by any regulation at all, since as Galbraith points out (1989, p. 3). „The lesson is clear. Neither regulations nor memory are perfect protection against the will to deceive oneself or others."

A series of conceptual clarifications about the nature of ethics and the financial system will help to focus the matter and will allow us to see to what extent some problems which we call economic are really ethical problems (although they are economic in the sense that they have to be resolved by professionals from the economics' world).

1. The Ethical Nature of Economic Decisions

It seems opportune to start by pointing out that there are no matters which are specifically ethical (or economic): something is not ethical (or economic) because it has or does not have certain properties, but rather something is ethical (or economic) if it is considered from a certain angle. In other words, ethical or economic considerations are a „viewpoint" from which a matter, an action or a situation are regarded, inasmuch as they depend on a free decision.

According to widely-held opinion, the object of ethics is to procure respect for fundamental human values in any decision that is taken, and in whatever may depend on this decision, in order to make it easier to reach human good. The object of the economy is to procure efficiency in the decisions on how to allocate scant resources between alternative ends, in a context of voluntary exchange.

In principle, an ethical decision would be a decision which respects the reality of people and things and is, consequently, the right decision (although it could be economically disastrous in the short term from a limited point of view).

There are two aspects to the ethical component of decisions:

3 Cf. Federal Trade Commission v. Standard Education Society (mentioned in L. Loss, *op.cit.*): „The best element of business has long since decided that honesty should govern competitive enterprises, and that the rule of caveat emptor should not be relied upon to reward fraud and deception".

a) One which is subjective and internal, inasmuch as these decisions affect the decision-maker (as a person and as a decision-maker). In this sense, there are decisions which bring moral perfection and make it possible to aspire to even better subsequent decisions: others, on the contrary, degrade the person and gradually make him incapable of taking ethical realistic decisions.
b) A second aspect which is objective or external, inasmuch as ethical decisions help man to achieve his social goal, cohesion through institutions. From this perspective, ethics has nothing to do with questions of conscience, and is only connected with the intentions, motives and attitudes of the subject inasmuch as these are manifested to others.

At the time of making the decision, not only does one have to bear in mind „the nature of the affair" and act accordingly (i.e. in the case of an economic action, look for technical efficiency in the allocation process), but also the „nature of the subject", his own perfection (which is moral). Thus, an overall consideration of the action is called for, a consideration of the action as a unit, because, in practice, an action cannot be considered as being separate from its agent (Koslowski 1988).

On the one hand, taking the internal side of ethics, the personal and social object of ethics is reached when *final* considerations are attended to, i.e. when the horizon within which the decision is made is extended to include the goal or good of man. Extending the horizon of the decision is not only a reference to time (which is also important), but, above all, to anthropological considerations (what man is, and what is due to him for being what he is) (Basáñez 1992, Possenti 1991).

On the other hand, considered from its external side, ethics is, in the words of Argandoña (1991, 1987), „the key to the analysis of institutions and social norms", and its specific function can be regarded as being to indicate „the conditions for the long-term stability and permanence of the institutions". This is doubly true of financial institutions, as stability is their particular condition for functioning.

In both cases, the instrumental function of resolving conflicts of action which require making a justified decision would correspond to ethics. The unquestionable fact that ultimate decisions have to be personal does not mean they cannot be shared or regarded as reasonable by other people. Indeed, the fundamental ethical requirement is that the decisions taken may be regarded as reasonable by any rational agent, taking concurrent circumstances into account. What is ethically correct or morally good, then, is identified with what is reasonable (from the formal point of view, ethics would be an ideal agreement or consensus on what is reasonable).

Thus, the „rediscovery" of ethics in economic life requires the prior rediscovery of practical reason and prudential decisions. This is the essence of practical reason, and in the words of Thomas Aquinas (*Summa Theologiae* I-II, q. 18 a 5 ad 1): „Only reasonable action is good; it only has to be on the borders of reasons to be bad". The only ultimate justification from the ethical point of view is: I did what was reasonable.

In turn, the foundation of any social justification or valuation is the conviction that one can reason why there are behaviours which are incompatible with a good life (one's own and other people's). Precisely because one can reason why there are behaviours which should be avoided, ethics is an objective science (it goes beyond the values of each subject, it is more than a feeling, more than a „I think that is good" or „that is bad")[4].

Referring ethics to action is immediate, as it refers directly to a subject's decisions and not to real situations or „structures" (although it is true that there are unfair situations and „structures", these can ideally be explained in terms of erroneous subjective decisions). In short, what ethics aspires to is to improve the decision-making process and the decisions themselves (Brown 1992), judging the reasonableness of these decisions and referring to the responsibility of those who make decisions (whether this be individually or corporately, and inside or outside a positively sanctioned legal framework).

All decisions (including economic decisions) effectively involve ethical responsibility, inasmuch as they involve a choice between what is good and what is bad, or between what is good and what is better. Or, to put it another way, opting for one alternative or another on the basis of preference. The economy itself studies how to organize certain alternatives (those which arise from the allocation of scant resources) over time, and this organization is carried out on the basis of valuations. Ultimately, ethical valuation is essential, because it is the valuation which takes human good into account, and considers it as the ultimate good or goal. As Polo (1991, p. 103) points

4 Over and above one's own moral ideals, one has to thus refer to a common ethical area which serves as mediation and ensures social cohabitation and market order (inasmuch as the market is an institution for social exchange) within real moral discrepancy. Consequently, the conflict between ethics and „many ethics" can only be resolved through common ethics which takes on a legal shape, and is obligatory inasmuch as it effectively contributes to social cohesion and the common good.

out: „Without the possibility of identifying the human goal, a practical science like economics would be perplexed by the alternatives on which it depends“.

Ethics has the last word in the practical application of any science, because if someone does not consider something preferable in itself or essentially valuable, they would never make a decision. Seen in this light, the whole functional régime of a society ultimately depends on the ethical nature of decisions, since the presence of alternatives is a characteristic of the social framework, and these cannot be structured coherently without ethics (i.e. without reference to human good, to what is preferable in itself) (Polo 1991).

If ethics is the science which studies practical human good in general, that is to say, how to live a good life inasmuch as this depends on one personally, then economics is an ethical discipline. Economics is part of ethics insofar as it studies the object of ethics from the specific point of view of the contribution made by economic goods (those obtained through the mediation of others) to the achievement of this good life (Garay 1994). Viewed from this angle, the demands for financial ethics are born of the need for the order of the financial markets to facilitate a good life for men, by functioning efficiently, and effectively meeting their own goals.

This leads to the ethical question of whether, and to what extent, one can separate the discourse on efficiency from the discourse on the means by which this efficiency is achieved.

2. The Time Horizon in the Financial System

The difference between a decandent society and a society which is progressing resides to a large extent in the time horizon within which decisions are taken. This horizon is represented by the preference for the short or the long term and by the degree of responsibility towards future generations. This preference is faithfully reflected in the functioning of the financial system.

The importance of the financial markets resides in their function of harmonizing and adjusting the different temporal preferences within society. This adjustment is effected by managing deposits and allocating capital to business projects, through products which are attractive because of the value added by intermediation. The specific characteristic of the (formal and informal) financial markets resides in this peculiar strategic nature of capital and that is why the financial markets have to be treated differently from other types of market.

The question of the time horizon is not just a case of preferring to seek financing through banking or the stock market. However, this has something to do with it, inasmuch as the stock market is acquiring increasing weight, in comparison with banking, in financing the economic system (which presumably reflects that temporal preferences incline towards the short term) (Mayer 1988, Boot, Thakor and Udell, 1987). As far as the process of allocating capital is concerned, all in all, it seems preferable to consider that the different markets carry out both alternative and complementary functions, and that these are not only related to temporal preferences, but also to the higher or lower quality of information and to the existence of more or less clearly defined corporate decision-making criteria (Allen 1994, 1990).

Thus, the financial system is closely linked to the model of society. If a capitalist society is theoretically founded on capitalization and the social function of capital, then the application of ethics to financial businesses is an imperative need, inasmuch as it lays the emphasis on opting for behaviour which can be sustained in the long term. It is not, then, simply a fashionable accessory, an aesthetic whim, but it is an element which is technically necessary for the markets to function well.

The dilemma or hypotethical trade-off between efficiency and ethics only exists in the short term, because what is ethical (respecting the reality of things and people) is what is efficient in the long term. However, unless ethics can be regarded as something that produces short-term returns, the economic agents will have no external reason to be ethical. And - here is the paradox - ethics cannot guarantee these results in the short term, because the effectiveness and fundamentality of ethics can only be seen in the long term[5].

The problem of the time dimension in financial activity is thus rooted in the ethical disposition of economic and political agents, and of citizens in general. To be more specific, it is related to the capacity of people and institutions to lend services, to inspire confidence and to make themselves worthy of credit (moral credit as much as financial credit). Economic interdependence is thus another variation of ethical interdependence.

---

5 Neither can ethics be considered in a purely instrumental sense (i.e. only with a view to a higher financial return), because it then loses its real meaning (ARGANDOÑA 1991).

From the strictly economic point of view, it is advisable to cooperate in the long term, but it may be - and usually is - convenient, to cheat in the short term. It is a problem of the breadth of the economic agents' time horizons. If these agents want to be genuinely economic, they have to look to the long term, as economics is not a science which deals with static atemporal balances, but with dynamic processes aimed at generating wealth, where the time dimension is a decisive factor. Only the pure speculator lives in the short term; he does not generate real wealth, but lives of zero sum games, and obtains his gains from other people's losses. On the contrary, the disposition to consider the long term is what defines business.

However, it should be pointed out that ethics alone is not sufficient: there has to be some authority to take coercive action against behaviour which goes against the system and which overlooks ethical considerations (that is to say, in a wide long-range context). In practice, if the State did not guarantee the rights and duties of the economic agents, or defend the „rules of the game“, the market would be dominated by the „law of the jungle“, and would become corrupt and disappear.

Thus, it is a question of establishing the „rules of the game“ which encourage - by means of incentives and restrictions - allocations of resources which are both efficient (incentive constrained efficient allocations) and ethical (although this does not normally imply that these allocations be „philanthropic“ or „disinterested“). In other words, the „rules of the game“ should foster cooperation and a long-term view. This is really what Adam Smith meant with his metaphor of the „invisible hand“: there is no room for gains without service, and one's own interest or private benefit should be made to consist of the effective - albeit unintentional - achievement of the common good. That is the difficulty. But equally it is the reason for rules and regulations in general (Brennan and Buchanan 1987).

As far as financial markets and institutions are concerned, this condition is largely fulfilled if both their stability and their opening up to competition are guaranteed. That is to say, if the necessary tension between security and freedom is succesfully maintained.

III. Regulation in the Financial System

As we said earlier, the general theory on economic regulation says that the market will simply become corrupt and disappear if it is not protected. To aim at a state of perfect competition in an intervention-free market is an illusion, as is reflected in all the economic literature on the regulation of competition. In fact, market functioning is always conditioned by State intervention.

These interventions take place at two different levels:

a) through the creation of a legitimate, fair, efficient institutional and legal framework (rules of the game);
b) intervention in the process of market exchange (administrative regulation).

The first of these can be regarded as legitimate intervention or regulation, and is part of the State's specific duties as regards economic affairs. The second is inappropriate interventionism, and has often led to appreciable distortions in the optimum allocation of resources and to economic inefficiencies, besides changing the very bases of competition.

Following Freixas (1990), we will now analyze the theoretical justification for financial regulation, and then go on to talk about the relations between regulators and those who are regulated.

1. Theoretical Justification for Regulation

In Spulber's view (1989, p. 37), regulation means „a set of general rules or specific actions imposed by the authority or by an administrative agency, which directly interfer with the mechanism of allocating resources on the market, or indirectly affect consumer and corporate decisions on supply and demand". For Mitnick (1980, pp. 1-5), regulation is „interfering in a process to direct it towards different results from those that would be obtained without intervention".

The object of any regulation of the financial system is to enhance its efficiency and efficacy, in order for it to achieve its goal in the best way possible (i.e. providing a country's economy with good cheap money, and obtaining profits by doing so). To do this, it must necessarily (although this is not sufficient) foment its stability, so that maximum security is compatible with maximum freedom, while also encouraging the different institutions involved to participate as far as possible in any decision-making that may affect them.

The problem with the regulation of the financial markets is a problem of second best: a choice has to be made between the deficiencies of the unregulated market and the alternative deficiencies of the regulated market. Thus, a cost-benefit analysis of the efficiency (or equity) of the results of regulation in will have to be compared with a cost-benefit analysis of the unregulated market, and the functional properties of alternative regulations will need to be considered. If alternative rules are studied, as we said, it is because different rules produce different results. Thus, here, according to McKenzie and Tullock (1975), it is a case of examining the „choice among constraints" and not so much the „choice within constraints", which is what makes for an orthodox economy.

The increase in regulation is generally linked to the presence of problems arising from irregularities in the „normal" state of competition. As Watrin (1989) points out, given a legal order for protecting property and contractual security, we know that certain „market failures" are almost inevitable (especially if market functioning is measured in terms of ideal criteria of equity or efficiency). But we also know that - measured with the same yardstick - „State failures" also occur.

The reasons for regulation may derive precisely from motives of efficiency („market failures", which explain the very existence of intermediaries) or from motives of equity (unfair positions of dependence, unequal starting or transaction conditions, lack of transparency or ethics).

For practical purposes, we can identify several situations which make market regulation advisable and which are totally applicable to the financial markets:

a) situations of market power or uncompetitive market structures (lack of competition, unjustified oligarchical or monopolistic structures, the existence of strong entrance barriers, collusive action);

b) situations where there are externalities: these occur when the action of one market agent has a positive or negative effect on other agents, outside the price mechanism, without there being any economic transaction between them and without the market mechanisms being sufficient to prevent them (lack of liquidity, systemic risk, „knock-on" or „contagious" effects).

The equitable or ethical reasons for regulation are founded on the fact that ethics is a condition for the stability of any system based on freedom, and especially the economic-financial system. The equitable reasons for regulation are related to the existence of situations where internalities appear (when a transaction generates costs or profits which were not included in the agreement).

Internalities appear when information is deficient, either because of inadequate publicity or because the information is asymmetrical or incomplete, and, as a result of this, an uninformed agent finds himself at a disadvantage in comparison with well-informed agents, or is unable to adequately evaluate the information he has at his disposal (this nearly always occurs in contracts between financial institutions and their customers): they appear in situations where an agent can influence a variable which determines another's gains, without the latter noticing this, such as in cases of „adverse selection" (for example, greater incentives for less solvent people to contract loans) (Hellwig 1987) or „moral risk" (for example, incentives for a bank to risk more if deposits are guaranteed) (Berster and Hellwig 1987): when transaction costs are very high (when there is distrust as to whether the contracting parties will fulfil what they have agreed to, or whether their credentials respond to reality, by generating procedures which make the market less agile), etc. A clear example of this is that of credit restrictions, or the credit crunch, profitable companies are subjected to in an environment of imperfect information.

Excessive inequalities in starting or transaction conditions, or situations of unfair dependence, show that some „market failures", supposedly attributable to lack of efficiency are really institutional failures attributable to lack of equity (for example, deficient assignations of property rights). In spite of the attempts to make the market an impersonal arena, where each is a „third party" for the others, some agents really have more power to manipulate the market than is supposed, and often act out of favouritism, favouring or granting privileges to some to the detriment of others (the typical case of insider-trading).

The solution to this favouritism should largely be in the direction of making the market more impersonal, which is particularly necessary in the case of the stock markets (for example, by encouraging unnegotiable contracts).

2. Relations Between Financial Intermediaries and Regulating Agents

It is worth commenting, albeit briefly, on the institutions involved in our analysis: financial intermediaries and regulating offices or agencies.

The basic methodological model for an economic agent is that of a coherent, rational „egoistical" opter, who is not benevolent, altruistic or cooperative in the short term. The key assumption is that individuals or companies, as economic agents, have different interests or, at least, consider their own interests as being different from the interests of others. In certain circumstances, this difference leads to a conflict of interests. This is clear if we simply consider how the time dimension influences exchange.

In the short term, the interests of two typical economic agents, the buyer and the seller, are necessarily different and conflictive, if we believe that the former will try to buy at the lowest possible price and the latter will try to sell at the highest (buy cheapest, sell dearest). The conflict will only be resolved when the law of supply and demand brings the two positions nearer together and both parties agree to a price which they consider to be advantageous. This is the basic condition for commercial transactions. Now, although the interests of the two appear to be conflictive in the short term, in the long term their interests are common and coincide: they both hope to repeat the exchange, as this is the condition for gains which are continual and steady, rather than one-off or occasional. This implies that each party will want the other party to feel that he is benefiting from the exchange, so that he will be open to further exchanges in the future.

This model, applied to two economic agents, can also be partially applied to the relations between regulator and the regulated, which manifests itself in the extreme strategies of opting for conflict (*adversial approach*) or cooperation (*cooperative approach*).

The „adversial approach" can be defined as „regulation + litigation" (the State imposes regulations and takes legal action against those who do not obey them) and the „cooperative approach" as „negotiation + incentives" (regulator, the regulated and, in general, all those affected help to draw up the regulation, and there are incentives to observe it). Besides its greater efficiency and lower cost, the ethical attraction of the „cooperative approach" resides in the fact that it gives those affected greater freedom, increases their sense of responsibility and foments cooperation instead of conflict. It most frequently materializes as self-regulation.

Obviously, conflicts exist (they are a basic condition for the model of economic exchange) and the only reason for considering alternative institutions is to find some criterion to resolve them. As we said, to discover guidelines, rules or regulations to convert the conflict into cooperation.

The regulating agent, like the economic agent, does not necessarily have to be particularly benevolent or altruistic, concerned with the general interest or the common good; it is not unusual for the regulator to seek to justify his own usefulness by generating maximum regulation. Besides causing problems of control in decision-making processes, excessive regulation has inevitable redistributive effects and tends to upset the relations between competitors, between customers and suppliers, etc.

Consequently, the relations between regulators and those they regulate, between regulating agencies and financial intermediaries, may not be relations of friendly cooperation (they may even be characterized by a degree of mutual distrust), since they generally have opposing interests in the short term[6]. Moreover, it is not unusual for regulated companies (which generally have better information than regulating agencies, and incentives to be opaque) to try to control the regulating process and change it in their favour, to obtain advantages from the political game which they are unable to obtain in the free market game. This encourages lobbying and directly unproductive profit-seeking activities.

Neither is the „cat-and-mouse game“ or the „dialectics of regulation“ infrequent between supervisors and financial institutions, as the latter attempt to get round some regulations and ordinances (without committing an offence). In this sense, it has been rightly said that „creative accounting“ (on the boundary of respect for generally accepted accounting principles, for example, playing with historical and market prices) and other activities which attempt to obviate certain regulations and get round „legal obstacles“ have always been extremely profitable.

---

6 R. ORTEGA, at the opening lecture at the „XII Jornadas sobre el Mercado Monetario“, Santa Cruz de Tenerife, 24.5.1985 (quoted in R. TERMES, 1992, p. 1159): „This state of affairs is the result of the fact that the public powers are totally convinced that (only) they know what is good for the markets and of the biased view of the majority of bankers, who feel that the market should function, but only if it does so in accordance with their own interests.“

IV. The Relationship Between the Ethical and the Regulative Approach

Although both ethics and regulation have rules, principles or norms which share the feature of exteriority, they have different functions. In fact, in practice they may be complementary (companies which try to behave ethically need regulations to protect themselves from those which do not), they may replace each other (the greater the ethical responsibility, the lesser the need for regulation) or they may not be related at all (purely technical regulations).

The need for Government intervention to regulate a market depends, as we said, not only on the existence of „market failures“, but also on the greater or lesser professional ethics of the agents operating on the market. If these ethics imply high levels of honesty, then efficient equilibrium can be reached on the market. If not, the only alternative is to regulate it. In the best of cases, as Schotter (1987, p. 71) says, the market „needs rather more than „short-sighted“ individual rationality to achieve optimum - or at least satisfactory - results“. In fact it needs ethics which should be shared by the agents operating on the market in question.

However, even if the approaches to ethics and regulation are not identical, regulation can be justified on precise ethical grounds. These are:

a) the State can (and should) establish regulations if these contribute to the general good of society;
b) the State's role as a regulator should be subsidiary (regulating only when companies are incapable of regulating themselves, or when there is free-riding);
c) the State should exercise special care when regulating, knowing that it is a question of second-best, and that regulations may have „perverse effects“;
d) regulations for reasons of efficiency must have a sound economic basis, and not simply depend on vaguely ethical motives („distributing work“, „one price for all“, etc.);
e) some regulations seem to be good substitutes for ethical duties which are sometimes not carried out (risk control, the company's duty to provide reliable relevant information), so that regulation can fulfil its function even if the majority are trying to behave ethically (precisely to prevent free-riding);

f) regulations should be also be observed for reasons of efficacy: obeying the regulation produces a positive external effect for everybody (although each company individually may have incentives for free-riding, universal observance of the regulation ideally benefits everyone);
g) if there is no positive regulation, in the end there will be some type of regulation based on custom, and, consequently, it is better to reduce uncertainty and offer some legal security from the beginning, through legal, technical and administrative rules.

In short, as we pointed out, regulation should aim to guarantee ethical (and efficient) behaviour even when the ethical intention is lacking.

Thus, a regulation brings an ethical obligation, not only if it is a legal mandate (and not merely moral), but also if it is prudent and reasonable (fair). In other words, if ideally:

a) it is justified by the common good (for reasons of efficiency or equity);
b) it is an acceptable solution (not necessarily the ideal solution);
c) it is generally formulated (it is not drawn up *ad casum*, but considers the circumstances);
d) it is applied non-discriminatorily (even if it treats unequals unequally);
e) it is specific enough to be observed without ambiguity (it offers security);
f) it is stable and easily accessible to those being regulated (there is no inflation or dispersion of the rules);
g) it is impartial (it does not unjustifiably benefit or prejudice any party);
h) it is proportional (damages are proportional to the benefits obtained);
i) it satisfies the needs of those subject to the regulation and the criteria of the experts in regulation;
j) it achieves its aim without producing „perverse effects" (even if it accepts some undesirable effect);
k) it does not restrict freedom beyond what is necessary to guarantee adequate security;
l) it does not introduce excessive costs into the system (unnecessary formalities, delays);
m) it does not discourage efficient and ethically irreproachable behaviour.

As a rule, a fair regulation makes its observance ethically obligatory (although the force of the obligation depends on the type of regulation, its scope and effects, etc.) However, a specific regulation may not bring an ethical obligation in certain circumstances, especially if the damage produced is untenable (*ad impossibilia nemo tenetur*), although the institution affected is not likely to be the best (impartial) judge of the circumstances (a possible drop in profits, for instance, is not sufficient reason to skip a regulation).

In any case, ethical principles must be respected over and above regulation, which is why the lack of a certain regulation does not justify unethical behaviour (one cannot expect regulation to cover every single case), nor can the observance of a certain regulation be an excuse for unethical behaviour (ethical obligations are broader than legal obligations).

Moreover, the regulation should be observed by paying more attention to the spirit than to the letter (although following the letter may normally be enough). Many ethical dilemmas as regards regulation arise as a result of not having a genuinely ethical attitude (which in itself eliminates many false „ethical dilemmas"), or of having made erroneous decisions in the past (it is still frequent, and perhaps inevitable, to try to palliate the effects of a past decision which was wrong because it was unfair with another unfair decision).

In spite of these principles, some problems are particularly difficult to solve:

For instance, if competitors do not abide by a fair regulation, is one obliged to observe it even if this means being at a disadvantage? Although it will depend on the circumstances in each case, one can say: (a) as a rule, the obligation to observe the regulation persists (the fact that others do not abide by it does not release one from the obligation of observing it); (b) the application of specific ethical rules has to be considered (such as the rule that refers to „a good or indifferent action with one good effect and one bad effect"); (c) ultimately, the dilemma can be resolved by a higher regulating body (the State, a regulating agency).

In the same way, if there is conflict between regulations because they operate in different territorial contexts, which regulation does one follow? In this case, respecting ethics can guide the observation of different regulations, which can be regarded as partial indicators of the common good, and not as definitive criteria for conduct (in the European Union, the solution is to grant a single licence, supervised by the country of origin).

Lastly, as not all regulations are equally efficient, nor are their effects on incentives and costs the same, it would also be interesting to consider the ethical aspect of the costs involved in certain regulations through an appropriate cost-benefit analysis (particularly, the costs deriving from finally obtaining an uncompetitive and inefficient market structure, and those deriving from the eventual elimination of the regulation). But without going into detail, it seems clear that there is no reasonable alternative: despite the costs involved in the short term, regulations which lack sufficient economic and ethical justification have to be dismantled.

To summarize what we have said so far, some generally shared opinions on regulation can be mentioned:

a) less regulation means greater flexibility (although this sometimes implies greater inefficiency, if market structures are not competitive, and entrance barriers are raised), while excessive regulation means inefficiency;
b) uniform regulation means greater inefficiencies, which is why it is preferable to try regulations that are as close as possible to each company or sector (yardstick regulations);
c) it is better not to regulate markets where the inefficiencies are small, since some regulations could be unnecessary and even counterproductive;
d) if there are few externalities, separation by function is the best form of regulation (it limits the moral risk, market power and the cost of regulation);
e) it is preferable to regulate the conditions of competition (structural regulation) than corporate activity (regulation of conduct);
f) it is worth trusting the market whenever possible, since experience shows that regulation is a poor substitute for competition (precisely because Government authorities and experts in regulation increasingly distrust the capacity of regulation to solve certain problems, they incline towards deregulation and towards extending market scope or favouring competition);
g) although regulation may be justified in cases of „market failures", „State failures" also exist (which requires particular perception as far as some regulations are concerned);
h) there are various private alternatives to State regulation, which should be investigated in each case (self-regulation, codes of conduct, competitive regulation mechanisms, competition between regulating agencies, licence tenders, etc.)

V. Forms of Regulation on the Financial Markets

Regulation of the banking sector and the stock market aims, respectively, to protect the saver-depositor, and to guarantee that the investor-shareholder has adequate information. In both cases, public confidence is unquestionably founded on security and stability (the latter understood as the harmony between the business objectives of solvency, liquidity and profitability).

According to Howells and Bain (1990, pp. 167-185), we can distingish between two types of regulation in the financial markets depending on the objectives they are pursuing:

a) macroeconomic regulation: its object is to help the public authorities to achieve „their" macroeconomic objectives, by facilitating a more effective monetary policy;
b) macroprudential regulation: this aims to ensure the smooth, efficient functioning of the market, by building up the confidence of intermediaries and the public.

It is particularly interesting to consider this second type of regulation, inasmuch as it requires special professionalism and an ethical disposition in those who actively exercise it. This type of regulation can, in turn, be broken up in terms of its scope:

a) structural or market regulation: this tries to create general conditions on the market which prevent undesirable situations and conducts, ideally by encouraging competition (property restrictions, entrance requirements, restriction of activities, separation of functions, etc);
b) regulation of corporate conduct or behaviour: this sets out the ways of carrying out an activity (price-fixing, establishment of standards and requirements, granting of licences and authorizations, publishing information, etc.).

The regulation of conduct is especially related to ethics, since its contents are clearly ethical (even if the regulation is legal). It includes rules of behaviour which are applicable to both financial intermediaries (rules for relations with the clientele) and to customers and any other individual or legal entity (norms of conduct).

From the point of view of legal regulation, macroprudential regulation is divided into prudential „rules" (aimed at protecting the stability of business) and „intervention" rules (directed at getting over business crises). Prudential rules are divided, in turn, into discipline and control regulations, and intervention rules into regulations for supervision and sanction. Here it is particularly interesting to look some of the rules related to supervision and intervention. The external supervisory régime may be complemented by internal supervision or self-regulation. In turn, self-regulation can be exercised both by means of general codes of conduct, such as internal rules of conduct, deontological codes which may be freely adhered to, codes of „style", etc. Moreover, discretionary mechanisms for resolving conflicts (arbitration and equity committees) can also be adopted.

1. Rules of Behaviour

These are legal rules (and must, consequently, be observed) which affect those involved in relations in the financial market. Consequently, they can be distinguished by the fact that they are legal (and not simply moral) mandates. However, they sometimes originate from principles of conduct found in professional deontological codes (and, in the case of the stock markets, linked to the typical codes of conduct on the Anglo-Saxon stock markets), which have acquired legal status.

A. In the case of the credit market, the rules of behaviour principally refer to the obligatory respect for the duties deriving from the (pre-contractual or contractual) establishment of a legal relation of confidence between a bank and its customer. Amongst these duties are:

a) keeping bank secrets: this duty is unlimited as regards other banks, limited as regards the Bank of Spain (which is, in turn, subject to the legal obligation of secrecy) and non-existent as regards the tax authorities. In fact, it seems that this right is only minimally protected in our legislation, there is no jurisprudence about it not being obeyed and, in practice, it is reduced to commercial use (and yet fulfilling this obligation is an unrenounceable ethical requirement);

b) giving loyal advice: this includes not giving false information or assessment and giving advice when the principle of good faith requires that customer be informed of the potential legal or business risks which he may incur, because of lack of experience or professionalism (fiscal benefits or damages from an investment, possibility of coverage or exchange hedge in foreign currency transactions, purchase of options or futures, etc.);

c) exercising no arbitrariness when granting loans: this implies abstaining from continuing a loan to a bankrupt company, giving the impression that the company is still solvent and inducing third parties to enter into relations with it in good faith. This especially affects the institution which is both a creditor and a shareholder or manager of the accredited (which obviously generates conflicting interests). This explains the need for an exhaustive study of the concentration of risks which financial institutions' ownership of non-financial companies may involve in order to avoid the former „capturing" the latter (in this case, Spanish legislation is even more demanding than E.U. legislation);

d) exercising no arbitrariness in obtaining guarantees: the bank may not ask for disproportionate guarantees (which are an excessive burden for the debtor or are excessively harmful for its other creditors) for the credit-risk it assumes.

Moreover, the bank user enjoys specific protection, which forbids banks to include certain „iniquitous" clauses in their contracts (Junyent 1989).

B. In the case of the stock market, behaviour rules are aimed at market transparency and equal opportunities. In view of the complexity of the interests involved, stress is laid on protecting investors (up to the point of defending the absolute priority of their interests).

Although this is not an exhaustive list, following on from Fernández-Armesto and De Carlos (1992, pp. 393-413 and 195-216) and the comments of Tapia-Hermida (1993), the following norms can be mentioned:

a) information related to the stock market must be kept secret;

b) „Chinese walls" must be established (to prevent confidential information leaking within the institution and producing conflicts of interests between its different functions);

c) privileged information must not be used (which would imply unequal opportunities and swindling the other party);

d) quotations must not be fraudulently manipulated;

e) the customer must be given honest advice (which implies complete transparency of information);

f) priority must be given to customers' interests before one's own (which materializes in different rules, precautions and limitations);
g) internal rules of conduct must be established;
h) there must be adequate means and capacities to carry out the activity;
i) periodic information, and information on important events must be provided (and on large stakes in listed companies, and on treasury stock).

2. Supervision and Regulation

In Spain, the two organisms which exercise administrative control and supervision on the financial institutions and markets are the Bank of Spain (credit market) and the Comisión Nacional del Mercado de Valores (stock market). They are both Government institutions, and are independent, with faculties for supervision, inspection and sanction (and with certain regulative power for promulgating circulars).

The purpose of supervision is to guarantee *ex ante* the stability and transparency of the markets and correct price-formation, and to protect investors and those using financial services. According to LMV 24/1988 (esp. arts. 38, 44, 78 and 86, and 1 of the Prologue), in performing their functions, the public authorities and supervisory agencies „should be guided" by criteria aimed at fomenting free competition, by encouraging the intermediaries to implement codes of conduct which work in favour of this. Indeed, free competition, together with transparent information, is the best way of guaranteeing the better functioning of the system.

The basic theoretical justification for the existence of supervisory agencies resides in the need to prevent „market failures" in the financial system (banking panic, systemic risk) and to provide protection for depositors and investors. Because of their numbers, small depositors (unlike big customers, corporations and institutional investors) do not have the capacity or incentives to adequately supervise banks, which means that they are generally guided by the bank's reputation. However, this is of no use if there is a deposit guarantee which is insensitive to risk, so that the only way they have of exercising their right to control and defend their interests is to turn to a supervisory agency (Diamond 1984).

Given the complexity inherent to the functioning of financial institutions, today bank monitoring, on the capital side, tends to be oriented towards the creation and maintenance of the conditions of solvency (capital and shareholders' equity requirements), liquidity (deposit guarantee) and profitability (dividend discipline). For its part, business management focuses on the definition and control of risk.

The supervision of the stock market is centred on protecting the investor, with the assumption that he is generally in conditions of asymmetrical information. The idea of a specific regulation on the transmission of information (periodic information on corporate business, information on alternative management projects implied in takeover bids, and on the use of privileged information on the part of insiders) is to restrict the consequences of adverse selection and moral risk.

In practice, the supervisory institutions have to deal with different demands:

a) efficiently supervising payment systems which carry very high risk;
b) identifying and evaluating growing risks at institutions which are less and less transparent and more international;
c) guaranteeing the liquidity necessary to the system;
d) objectivizing crisis situations (which affect one or a group of institutions, a whole sector or several markets), intervening to reduce their effects (by supplying liquidity to the institutions which deserve it, but allowing the others to disappear).

It is worth asking whether a single agency or institution can be responsible for both supervision and intervention. In our opinion, the general answer is no, as confusion could arise in regard to the activities it is responsible for, and lead the institution to undertake functions which make it incapable of effectively performing any of the other functions it has been charged with. Indeed, there is the danger of a supervisory agency which is responsible for both supervision and reducing a crisis (like the Bank of Spain), intervening to prevent a crisis at an institution (for example, a bank which is „too big to be dropped") where its supervision was not efficient enough. In a case like this, one can only say, as Ortega (1993, p. 10) says, that „the credibility of a supervisory institution will be considerably undermined" and that „its action cannot be judged favourably".

However, dividing functions into different agencies can imply a „team's moral risk", i.e. that none of them may want to take the responsibility for an institution's bankruptcy (*regulatory cover-up*). When a private agency is responsible for the rating, the incentive to supervise effectively (without giving unnecessary warnings about danger nor ignoring real dangers) tends to be greater than in the case of an official agency, since it has a reputation or goodwill to keep up (if it loses it, it may lose the public rating contract) (Dewatripont and Tirole, pp. 36-37). However, sometimes this is not a sufficient guarantee that it is performing its task efficiently, or that external audits are reliable (which is particularly serious as these are directly responsible for truthfully informing the supervisory authorities about an institution's financial statements).

Moreover, the innovations on the markets often require that the supervisory authorities not only thoroughly examine the way in which they exercise control, but also their very capacity to do so (cases like BCCI, Continental Illinois, Savings & Loan, etc. show the mistakes that can be made).

3. Self-regulation

The aims of regulation can be achieved more easily, more reliably and more effectively when the market agents realize that the rules agreed to are in their interests. These interests can be guaranteed by means of a „cooperative approach“, by creating self-regulation agencies and by drawing up codes of conduct (Boot and Thakor 1993). We are now going to mention a few general ideas on the relevance of self-regulation and codes of conduct, and some of their ethical implications.

A. Self-regulation is the mechanism or process whereby economic agents affected by a conflictive situation (for reasons of inefficiency or injustice or, more specifically, tension between profit-seeking and ethical behaviour) decide to take responsibility for establishing and demanding the observance of certain principles and rules aimed at resolving the conflict.

The way in which self-regulation is carried out may be by adopting internal codes of conduct or „ethical codes“ (specifying the mission, principles and values which should guide the company and encouraging its members to put these into practice), by voluntary submitting oneself to an arbitration committee, by creating a self-regulation agency, or self-regulation agencies which compete with each other (like the British SROs), etc.

In principle, self-regulation does not necessarily guarantee that the mechanisms adopted or the results obtained are more ethical, but it does reveal a more ethical disposition in those who adopt it (as they are taking on greater responsibility and are becoming more involved). For this reason, self-regulation is generally preferable to regulation from the ethical point of view.

From the point of view of efficiency, although there are many arguments in favour of self-regulation, how effective they are in the end depends on the possibility of setting up mechanisms which are simple, efficient, reasonably-priced and unanimously accepted. However, the danger of relying exclusively on self-regulation institutions resides in the fact that these may become more like business associations than agencies protecting consumers. In order to prevent „cartelization" of *clubs* and possible „capture", there is a need for a superior supervisory institution or agency whose decisions are binding[7].

B. One way in which self-regulation can be implanted is by drawing up and establishing codes of conduct, both in the market involved (general codes) and in the institutions which operate on this market (internal codes). Indeed, in the view of Sánchez Asiaín (1992, p. 132), „until there is a new efficient framework for control, it is increasingly advisable for the institutions to self-discipline themselves, by providing themselves with instruments like codes of conduct which oblige them to behave ethically and with a social conscience on the market".

General codes of conduct contain a list of principles (which lack legal value, but not ethical value) to guide the behaviour of the intermediaries, in order to ensure the correct functioning and transparency on the markets, generate confidence and prevent fraud and wilful misrepresentation. They generally find their inspiration in the agreements and recommendations of international institutions (for example, the OICV-IOSCO) or in rules of behaviour drawn up by the legislator.

According to the „Código general de conducta en los mercados de valores" (Appendix to Royal Decree 629/1993 of 3rd May, „on the rules of behaviour in the stock markets and obligatory registers"), the following principles should be observed on the stock market:

a) acting impartially and in good faith, without putting one's own interests before customers' (honesty and fairness);

b) acting with the care and diligence to be expected of an expert professional (diligence);

7 Although it seem clear that an external controller is not sufficient to (because *Quis custodit ipsos custodes?*), neither is it really enough to rely on self-control alone, because this, quite simply, does not work.

c) using the right resources to efficiently carry out intermediation (capabilities);
d) being aware of customers' circumstances (information about customers);
e) adequately informing customers (information to customers);
f) resolving conflicts of interest between customers (conflicts of interest);
g) collaborating in the task of supervisory agencies.

It can already be noted that, precisely because of their ethical nature, these principles also include demands that immediately affect competition and efficiency in carrying out business. The commitment to respect the legislation in force, to apply the principles of professional ethics which correspond to financial intermediaries, and to orient action towards service to both customers and society as a whole are really no more than the materializations of superior ethical principles.

Besides the general codes of conduct, internal code and rules of conduct which must be fulfilled at each institution „can" be drawn up (although on occasions this is prescriptive). Precisely because this is discretional and internal, not observing this type of code cannot lead to an administrative sanction (but it can have consequences for one's job if it implies transgressing contractual good faith).

Deontological codes which may be freely adhered to (codes of „style") may also be established; these codes are founded on the importance of people participating in decision-making when the decisions being taken might affect them (if they do not participate in the decision-making, the commitment would be weaker and the people affected by the decisions would do no more than formally fulfil what has been established).

VI. Regulation and Risks

Of course, one thing is supervision, and another is expecting regulation to eliminate the risks inherent to any investment process (especially considering the predominant tendency to securitize bank deposits). There is a danger that, because supervisory agencies and deposit guarantee mechanisms exist, the public might not worry about obtaining and evaluating the relevant information, but build up a false idea of security, and then use this as a basis for claiming compensation when things go wrong.

In a sophisticated market where services and products are essentially based on information and related technologies, the risks reside to a greater extent in the financial instrument itself than in management by the intermediary. However, it is good that the intermediation institutions themselves are aware that they may have to pay an untenable price in terms of prestige and prices for capturing funds if they do not correctly evaluate the risks implied.

Diversifying risks is an elementary precaution. It is important that credit risks (market, interest rate and others) be broken down and evaluated separately according to the contracts each institution makes, but they should be considered globally to establish the risk the institution is carrying as a whole (since risks can offset each other). In any case, in spite of all the techniques for calculating risks, the limits that can be taken on should finally be established by the chairman of the board of directors. Thus, ultimately, a prudential decision is what determines what is reasonable and what is feasible.

To be specific, the fact that some bankers did not understand the risks inherent to certain instruments obliged regulators to ask for stricter coverage conditions and requisites (such as the „Cooke" ratios). Paradoxically, the „reputational risk" seems to increase with the imposition of capital requirements, since these lead to a reduction in vigilance, and, consequently, in asset quality (Boot and Greenbaum 1994).

Similar effects derive from the „moral risk" in banking as the result of a system of guarantees or deposit insurance which is insensitive to risk (at a fixed premium or flat rate), together with the excessive presence of risk-carrying debt, or the assumption that the bank is „too big to go bankrupt"; all of these circumstances propitiate more risky management. It seems that the existence of a deposit guarantee or insurance mechanism should be complemented by a stricter requirement as regards risks carried, in order to minimize or eliminate the risks associated with the guaranteed deposits.

If this is not done, this moral risk inevitably lead to conflicts of interest between the bank's managers and the supervisory agencies, between the bank's creditors and its shareholders, and, ultimately, between these and taxpayers as a whole (in the last instance, public money is risked when a central bank exercises the function of lender, or when a bank which is „ill", and whose managers have preferred to „seek ruin", is „resurrected" at the expense of the deposit guarantee). Indeed, more and more people are questioning the special nature of banking businesses and the assumption that this „speciality" justifies equally special protection, i.e. directly at tax-payers' expense and at the expense of the intermediaries and their customers.

Obviously, one should not confuse the special nature of the function of banking (which may well justify special protection) with that of the supposed special nature of private institutions. Banks should be regarded, *tout court*, as companies like any others, without privileges or „private laws". In short, as those who advocate free-banking point out, it appears to be more important to guarantee that the function is exercised rather than the to guarantee the actual subjects who perform this function (Fama 1985).

As far as systemic risk (or the risk of generalized bankruptcy caused by situations of panic or fraud) is concerned, a widely-held opinion is that its prevention should take absolute priority inasmuch as it affects the function carried out by the system. In fact, it seems that combining deposit insurance with the intervention of an ultimate lender eliminates the risk of a banking crisis and systemic risk. But this security system should not prevent less efficient institutions (because of bad investments, poor management or even fraud) from disappearing, although the monetary authorities must try to ensure that the readjustment process is orderly and not too onerous for society.

Moreover, if we know that a deposit guarantee like the present one (at a fixed premium or flat rate) creates occasions of moral risk (by encouraging lack of prudence when taking on risks) and adverse selection (encouraging opacity in the information the insurer is provided with), and distorts competition to benefit of the least solvent or most inefficiently managed institutions, according to Ronn and Verma (1986) (and all the liberal school), the reasonable thing to do would be to apply premiums which are in line with the risk carried and pass the assumption of risks on to depositors.

But, this does not seem to be viable at present, and so a demanding regulation on capital-adequacy requirements is still necessary, as is strict supervision on the part of the market authorities (Middleton 1992).

VII. Conclusions

Although they are drawn up in a different conceptual framework and have different immediate objectives, ethical theory and regulative theory are not in opposition to each other. In fact, as we have seen, the demands and effects of the specific market regulations and of the ethical principles applicable to financial intermediaries generally tend to be complementary (and, on occasion, may replace each other)

Certainly, as is generally said, ethics is „above all that“: regulation tends to be minimalist, while ethics seeks excellence, the optimum. But the fact that ethics considers superior values does not mean that it does not assume other values as well. The strict obligation to „always do what is reasonable“, as a fundamental ethical rule, implies a balanced idea of rationality (which obviously includes efficiency considerations, but, necessarily, other considerations too). Thus, this means that the dilemma or trade-off between efficient behaviour and ethical behaviour which sometimes arises in practice derives from erroneous perceptions of the meaning of „what is reasonable“ (and, consequently, of the content of ethical values and efficiency).

Sometimes this dilemma arises precisely as a result of an inadequate regulation, i.e. an „unreasonable“ regulation. It is true that there has never been a spontaneous disposition to obey the laws; but as Garay (1994, p. 224) rightly said, „obeying the market authorities is currently one of the most neglected ethical duties“. However, if there is disobedience, then this is partly because the legislation is bad, either in its design or its application (Neven and Mayer 1990). To quote Aristotle (*Política* VI. 8 1294a3-6): „Good legislation does not consist of having well-established laws that are not obeyed. Good legislation means that the established laws are obeyed and that the laws are good“.

The first requisite for any regulation is that it be governed by the common good and favours social cooperation, which implies that it encourages everyone to broaden the horizon of considerations on which their decisions are based. At this point, as Hazlitt (1973, pp. 11-13) points out, ethical, legal and economic considerations coincide in opposing „the tendency to only consider the consequences and effects of a decision, a regulation or a policy on a particular group at a certain moment in time, and to neglect to inquire what the long-term effects will be for society as a whole“.

A „reasonable“ regulation will thus favour reasonable allocations of resources and will encourage positive sum games, while discouraging playing zero or negative sum games. Today, for instance, as Tobin (1993) says, „enormous quantities of intelligence and work are misspent on financial speculation, with final results for society which are equal to zero“, when the fact is, according to Ortega (1993, p. 11), that „the financial markets provide legal and economic mechanisms to facilitate positive net transfers of welfare“. The problem of zero or negative sum games sometimes being played, thus, normally originates more from a deficient ethical disposition than from deficient regulation (generally speaking, regulations incorporate the principal ethical demands at their own level).

However, as we said, some regulations can be „unreasonable“ (i.e. inadequate from the ethical or economic point of view). And they may be unreasonable precisely because of their incapacity to adequately balance freedom with security, maintaining the tension between the two. The solution to this, as we saw, depends directly on how some requirements - mainly related to risk and information - for the correct functioning of the financial system are satisfied.

What does seem clear is that, in view of the need to resolve functional disadvantages in comparison with parabanking financial institutions, the immediate future of banking will increasingly depend on diversifying not only risks but also functions (providing other services with higher added value than lending) and on the balance between intermediation and securitization. To be specific, it will be through the more objective identification of risk that the price of capital can be more accurately established, and this should lead to it being allocated more efficiently.

The trend on the most highly-developed markets seems to be to live with risk, i.e. for bankers to become more like entrepreneurs and businessmen. In Spain, on the contrary, the predominant opinion still favours „boring banking“ - that is to say, getting more deeply involved in the original function of banking and in the basic principles of the banking business. But improving solvency, the quality of service and staff training are no longer characteristics exclusive to this type of banking, and now, quite rightly, seem to be insufficient conditions for maintaining or increasing profitability.

For their part, like the intermediaries, regulators will have to be even more market- and competition- oriented, if they wish to successfully design and apply a suitable regulation for the financial system.

In sum, since „reality is ahead of the law“, both regulators and intermediaries will need to be more market and competition-oriented, and to adapt to the evolution of the financial markets, if they wish to be not only competent, but also competitive. And this too as an elementary demand of their professional ethics.

References

ALLEN, F. (1990): „The market for information and the origin of financial intermediation", *Journal of Financial Intermediation*, 1, 3-30.

ALLEN, F. (1994): „Mercados de valores y asignación de recursos" in: C. MAYER and X. VIVES, 95-125.

AQUINAS, THOMAS: *Summa Theologiae* I-II.

Argandoña, A. (1987): „Trabajo, economía y ética", in: F. FERNÁNDEZ (coord.): *Estudios sobre la Laborem exercens*, Madrid: BAC.

Argandoña, A. (1991): „Values, Institutions and Ethics", *IV European Conference on Business Ethics*, London.

ARISTOTLE: *Política.*

BASÁÑEZ, F. (1992): „Una fundamentación antropológica de la economía de mercado", in F. FERNÁNDEZ (Ed.): *Estudios sobre la Centesimus annus*, Madrid: AEDOS-Unión Editorial, 475-516.

BECKER, GARY S. (1994): „Cuanto más control, más corrupción", *Actualidad Económica* (14.2.1994).

BERSTER, H. and M. HELLWIG (1987): „Moral hazard and equilibrium credit rationing", in: G. BAMBERG and K. SPREMANN (Eds.): *Agency Theory, Information and Incentives*, Berlin: Springer Verlag.

BOOT, A., A. THAKOR and G. UDELL (1987): „Competition, risk neutrality and loan commitments", *Journal of Banking and Finance*, 11, 449-471.

BOOT, A. and A. THAKOR (1993): „Self-Interested Bank Regulation", American Economic Review 83, 206-212.

BOOT, A. and S. I. GREENBAUM (1994): „Regulación bancaria, reputación y rentas: teoría e implicaciones de política económica", in: C. MAYER and X. VIVES (1994), 303-331.

BRENNAN, G. and JAMES M. BUCHANAN (1987): *La razón de las normas. Economía polìtica constitucional*, Madrid: Unión Editorial.

BROWN, M. T. (1992): *La ética en la empresa*, Barcelona: Paidós.

COOPER, K., and D. R. FRASER (1986): *Banking Deregulation and the New Competition in Financial Services*, Cambridge Mass.

DEWATRIPONT, M. and J. TIROLE (1994): „Estructura eficiente de gobierno: implicaciones para la regulación bancaria", in: C. MAYER and X. VIVES (1994).

DIAMOND, D. W. (1984): „Financial Intermediation and Delegated Monitoring", *Review of Economic Studies*, 51, 393-414.

FAMA, E. F. (1985): „What's different about banks?", *Journal of Monetary Economics*, 15, 29-39.

FERNÁNDEZ-ARMESTO, J. and L. DE CARLOS (1992): *El Derecho del Mercado Financiero*, Madrid: Civitas.

FREIXAS, X. (1990): „Fundamentación teórica de la regulación de los mercados financieros“, *Moneda y Crédito* 190, 11-33.

GALBRAITH, J. K. (1989): *El crac del* 29, Barcelona: Ariel.

GARAY, J. de (1994): *El Juego. Una ética para el mercado*, Madrid: Díaz de Santos.

HAZLITT, H. (1973): *La Economía en una lección*, Madrid: Unión Editorial.

HELLWIG, M. (1987): „Some recent developments in the theory of competition in markets with adverse selection“, *European Economic Review*, 31, 319-325.

HOWELLS, P. G. and K. BAIN (1990): *Financial Markets and Institutions*, London: Longman.

JUNYENT, J. (1989): *Usos y abusos en la banca española*, Madrid: Pirámide (Informe de la Asociación Española para la Investigación y el Control Financiero - ICOFIN).

KOSLOWSKI, P. (1988): *Prinzipien der Ethischen Ökonomie. Grundlegung der Wirtschaftsethik und der auf die Ökonomie bezogenen Ethik*, Tübingen: J.C.B. Mohr.

LOSS, L. (1988): *Fundamentals of Securities Regulation*, Boston and Toronto: Little, Brown and Co.

MAYER, C. (1988): „New Issues in Corporate Finance“, *European Economic Review*, 32, 1167-1188.

MAYER, C. and X. VIVES (eds.) (1994): *La intermediación financiera en la construcción de Europa*, Bilbao: Fundación BBV.

MCKENZIE, R. B. and G. TULLOCK (1975): *The New World of Economics: Explorations into the Human Experience*, Homewood, I1.: Irwin.

MIDDLETON, P. (1992): „Does investment banking need greater supervision?“, Barclays Briefing 88.

MITNICK, B. M. (1980): *The Political Economy of Regulation*, New York: Columbia UP.

MULLER, D. (1984): „A Legal Framework for International Supervision. The EEC Model“, *Issues in Bank Regulation*, 8/1, 36-42.

NEVEN, D. and C. MAYER (1990): „The design and implementation of financial regulation“, *Documenta* (Fundación BBV), Bilbao: Centro de Estudios Bancarios.

ORTEGA, R. (1993): Crónica de doce años de cambio“, *Papeles de Economía Española*, 54, 2-14.

POLO, L. (1991): *¿Quién es el hombre?* Madrid: Rialp.

POSSENTI, V. (1991): „Presupuestos antropológicos de los sistemas económicos“, in AA. VV., *Doctrina Social de la Iglesia y Realidad Socio-económica*, Pamplona: Eunsa, 475-493.

RONN, E. I., and A. K. VERMA (1986): „Price risk-adjusted deposit insurance: an option-based model“, *Journal of Finance*, 41, 871-895.

SÁNCHEZ ASIAÍN, J. A. (1992): „El sistema financiero español ante la unión económica europea“, in AA. VV., *España y la Unión Europea*, Barcelona: Plaza y Janés.

SCHOTTER, A. (1987): *La economía de mercado. Una valoración crítica*, Barcelona:Ariel.

SPULBER, D. F. (1989): *Regulation and Markets*, London: MIT Press.

STEINHERR, A. (1990): „La intergración de los mercados financieros europeos: cuestiones e implicaciones de regulación", *Moneda y Crédito*, 190, 83-127.

TAPIA-HERMIDA, A. J. (1993): „Las normas de actuación en los mercados de valores", *Revista de Derecho Bancario y Bursátil*, 50, 315-360.

TERMES, R. (1992): „Efectos de la regulación financiera en el negocio bancario", in *Desde la Banca*, Madrid: Rialp, vol. 2.

TOBIN, J. (1993): „Grávense los especuladores", *Papeles de Economía Española*, 54 (from *Financial Times*, 22.12.1992), 309-310.

WATRIN, C.(1989): „Fallos del mercado" frente a „fallos del Estado", *Cuadernos del Pensamiento Liberal*, 10, 39-66.

ZUNZUNEGUI, F. (1992): *Ordenación bancaria*, Madrid: Espasa Calpe.

Chapter 3

Social and Institutional Responsibility in Banking

JOSÉ MARÍA ORTIZ and NEKANE ECHEVARRÍA

I. Two Conclusions to Start with

I am going to start with the conclusions to be drawn from this paper, just in case they are not very clear at the end. The initial reaction - which is psychological, but real all the same - to abstract concepts such as „social responsibility" could be as follows: a difficult idea to put into practice, a nuisance to business which might, at best, serve to clear consciences. However, emergency situations arise in society which may justify anyone moving into the front line who is capable of doing so. In other words, if I can help to prevent wrong from being done, then I am obliged to act. Power becomes duty when the wrong is profound.

The need to accept responsibility does not only arise from seeing something that must be done, and volunteering to undertake the task; it may be that the institutional situation of a certain activity is so important that one must feel responsible not only for one's own acts, but also for many of other people's acts.

This is the price of social importance: power brings obligations, omissions are more serious, and a bad example may have disastrous consequences. To put it positively, one is in a position to breathe hope and new life into society.

The second basic idea I would like to underline is that many evils come from the systematic confrontation of realities which have no reason to be in opposition with each other. Private interests are not the antithesis of public interests, and the individual good does not have to be interpreted as being in conflict with the common good; what is good for me does not have to be precisely what is harmful for someone else. Confidence is not in opposition to risk, nor transparency to fluidity. The past is present in the future. And the good of institutions does not necessarily imply misfortune for the State. In the same way that the „social function" mentioned earlier does not necessarily involve a decline in business capacity.

This presentation of conclusions may well have been too hurried. But rather than telling you how the film ends before it starts, my intention was simply to indicate the most important points I will be making. When analysing some of the ethical problems which arise in the banking business, I will try to explain why contributing to the common good should always be one of the coordinates in the search for profits; in other words, the responsibility of maintaining an institutional identity necessarily involves social responsibility.

II. Between Confidence and Risk

Banks are probably the most important financial intermediaries for savers and borrowers. Banks bring two types of people together; on the one hand, those who present the accumulated result of work done; and on the other, those who are planning activities which require credit, financing, etc. Banking reduces the distance between the past and the future, in the present. And it reflects the temporary nature of money.

Money tells us what it cost to obtain it and the work that can be undertaken with it. It tells us about savers and investors. These two types of people need each other, just as they need someone else to bring them together. Just like the past and the future. The future would not exist without the past: nothing can be undertaken without having first saved for it, or without someone having saved previously; but the past is meaningless without the future: there is no sense in storing for the sake of it, without investing, without plans.

The process of allocating resources undoubtedly has its risks: collecting and distributing funds, managing the accounts and the administration of operations, customer service, storing information... But it is true that there are many opportunities for corruption - the more important the business, the greater the danger of corruption -, and the extremely important social function banking plays in a market economy should not be forgotten.

Firstly, banking has the capacity to be the risk-taker in the last instance; and, secondly, it generates confidence in the system. Financial crises are crises of confidence (J. A. Sánchez Asiaín, „Reflexiones sobre la Banca. Los nuevos espacios del negocio bancario").

Only confidence can prevent an alarming withdrawal of deposits. And how easy it is for confidence to be lost, when there is uncertainty about the future, when doubts arise about how far certain operations are licit... Banking is based on confidence, and reputation is one of its main ethical problems.

III. A Case of Reputation: Money-Laundering

Banks may unwittingly serve as intermediaries in transferring and depositing funds of criminal origin. Arms and drug-trafficking, kidnapping and other terrorist actions involve payments and transfers, but also need to conceal the origin of the funds and the identity of their owners, to store bank notes in safe boxes, etc.

Are police vigilance and legal supervision sufficient to prevent this financial support being given to crime? It is becoming more and more necessary for financial institutions to lend their support in reporting operations that have criminal ends. But some questions necessarily arise: what right do banks have to judge the legitimacy of the transactions carried out by their customers? When are suspicions about a customer sufficiently well-founded to justify reporting him to the authorities?

The measures to be taken seem clear enough: proven identification, a file of references and documents, special attention to transactions with countries where the legislation is more relaxed. But can the duty of lifting bank secrets be justified without informing the customer?

It seems to me that this relationship with the customer - the unwritten pact which assumes that the bank will keep the secret - can only be broken through recourse to a good which is superior to the parties involved. In other words, the justification for the necessary collaboration with the international, legal, and political authorities, etc. cannot simply be that the public would lose confidence in banks as a result of their involuntary association with delinquents.

A series of suspect activities - transfers, cheques, loans, deposits, movement of bank notes, handling of disproportionate funds - may justify the betrayal of something as essential as the confidence of a customer, who will only be reported to the authorities if one is considering the social good, but not if one is only considering the good of the bank in question. Otherwise, it would be sufficient to use the capacity of accepting someone as a customer or not.

In short, the fight against crime could override confidentiality if banks sees themselves as having a social responsibility.

IV. What Is Wrong Will Eventually Be Forbidden. The Fight Against Fraud

Not all money-laundering is related to criminal activities. At least, interestingly enough, that is how the States involved in attracting black money and in drawing up legislation on securities which are fiscally opaque seem to view the matter. And this makes us wonder how certain situations are justified before they are forbidden.

Some things are wrong, because that is what a certain law says. And there are laws which forbid things which are wrong. In many cases, reality is ahead of the law and, while it is desirable for laws to regulate the new problematic aspects of economic activity, it is no less true that a situation is not necessarily good or desirable before it is made illegal.

The capacity for inventing new a-legal situations is infinite. For this very reason, when regulating the financial markets, attitudes should be based on a criterion of right or wrong, and not only on permission or prohibition. Before a law appears, the situations themselves are already calling for a judgement on their desirability. From this perspective of the social good, there can be no doubt that ethics and legality are perfectly harmonious.

In Spain tremendous effort is being made in the legislative sphere to regulate activity on the financial markets; as happens with everything, the first steps will be hesitant, with inaccuracies, errors, imprecisions... But it is important that good intentions be reflected in norms of conduct, and that these can be demanded with the force of the law. A society is much more culturally mature when the protection of its markets is not left to the goodwill of its agents, when the norms become regulations, which could in fact give rise to sanctions. Equally, it is more mature when it manages to foresee problematic circumstances, which are difficult to envisage, before they occur. And perhaps political party financing is connected with this.

In my opinion, the development of a legal framework is good news from the ethical point of view. It would be short-sighted to believe that advances in legislation imply that ethics is taking a step backwards. On the contrary. If ethical activities do not materialise in the culture of society - and laws are one of the main elements in any culture - these activities are ineffective; moreover, the idea that the desire to obey the laws is essentially an ethical stance still remains.

In the same way, the principle that taxes should be paid can also be viewed as being very much an ethical stance. In principle, to call the underground economy and tax fraud „necessary evils“ is, at the very least, to set oneself up as both judge and defendant in a conflict. And being responsible for the exception becoming the rule is an extremely serious matter.

Just as the choice between the fight against crime and confidentiality is resolved by turning to the social good, which justifies actions such as confiscating property, blocking accounts, reporting suspicious individuals - with all the risks to reputation involved in this -, so the social good makes it advisable to obey the law, pay taxes, and fight fraud. However, it may be that Spanish society still has a long way to go culturally before it accepts that banking should collaborate in the fight against tax fraud.

V. Transparency vs Fluidity

There is a risk involved in this cultural progress which should not be overlooked, and that is how rules of conduct are developed; at the outset, until all the elements are firmly established, practices or activities could arise which involve excessive control and are a hinderance to the mobility the market requires.

In short, until the rules which will give the financial markets the desirable transparency are established, there is the risk of the natural flow on these markets being obstructed.

In banking, money is more than ever information. The speed and versatility of movements increasingly require regulations and laws. But common sense is needed more than anything else. Banks are really information manufacturers. A current account is no more than information.

In my opinion, this is one of the points which best serves to exemplify the tightening up which would come with a pedantic maximalist approach. To try to chase up all the privileged information on the financial markets would be equivalent to stifling or destroying these markets. What is more, there is no organisation which does not mainly function on the basis of privileged information.

There is some information which loses interest once everyone has it at their disposal. Moreover, it can be grossly unfair to give information to people who do not have the right to it. This is true for any organisation and any market, and, of course, for the financial markets.

How, then, can we translate that unfortunate American expression „insider trading“? I think that Spanish has plenty of good expressions of its own for there to be no need to enter into a long discussion about when trading can be done from inside. Negligent, thief, liar: these are expressions which are clear to our culture; and perhaps there is no need to invent any others.

On every market some agents are sharper than others; and the least talented are always those who try to obstruct others' progress by asking for extra time. To expect information not to be used until all the members of the market have it would be to give too great an advantage to its most inept members, and would undermine the essence of a competitive market.

Thus, it is extremely difficult to decide when information should be considered as being available to the public, and ready to be used on the market. What is common knowledge is no longer interesting. And when something is already news on the financial markets, then what one has to do is to sell: buying happens before, when the information is still no more than a rumour.

There will always be privileged positions on the financial markets; people whose intuition enables them to foresee trends; people who are capable of reading between the lines. And these people cannot be asked to stop using their talent, in the same way that a person who sees a business opportunity is not asked to make this public knowledge before following the opportunity up.

Consequently, what has to be done is to define more and more precisely which privileged positions are legal and which are not. To define what handling of information constitutes a criminal offence - not because it is a crime to handle information but because some uses of information can be regarded as theft, lying, extortion, damage to third parties, etc.

VI. He who Has Money Has Power

Irregular behaviour gradually undermines the prestige of any institution. But, naturally, this applies to some types of behaviour more than others. Thus, at the smaller banks the ethically incorrect types of behaviour which are most frequently detected are interest fraud, theft committed by staff, lying and internal manipulation, while bribery and irregular handling of information top the list at large corporations.

When a person or an institution is perceived as being responsible for reprehensible conduct, the person or institution will undoubtedly lose prestige and authority. Disrepute and mistrust would finish the institution of banking, and this makes us reflect on the following: banking not only needs to preserve its power, but also its authority.

Money is information. And its power comes from the future, from the capacity to project. Authority is different: it comes from the past, from its establishment as such. Banking is risk and, at the same time, confidence, power and authority. Thus, it can never forget that - because of its very nature - it needs to maintain not only its strength, but also its prestige.

And when do power and authority coincide? We generally say that the one who has the information has the power. In the banking business, the one who has the money has the power. But that is not enough. The one who has the information may view it as a value to be shared, and may distribute it fairly; or he may see it as a value which implies that as he has it, others do not. In any company, those who know how to distribute information and responsibilities not only have power, but also moral authority and prestige. Those who remain at the top because others have no access to what corresponds to them may have power, but will lose their authority. Thus, then, the institution of banking needs to show that not only does it accumulate large quantities of money - that it has power - but that it really knows how to use it fairly, by providing opportunities for those who wish to start businesses, by using it for the good of society - and then it will have authority besides power.

This is where banking needs to show that it is not turning its back on society. The more power it has, the more it will need to gain citizens' confidence; the financial markets are not a game: in other words, they are not an end in themselves; they cannot lose their footing, they need to maintain their connection with the „other“ real economy.

The financial economy is also real and, although its objects are not physical like in industry or agriculture, they are subject to natural laws, and not simply to positive legal regulations. Ethics has an intrinsic effect on the financial economy, because it is also a real economy.

VII. The Responsibility of Investments. Who's Boss?

Should banks become owners in industry? What is to be done when there is no alternative but to become a shareholder of a company? Are there any enterprises or sectors which have special ethical significance? Do banks have any responsibility when they take part in - or finance - businesses which are dangerous to the environment?

It seems clear that the corporate model is changing. No one sees the relationship with customers as being conflictive; on the contrary, they are the main source of information. And that is how the complaints made through the „customers' ombudsman“ should be viewed in banking - not as a nuisance to be silenced, but as the main source of opportunities for improving the business and enhancing customer loyalty. That is why they should perhaps be called „customer *participation* departments“.

Moreover, the concept of distributor and competitor is also changing in the world of business, since it is perfectly possible to regard the relationship with them in terms of mutual cooperation. The ideal is no longer independence. And this is also changing the role of shareholders.

Every institution needs to be clear about who is the authority, who is the owner. We human beings need to have this very clear. And, indeed, one of the worst social crises occurs when citizens discover that those who should be looking to the general good are using their positions for their own personal enrichment. Because this situation is demoralising. Now, excessive division of ownership may involve this risk, the risk that those who represent the authority make decisions behind the backs of the real owners.

Should shareholders be informed about the company's most important plans? Can the concealment of information or projects be justified by claiming that this is for the good of the business, i.e. of the shareholders? Who is boss then? And for how long?

The boundaries between the different parties - manager, shareholder, customer - are becoming increasingly nebulous. When this occurs, when flexibility and mobility increase, one thing is clear: the most important qualities are ethical. If I want a very high degree of staff mobility, I will have to foment qualities such as fluid communication, confidence, increased responsibility; while, if I opt for more rigid relations, the variables to take into account will be much easier to quantify. In short, as the market demands a more virtual - relational - type of corporation, then the most important thing to be done is to promote the variables which are the most difficult to quantify.

It is essential to try to do what one does well even better, without seeking to move unnecessarily into other fields. In the case of a bank, this principle may be limited by the size which is desirable for the bank to reach. Because, obviously, a society cannot be purely a society of services.

Loans which are not repaid, for example, mortgages, sometimes put banking in the role of entrepreneur. The solution to these cases may be to sell or to govern. That is the decision of the bank that finds itself in this situation, and a decision that is made taking a variety of parameters into account.

But it is also important to ask ourselves when, and to what extent, banking should play the role of capitalist partner. It may well be a necessary function inasmuch as a capitalist society has no other large capitals, provided that it stimulates the creation or existence of real industrialists.

As regards encouraging investment in sectors of particular significance or importance, it is clear that, first, support must be obtained from those entrepreneurs who will help to cope with the most urgent needs. Today, thanks to the more general phenomenon of globalization, we also believe that all activities should respect the tenable - sustainable - nature of development.

Environmental demands have revealed the united conscience of the human race, the need for global solutions, and the desirability of discussion which is not purely strategic; and the undeniable responsibility of all the economic agents. Apart from making the odd gesture or taking specific care with noise, pollution, paper consumption and energy, banking is beginning to consider the desirability of demanding - where possible - ecological audits from companies.

Any institution which can help to prevent the destruction of the environment, water contamination, the issue of toxic gases, massive deforestation, the destruction of the ozone layer, etc, should do so. And banking may be best able to collaborate in this by controlling its stakes in companies.

Another aspect of the connection between the worlds of finance and industry is the harmonisation of stock market information with information about the real situation of companies.

Financial data should be supported by the appropriate information: on the business the company and its subsidiaries are involved in - products, services, staff, the competitive conditions of the business, fixed assets, the decisions subject to shareholders' votes, capital, tax, financial figures - on audited financial statements, cash-flow, goodwill, sales, liabilities-, and on its managers, etc. This transparency is not merely a question of commercial scruples or image-seeking; the connection with economic life, in which the financial market plays the role of intermediary, is necessary to understand what forecasts are really based on.

The relationship with investment companies brings us to the chapter on stock market regulation. As we shall see, this is linked to the more general approach of whether or not it is appropriate to put a conflictive focus on the relationship between companies and their customers.

VIII. Conflicting Interests and Customer-Tailored Banking

An important step in the defence of investors was Decree Law 629/93 of 3 May whereby all the broker-dealers on the stock markets have to comply with certain rules of conduct. The General Code of Conduct in the appendix to the Royal Decree sets out the measures to increase protection for the customers of stockbroking companies.

This is the perspective which gives unity to the articles in the law. The very first article states that „all persons and entities should exercise their activities impartially, without putting their own interests before those of their customers, to the benefit of these and of the correct functioning of the market."

The stance taken is clear: what is good for the market is good for investors. For this reason, manipulation of the performance of quotations, and privileged treatment of important customers must be avoided; the market must diligently follow its customers' instructions; fraudulent activities and undersupported expansions should be avoided; attempts will be made to provide the means so that the customer does not suffer from the interruption or termination of business; everything will be done to prevent one person's operations benefiting others.

On the subject of information, it states that the customer should be adequately identified, but without any loss of confidentiality. He should be provided with relevant, clear, precise, sufficient up-to-date information. Assessment should be impartial, without considering the stockbroker's interests. And customers' transactions will not be revealed to other customers.

What is beneficial to the customer is beneficial to the market. When information is being handled, immorality is equivalent to inefficiency because the lack of ethics destroys confidence. And if anyone is still thinking that there are „opportunities" which cannot be missed, or that if „everyone else acts incorrectly". I cannot act differently, then it is worth remembering that this is only a psychological „tic". In the same way as when we ask someone „How's everything going?" and walk straight on, we show that we are not expecting a reply. When we start a sentence by saying „what is true is that..." it is because we are convinced that we do not know how to support what we are going to say. Thus, then, when we do something because „everyone else does it", it is because we know that it is wrong.

However, the approach of the General Code of Conduct for the stock markets involves a certain risk, because of its maximalist nature: believing that the relationship between customers and companies is basically conflictive; not understanding that the good of the stockbroker is not incompatible with that of its customers. It is impossible for a stockbroker firm to benefit anybody if it does not benefit itself at the same time, in the same way it is impossible for a human being to love something without loving himself at the same time.

Beware then, because what is worse is the enemy of what is good. When a quotation cannot rise any more, it has to fall. And a silk purse cannot be made from a sow's ear. The investor does not have to be in conflict with anybody to be protected.

The same reasoning can be applied to customer-tailored banking, when funds contribute to the activities, companies or sectors the customers desires. It is true that the customer will choose what the bank offers him, and that he will be offered something which is of interest to the bank. But that is no reason to assume that what benefits the bank works against the customer. Moreover, no citizen is obliged to use the services banking offers. Like anyone lending services, neither are banks obliged to treat all their customers in the same way, and it is logical enough that they be treated differently according to the volume of business they do with the bank.

IX. Fulfilling the Corporate Role. The Public Deficit

Altruistic behaviour and charity cannot be required of banking, simply because that is not what banking is about. It is good that banking sees that it can return part of the profit society provides it with in the form of charity and patronage. But this subtle form of publicity is not the main social benefit that banking can provide.

The most important thing is for banking to play the role which corresponds to it within the market economy. It should promote equal opportunities, free initiative, private property, free price formation on the market, the protection provided by contracts. This is indeed contributing to the common good as an institution.

The processes of globalization and internationalisation, together with the unsuccessful interventionist economies, bring a risk with them, namely that big capitalist alliances simply mean that monopolies change hands. The cost of infrastructure means that there are indeed fields where one can only be competitive through alliances - air travel, motor companies, health, telecommunications - and there is no doubt that banking will play an extremely important role, since the prevention of cartels or monopolies which would work against the free market is in its hands.

To be concerned about the common good and the health of society is not the exclusive task of the State. The Welfare State is fictitious, because the relationship between private and common good is not essentially conflictive either. It is enough to believe that honesty, good faith, the correct functioning of the legal system, etc. are aspects of a society's common good, and are also essential for the banking business to function. In other words, social responsibility is an essential part of the banking business because it is an activity which is not exclusively interested in the short-term future. Charitable activities are voluntary for the market agents. But their contribution to justice is not voluntary.

What happens when it is the State that does not fulfil its role as an enterprise? There will always be activities necessary for the common good - health, territorial defence, infrastructure, preservation of the artistic and cultural heritage, primary education - which are a burden for all the citizens. Now, this is not the same as when the State competes with private companies in certain sectors, and especially when these activities are unprofitable. If it is already a problem if someone lays down the rules of the game and, on top of that, plays it, it is even worse if they lose and others have to cover their debts.

How far are banks obliged to finance the public deficit? And to subscribe to or place public debt? In fact, they cannot ignore the State's financial problems; first, because it is in their interests to capture public funds in their operations, and public institutions will ask for something in exchange; and, second, because foreign debt and the public deficit closely condition the economic life of a country and its commercial transactions, and banking is not uninvolved in these matters.

The decision about what intervention is reasonable will depend on the risks that can be taken on, on how the situation is valued and especially on the capacity for discussion. A person may ask for help to solve a problem if he is prepared for the person who is going to help him to palliate the consequences to also intervene in correcting the causes behind the situation.

Banking can be asked to facilitate the funding of the deficit to the extent that it is allowed to intervene in reducing it.

X. Bridging the Gap Left by the State

We have the impression that history is speeding up as we draw near the end of the twentieth century, with the danger of catching us without many new ideas or with ideas that have hardly had time to settle. The loss of prestige of State interventionism must be accompanied by the progressive maturing of the institutions that could eventually fill this gap.

Those who can do it, should do it. They have a moral obligation. And it is urgent because a crisis of values is rocking the foundations of society.

Breathing new life into society, making demoralisation a thing of the past, is in the hands of institutions which have sufficient power to do this at any particular moment in time. And, in my opinion, not too many institutions have this capacity in Spain, apart from banking. This concentration of power is an advantage and a risk. But, as I said earlier, risk is part and parcel of the banking business. The opportunity is undoubtedly historic.

Chapter 4

On the Social Responsibility of Banking

LUIS A. LERENA

I feel that a precise definition of the „abstract concept" of social responsibility is all the more important when we are talking about social responsibility in banking, because there is a sort of oral tradition in banking which suggests that banking fulfils its social responsibility by supporting and promoting certain artistic and cultural activities. Thus, financing exhibitions, purchasing works of art, or providing economic support for scientific research are the material manifestations of what could be interpreted as social responsibility. This idea probably originates from the behaviour patterns of some American banks, especially Chase Manhattan in the glorious days of the patronage of the Rockefeller family. Our own Banco Urquijo was, at one time, another brilliant characteristic example of this type of action („a humanist bank"). However, it is - at the very least - risky to believe that this type of action covers the social responsibility of financial institutions.

First, it should be pointed out that, although we may not accept that action in the field of art or culture serves to define social responsibility in banking, by no means is bank activity in this sphere being questioned. But these activities seem to correspond much more closely to a policy on image and, consequently, all the financing for these could come under advertising expenses. Investment in cultural activities is totally justified, and should be included under operating and marketing expenses, although social responsibility is not necessarily being fulfilled through these activities. The dictionary definition of responsibility is *„obligation"* to another party, which suggests that unilateral altruistic or generous action does not tally too well with what is called social responsibility.

For the economist, the definition of social responsibility best suited to his professional sentiment is along Friedman's liberal economicist line. We can start the discussion from Friedman's idea that a company has one, and only one, social responsibility: to use its resources in activities aimed at maximizing profits, provided that it keeps to the rules of the market game; in other words, it takes part in free open competition without deception or fraud. In short, the company fulfils its social responsibility by performing its function as an economic agent responsible for organising and managing the production factors necessary to obtain a volume of production that brings it maximum profits. This is to be done according to the rules of the market economy.

Banks, like any other companies, assume a series of responsibilities towards other economic agents which form part of the society in which they operate. The most direct of these are the shareholders, staff and customers, while the citizens who constitute the social environment in which the financial institution moves or operates are also indirectly involved. The question we must ask is whether the responsibilities the company has towards these groups of people are also fulfilled, by meeting the economic objective of maximizing profits.

There is no easy answer to this question and the criticism levelled at Friedman's position is justified. Its justification resides more than anything in the fact that Friedman's view is - or is interpreted as being -a view of what short-term profit is. The problem is especially important in the banking sector, because banks work with a view of their tasks and of the effects and range of their decisions which does not generally go beyond the short term.

This view, which may quite rightly be regarded as short-sighted, does however have its justification. Public confidence is essential for a bank to function, but this confidence can be lost in a moment. Consequently, banks always have to see that their decisions serve to guarantee public confidence both immediately and in the short term. The constant attention that has to be paid to the immediate consequences of their policies involuntarily leads to little or no attention being paid to the long term.

When a bank concentrates exclusively on maximizing profits in the short term, it may, first of all, miss long-term business opportunities. The banking sector faces this dilemma every day. When programmes are designed to reduce operating expenses and, to do this, staff reductions are planned, there can be no doubt that the objective is short-term: to reduce costs and, thus, obtain higher profits. This has the immediate effect of increasing the confidence of shareholders, customers and the society as a whole, and will prevent any risk of a bank crisis due to lack of confidence. However, the indiscriminate reduction of expenses or staff could jeopardize the institution's profitability in the long term. For example, staff reductions made under the pressure of urgency could bring the loss of those with the capacity to develop new activities, which the changing banking business may make it necessary to undertake in the future. Thus, the bank's long-term profitability may be negatively affected, even though profits are improved or even maximized in the short term. The conflict between the long and short term as regards fulfilling social responsibility is clear, according to the Friedman model. Unfortunately, as commented earlier, the pressures and urgency of the banking business often mean that long-term concerns and views are relegated to second place.

The fact that the short term takes priority also brings risks of conflict between the different groups affected by the company's action. The disparities between long and short-term results have a different effect on the commitments the company has to the different groups of people. It could be claimed that the conflicts between the long and the short term conceal possible conflicts between the social agents involved. Thus, the concern that shareholders never lose confidence would lead to a policy whereby dividends never fall, come what may. With this end in view, besides reducing staff, assets may be sold in order to obtain capital gains (hidden reserves) so that dividends can be paid. The company becomes weaker and the risk for customers and employees increases. Not to mention the problem of the moral risk which could arise as a result of using guarantee funds to cover deliberate „taking a gamble“ policies.

Note that this is not to suggest that the public and private interests of the bank or company are in opposition to each other. There is no need to pose the problem of social responsibility in terms of the conflict between public and private interests. The point I am trying to emphasize is that the adoption of a policy or strategy in a institution with a short-term approach could make it more difficult to fulfil other important long-term objectives which form part of what constitutes social responsibility in banking. From a strictly short-term point of view, no bank, nor possibly any private company in any productive sector, would be likely to adopt a policy to defend the environment. However, from a long-term perspective, the respect and defence of the environment guarantee the future profitability of the company and its survival, which in turn ensures that it will be in a position to fulfil its social responsibilities better over a longer period of time.

My first conclusion here is that, when a bank maximizes its profits, it can better fulfil its social responsibility, if its objectives adapt to criteria and views of long-term profitability. Thus, the Friedman idea is easier to defend, although we may never feel satisfied about the extent to which we fulfil the obligations imposed by social responsibility. In any case, it is a question of drawing up an economic- rather than economicist - principle, to help us to obtain a concrete idea of so-called social responsibility.

Another conclusion is that the long-term criterion or view must be accepted and adopted by all the social agents. The shareholders, for example, must not see the company as a source of short-term profits. They also have to understand that certain interruptions in the generation of large profit flows and, even the reduction or suspension of dividends at certain moments in time, could be the guarantee that the company will survive and will be more profitable for them in the longer term. They have to accept that their real interests are being defended by these actions. However, this is not the general criterion of shareholders nor, above all, of the markets. The shareholder should not have the mentality of a pirate who goes to the company to grab the dividend and run. At least, this type of shareholder should not receive any special protection from the managers of a company which has a social responsibility. Naturally, the employees of the institutions and their managers must also have the same view.

The view I have just described leads us to the conclusion that social responsibility is closely linked to banks' capacity for generating profits. Banking cannot be expected to undertake activities which reduce its profit-making capacity and which, consequently, jeopardize the institution itself, and the interests of other groups related to the banking business. The shareholders have the right to demand prudence as regards all banking expenses to prevent their interests from being harmed. The expenses or investments which may be made in order for banks to become involved in the interests of the population or of the geographical areas where they work should not reduce their profit-making capacity, but, on the contrary, should be made on the principle that they may serve to increase profitability in the future.

In short, a clear distinction has to be made between what is purely altruistic activity in banking and what is genuine social responsibility. It may be that part of the social responsibility can be fulfilled through altruistic activities. However, extraordinary or constant altruistic initiatives cannot be expected, since these must necessarily be first voluntary and always limited by company profits. On the other hand, it would be reasonable to ask for the economic activity of profit-making to consider the interests of all the groups involved and for social responsibility to adjust to profit performance above certain minimum levels, which must necessarily be maintained.

Many of the requests for altruism or generosity made to banking arise from a sort of inappropriate social contract which has prevailed for years and which has been particularly characteristic of the Spanish banking system. Indeed, in our case, when Spanish banking was subject to intervention and protection, it was capable of generating a considerable volume of extraordinary profits, because of the lack of competition. It was implicitly accepted by everyone that banks had the obligation to put part of their extraordinary profits into fulfilling certain responsibilities towards the communities in which they did their business. What is more, the Government had the implicit right to ask banks for attitudes or conduct which favoured public interests in exchange for the privileges it had granted. Thus, banks were obliged to subscribe to public debt or to charge low interest on loans granted to those sectors of the economy which were regarded as priorities in Government policy. Social responsibility was defined in an unwritten bilateral contract which obliged the parties involved to lend each other services.

However, now that this protection has disappeared and banking has become a business subject to tremendous competition, with limited profit margins and a tendency for the prices of services to be the same as production costs, activities which are altruistic, or simply unjustifiable according to business principles, are unfounded. The implicit social contract has been broken and the privileges have disappeared. Banks cannot be expected to make this type of sacrifice, because their profitability would be put in jeopardy and, consequently, so would their capacity for survival.

Some of the demands for social responsibility come from attempts to prolong this situation. Thus, a burning problem in Spanish banking is, for instance, that of its participation in industry. As a result of the industrial crisis, Spanish banks have withdrawn significantly from industry and do not play the same part in promoting these businesses as they did in the past. The risks involved in industrial activity have increased. The legal requirements for provisioning and allocation of capital for this activity make it almost untenable in today's competitive environment. European Union regulations are very tough and restrictive on this matter. The returns that can be obtained are very low and certainly do not guarantee maximization of profits. All of this has led banks to reduce their positions in industry. The banking sector is frequently accused of not fulfilling its social responsibility towards industry. But the situation has changed and this must be understood. Today, banking has to approach its participation in industry in the same terms as its participation in any branch of business. If the business is profitable, then it is involved. If not, it keeps out. In this sense, some will say that the social responsibility of banking has become economicist and that any desire to create or support business ventures has been lost.

The economic treatment of these problems of social responsibility puts them in an objective context and surrounds them with cold criteria that put an end to any call for sentiment. The introduction of a market economy can indeed alter the meaning of many altruistic attitudes. Singer reminds us that, when blood cannot be bought, blood-donning implies giving something priceless, and the doner himself sees it as giving the „gift of life". But, when blood can be bought at $50 a bottle on the market, giving blood has no more significance than giving $50. The introduction of the market and of the idea of profit undoubtedly restricts the value and the meaning of many altruistic attitudes. But the economist must always question the economic sense of these attitudes.

Chapter 5

Ethics in the Management of Financial Institutions

JESÚS DE GARAY

I. Economic Goods and Ethical Goods

We sometimes forget that ethics and economics have something in common: they both deal with goods. Ethics deals with goods in general, while economics is restricted to a certain type of goods. That is to say, ethics studies goods in its broadest sense, i.e. not only economic goods, but goods of all types (Garay 1994b, pp. 1-19).

This means that ethics belongs to the foundations of the economy. Ethical questions are not alien to economic activity, but are in fact its source of inspiration. Economics aims to identify, produce and distribute goods. And in this sense it is an ethical discipline (Sen 1989, p. 20).

To overlook this point is to ignore the ethical assumptions which are inevitably behind every economic theory or activity. One example may suffice: today, the market economy is based on the idea that freedom -and economic freedom specifically - is a good; secondly, it assumes that wealth is a good; and thirdly, it accepts that this good of wealth should be distributed fairly amongst all men. If any of these assumptions were denied, the result would be a different type of economy.

Another thing that ethics and economics have in common is that they try to discover which goods are real and which are apparent. In other words, both attempt to look beyond appearances to discover the causes, the reasons, the bases for goods. Perhaps economics uses mathematics while ethics does not, but the same rational effort is made in both cases to discover real genuine goods.

But do ethics and economics both talk about goods in the same way? Or, to put it another way, is there anything in the ethical point of view which distinguishes it from the economic point of view? In short, it is a question of finding out whether good management of a financial institution is the same from the ethical view point and from the economic viewpoint.

Now, the ethical treatment of goods is characterised by the fact that it alludes to absolute or unconditional goods. That is to say that ethics studies goods, but from the point of view of absolute goods. It examines which goods should be sought and which should be avoided: everywhere and all times. What is peculiar to ethics is precisely that: analysing which are primary goods, since all others are subordinate to these. In other words, ethics deals with universal goods, i.e. the goods which are truly good in any circumstances.

For example, a theory that is typically ethical would be: man is preferable to things (Kant 1983, pp. 91-92). That is to say, man is a better good than things whatever the circumstances and conditions. This is an ethical statement, which is almost unanimously accepted in our culture, and which establishes a primary good, namely man.

In this sense, modern ethics is humanist, because human dignity is one of the central values. Consequently, economics is also humanist, since an economic good is by definition a good belonging to man.

Thus, the first thing to be said is that the management and administration of a financial institution is essentially an ethical task. Whether we like it or not. Because it deals with goods. Consequently, all decisions, all strategies, all policies have a fundamental ethical component.

What is more, this is true of all the facets of the people who work for a financial institution: their intentions, which materialise in specific decisions; their actions and their omissions; their characters, or, as we tend to say, their virtues and their vices; and, of course, the customs and habits which define human relations.

II. Wealth, an Ethical Good

The difficulty, quite obviously, is in being specific. To talk about man in general is still very vague. However, it is difficult to establish a hierarchy for the goods belonging to man. For example, physical well-being is a good which belongs to man. So is health. And the survival of the body. And freedom. Perhaps - at first sight - the survival of one man would appear to be preferable to another man's headache, or to larger profits on a company's books; or even preferable to a building or a car. But it is precisely here, in trying to be specific, where the difficulties of ethics reside.

A hierarchy of values is absolutely necessary for the management of a financial institution. It is essential to be quite clear about which good is regarded as being the most important, which comes second, which comes third. and which comes last. A clear sign that the institution is managed with a sense of ethics is when this order of values exists. And vice versa: when no attention is paid to this point, it is sure sign of an institution's contempt for ethics.

It is not easy to order economic goods within the set of goods. For example, assuming that wealth -in general - is the object of the economy, then the question is to examine whether wealth is the primary good or whether it is subordinate to other goods.

Of course, it would indeed seem that wealth is a good belonging to man (Hernández Pacheco 1991). The problem is not so much this, as knowing what other goods belonging to man it is subordinate to, if it is indeed subordinate to others. And in what circumstances.

Wealth indeed appears to be a good: it is an apparent good for men, since there can be no doubt that men wish to be rich. However, there are men who claim that this desire for wealth should not be seconded on certain occasions because, although it is an apparent good, it is not always a real good; although it appears to be a good, sometimes it is not. There are even those who consider that the real good is not wealth but poverty.

In my opinion, this is the crux of the question which should be posed when talking about ethics in the management of financial institutions. We need to know whether the acquisition of wealth - a good for man and obviously the goal of any company, and also of financial institutions - is a primary good or not. And when and how. In other words, it is a question of considering what place profits have within the set of goods provided by the financial institution.

What is undoubtedly true is that profits are an apparent good. To put it more crudely, everyone likes making money and considers it as being a good. And the more, the better. The problem resides in knowing the place of these profits within the set of goods: in other words, whether it is preferable for a company to make less money if these means achieving better goods.

Now we can make the first clarification: at a financial institution, profit and profitability are goods which condition other goods. It is not that they are the most important goods, but, without these, there can be no other goods.

In a market economy, if a company is not profitable, it will soon or later disappear. The condition for all the goods which come from a company is that the company survives. This seems obvious, but it is important: if a company is not viable, then few or no goods can be expected of it.

In this sense, profitability unquestionably has an ethical value in a market economy. Perhaps small profits on the income statement do not have much ethical importance in themselves. But they are important, inasmuch as they are the condition for many other goods with great ethical value, such as a series of jobs in which the lives of families depend.

Thus, then, the ethical question as regards profitability is not whether or not ethics is profitable: that is an economic problem. What is decisive ethically speaking is that profitability is an important ethical good in business, because it is a prerequisite for many other goods, such as the physical survival of the people who work in a certain company.

Business is said to create wealth. Generally speaking, creating wealth is the same as producing goods or making profits. The problem is that the concept of wealth is ambiguous, because it includes different meanings of good.

In the first place, the notion of wealth refers to the profits which enable the shareholders, managers and the company's staff in general to become richer. But behind the idea of wealth there is a second meaning that refers to the goods created by the company which benefit society as a whole, and not only those people who belong to the company in one way or another.

Consequently, the question is whether it is preferable for only the members of a company to benefit, or whether it is preferable for the society as a whole to benefit. Generally speaking, it would appear to be preferable for the whole of society to benefit rather than just a part of it (i.e. only those people who form part of the company). However, the only way society as a whole can benefit is if the people who comprise the company benefit first, because - once again - if the company is not profitable, it will disappear and any subsequent benefit to the society as a whole will simply not exist.

III. The Different Interpretations of the Goods of Man

A serious ethical problem is that not everybody interprets goods in the same way. There are discrepancies as regards real goods. However, this is not such as serious difficulty for the market, because those who operate on the market accept the freedom of trading. And, consequently, they assume that the goodness of the goods is marked by their price. Thus, the different interpretations of a good are negotiated until a price which is valid for both parties is determined. It is not that everyone agrees that a certain price denotes the real goodness of the good. But the price is fictitious in terms of the real price of the good, and this fiction is freely accepted by both parties. In this sense the market is an excellent means of getting round divergencies about the real value of things.

However, ethical discrepancies exist, even though the market makes them less rigid and smoothes them out. That is why there are many markets; that is why there is also a wide variety of legislation on economic activity, and that is, of course, why so many different business cultures exist

Different markets are born when there are people who consider certain goods as being valuable, whether these be paintings, books, cattle, shares, metals, etc. When a group of people interpret that certain realities are a good, then markets for these goods are easily created. In the same way, the legislation of different countries governs certain goods and ignores others, precisely because they value some goods more than others.

Companies also act in the same fashion. A company assumes that manufacturing or distributing a product is a good that is preferable to other goods. And it also assumes that the work of its staff should be conducted in one direction and not another. In general, the managers of a company believe that there is one good way of running a company as compared to others. All of this implies a company culture: corporate philosophy, as it usually called.

In other words, each company has its own culture, which defines its own way of interpreting goods. The culture of a company is an ethical concept: it involves certain theories about what is good and what is bad.

A financial institution's ethical code is not a minor matter in management and administration. On the contrary, it is like the ultimate nucleus of values around which all the institution's business revolves (Garay 1994a). It explains which primary goods the institution is pursuing: its ultimate objectives. And it explains how the other goods are subordinate to these final goods. An ethical code states whether there are any absolute and unconditional goods which may not be neglected under any circumstances.

How a corporate culture - and especially its ethical code - materialises in practice is a different matter, but the most important thing is undoubtedly that a company knows what criteria govern its movements, what its objectives are, what its strengths and what its weaknesses are. It is different, for example, to consider that everything is negotiable or, on the contrary, to declare that there is a set of absolute values which will never be changed. There are companies which are not too concerned about receiving gifts from customers, while this practice is strictly forbidden at others. Knowing - simply knowing - what one's culture is, the conduct peculiar to a company, is already a big step in this institution's ethics.

Generally speaking, many values in the cultures of financial institutions, and of the majority of companies, tend to coincide (for instance, free contracting, profitability, work as a means of enrichment, equality, etc). But the points which distinguish one from another are those which give each institution its own particular identity (the emphasis on aggressive policies as regards competition, the interest in training people, the rigour or laxity in obeying legal regulations, the concern for profits, etc). According to the good which is considered to be more important than the others -and not so much in theory as in practice, in decisions and actions -, the culture and ethics of one institution differ from the culture and ethics of other institutions.

IV. Real Goods and Apparent Goods

It is easy enough to simply conclude that financial institutions as a whole have different ethical conceptions. It is much more difficult to pinpoint which goods are really - and not only apparently - the most valuable in absolute terms, and consequently should be included in all their cultures, their styles of conduct and their ethical codes. It is difficult to discover the truth, especially as far as ethics is concerned. And because error exists, so does truth. Mistakes are made in both economic management and in what could be termed ethical management.

Thus, the question is to clarify which goods a financial institution should propose as objectives in management and administration. This is relevant to a market economy, since the market is a form of democracy, where the tastes and preferences of consumers (of the „people“) determine that a certain product is manufactured. Logically enough, the manufacturers try to persuade the public to buy their products, but the customer always has the last word, since he is the one who decides whether or not to use the product.

To put it another way, the market produces and sells what people see as being good, although it may not necessarily be what really is good. This means that a company may get rich by distributing products which appears to be goods but which are really evils: this is the case of drugs, white slave trafficking and antiecological products.

If the owner of a company orients his business exclusively according to the dictates of the market, then he will have no compunction about distributing products which are really bad, provided that they respond to demand which brings profits. For example, he would not mind trafficking drugs or slaves - if this were, legal -, if it brought profits. There can be no doubt that profits are apparently a good, but, in these examples, they are really an evil, because they are obtained by, destroying more important goods, such as, for example, health and personal freedom. In other words, an ethical view of the market means that not only must people's preferences be taken into account, but also what is really a good for them.

We could also say that, if market flows are determined by people's tastes, then any entrepreneur who wishes to behave ethically should provide consumers with not only the goods they are most interested in having, but, first and foremost, with the goods that, in his opinion, are really good for them. That is to say that arousing dormant tastes for real goods is ethical conduct, to be recommended for any entrepreneur in a market economy.

For instance, granting a loan is not an aseptic matter, exclusively governed by the economic return on the operation. Many things are in play, such as developing a certain company, the future of a people, the political stability of a country, etc. Investment, saving or consumption are not indifferent matters in ethical terms. Certain trends in society can be fostered or prevented by the financial powers. What is more, they are effectively fostered or prevented, even if one has no desire to consider the consequences of one's decisions.

If freedom were man's only good, then this problem would not exist. Satisfying people's desires would always be licit, even if we were convinced that it was harmful for them or for other people. But, in my opinion, freedom is not man's only good. Of course, freedom is an important good for man: so much so, that if it is lacking, there are no specifically human goods. Without freedom, man only has access to goods which are common to animals, plants or stones, but not peculiar to him.

Freedom is an important ethical good, because it is the condition for everything else. But it is not the only good. For example, the good of freedom is not the good of sexual pleasure or the good of friendship, but, without freedom, there is neither human sexuality or friendship (Garay 1994b, pp. 227-230).

Freedom is ethically a basic good, and perhaps the most elementary of all in human life. If there is no freedom, then there is not even morality. When one acts out of violence, there is no moral responsibility. In this sense, there is no specifically human good which can be obtained without freedom. The greatest goods are no longer the greatest if they are not freely desired; there is no good for man without freedom.

But freedom alone does not automatically make conduct good. The voluntariness of the contracting parties is not enough for the result to be a good. The justice of a contract is a question of more than the willingness of the parties. A financial institution should not simply assume that the freedom of the contracting parties makes all its actions just. There is no justice without freedom, but neither is there justice with freedom alone (Hayek 1991, p. 35).

In short, it is important to identify the real goods a financial institution should be looking for, as its managers will be systematically tempted to satisfy market demand, without asking themselves whether the preferences of possible customers are really a good or an evil. The management and administration of a financial institution should revolve around these real goods.

V. The Power of Financial Institutions

Some of the real goods of financial institutions have already been mentioned. Firstly, we have stressed that freedom is the prerequisite for every specifically human good, and, consequently, people's freedom must always be respected when managing and running the institution. Secondly, we insisted that profitability is equally a real good for the institution, because it is a necessary condition for the other goods it may provide. Now there is another real good for a financial institution to add to the list, and that is power.

Generally speaking, a financial institution has power, capital, resources, and assets. Wealth is power (Smith 1988, p. 166; Hobbes 1987, p. 69). Every company has initial power which, when invested in a certain way, will bring it certain benefits. These assets are extremely varied: from human capital to property, money or securities. In other words, it has wealth - power - at its disposal. Capital which is invested or spent. And precisely what it attempts to do is to create new wealth, from this initial wealth.

However, the power of financial institutions has its own particular features. To be precise, the first thing that strikes one is that it is great power. Financial institutions are large companies. They are institutions which carry weight in the life of society, like any other large company.

It may be argued that having great social power is not in itself good or bad. Power is only a means, and consequently, its ethical value does not depend on the power itself, but on the ends to which it is used. That is to say, power is good or bad depending on how it is used. It is better for an infinitely good God to be all powerful rather than weak; and the contrary is also true.

Now, a financial institution can only fulfil its function if it has sufficient power to provide the resources required on each occasion; and it is obvious that some investments require large volumes of resources. Moreover, sufficient resources are also required to control the risks which necessarily arise from lending operations.

Thus, then, having great power at one's disposal is not in itself good or bad. It depends how it is used. But a financial institution can only generate goods, do something good if it is very powerful, if it has great power. This is a condition which is necessary for it to fulfil its function. If it is not powerful, then it simply cannot exist. Consequently, in the case of a financial institution, having great power is effectively a good. What is more, it is a great good, because it is the condition for all the goods a financial institution can produce. Only if someone were to completely deny the fact that a financial institution generates wealth, would it be meaningful to argue about the need for it to be powerful.

Consequently, ethically speaking, the management and administration of a financial institution necessarily involve seeking and preserving great power. Or, in other words, the institution must be solvent, and must have sufficient liquidity, etc. If a financial institution is weak, then it is ethically bad, because it can hardly provide goods, or can only produce goods inconsistently or in small quantities. To put it another way, the good economic management of an institution is ethically important inasmuch as it makes it stronger and more capable.

So, then, in terms of ethics, the accumulation of power at a financial institution is positive. This is a simple statement; it is the same as saying that it is better for a hospital to be powerful, in the sense that it has the most modern instruments, the most highly-skilled doctors and the best-equipped buildings. The more power the better, as the goods that can be produced will also be better.

The power of a financial institution comes, first and foremost, from the fact that it deals with money, and money is the means par excellence. In our society hardly anything can be done without money. It is an instrument which is absolutely necessary. Perhaps money in its physical form - notes and coins - is not so necessary, but at least the reference to money is constantly required in everyday life.

Thus, being involved with money brings particularly strong power with it. If anyone were to have absolute power over money, they could manipulate any of today's societies at will. Money gives its owner very extensive power; money buys education, status, knowledge, experience... Many human possibilities are realized thanks to money. Perhaps not all of them, nor the most important, but certainly many quite important ones.

Other powers are more limited. It is difficult to find such versatile and universal power as money. The versatility of money is what makes bankers and the managers of financial institutions in general so powerful. Even political power does not go as far as the power of money, which even controls the smallest trivialities of everyday life.

Everyone needs money: the State, pensioners, political parties, newspapers, trade unions, televisions, churches, companies. And they need it constantly all day long. Thus, in comparison with the different powers in society, the power of financial institutions appears as a fundamental power sought by everyone.

This power is exercised, above all, by fixing a price for this money which everyone desires so fervently. And as the demand for money is intense, the result is that profits in the money business -profit margins - can be particularly high.

However, the power of a financial institution does not only reside in its power over money or over securities. Its power includes a whole range of assets, from something as tangible as the branch network to something as intangible as the confidence customers have deposited in the institution, and includes the people who work for the institution in one way or another. If you like, these powers are common to all types of companies, not only to financial institutions. But, even so, as it is a large company, the sum of powers gives it great power.

In any case, power should not be confused with the violent domination of others. There is a certain tendency to identify power with violent domination. According to this, a powerful person would be one who dominates other people with violence. This is a serious mistake. It is true that a person with power has the possibility of abusing his power and thus dominating others. But this possibility is no more true than the opposite: not dominating others. And in fact there is a third possibility: using the power to benefit others, as a service to others. If this confusion is not cleared up, power will always be viewed as criminal, when really it is a condition for all good.

VI. The Abuse of Power

However, many of the ethical problems affecting financial institutions undoubtedly arise from the abundance of power. On the one hand, as mentioned earlier, abundant power is not in itself negative, but, on the contrary, it is a good. But, on the other hand, it is true that corruption generally goes with excessive power. The tendencies and desires of men are not always honourable. Quite often they want to do things which they themselves - or other people - regard as wrong. And if they have the power to do these things, their desires carry more weight than any possible moral objections. That is why some say that corruption always accompanies power.

Unfortunately, the abuse of power is a very human way of using power. However, logically enough, power can only be used when someone has more power than others. Only if power is great, can it be abused. For this reason, the abuse of power is a type of corruption which is typical of financial institutions.

But, I must insist that this does not mean that great power is negative in itself. If the State is not powerful, it cannot fulfil its function, in the same way that a financial institution cannot if it is not strong. The weakness of a financial institution is an evil, not a good.

Can the abuse of power be avoided, or does it have to be tolerated, as a sort of lesser evil? Up to now, different ways of controlling this type of abuse have been discovered. Perhaps the first of these was to establish other equally strong powers, together with the financial powers, which balance out possible abuses. In other words, society does not only need a strong financial power, but also a strong judicial power, and strong executive and legal powers. And a democratic society also particularly needs the equally strong power of the media.

These different powers should be controlled by different bodies. Not to foment conflict and to divide effort, but to prevent abuses. If the financial power becomes so strong that it controls the media, for instance, then abuses of power will easily multiply.

The balance of powers does not, of course, guarantee ethics, but it is a strong obstacle to immoral conduct. Consequently, if a financial institution aspires to controlling the media, or if banking is subjugated to political power, it is difficult to control corruption. From the point of view of the general strategy of a financial institution, it is tempting to control the media, but -no matter how profitable the institutions is- it is harmful to society as a whole.

Consequently, from an ethical point of view, the strategy of a financial institution should not be aimed at controlling other social powers. Anything that involves concentrating the power of society in very few hands facilitates corruption and is, consequently, an evil. In short, aspiring to tyranny is ethically an evil.

Another way of reducing the risks of abuse of power is free competition on the market. When different entities are competing for demand, it is more difficult for there to be abuses. For this reason, trying to monopolise is equally harmful for society. The balance of powers should not be only between financial powers and other powers in society, but also between different financial institutions, which are really different powers that balance each other out.

A third way of correcting abuse of power is transparency. Of course, a financial institution cannot indiscriminately publicise all of its operations, because confidence- on which it is founded - is fragile and a degree of discretion has to be exercised in some operations. But, insofar as the shareholders are the legitimate shareholders of the bank, or, in general, inasmuch as the institution has owners who are not the people who manage it, these owners deserve to receive sufficiently detailed information about the situation of the institution. Similarly, customers should receive sufficient information about the institution to which they trust their deposits, in the same way that a worker has the right to certain information about how his company is progressing. Thus, the transparency of balance sheets and contracts is important for correcting abuses of power.

Careful transparent accounting at a financial institution is not only an efficient instrument in good economic management, but also an essential requirement for the good ethical running of the institution. Great transparency for shareholders and customers is not necessary for its own sake: and it may even be counterproductive from an exclusively economic point of view. However, bearing in mind that corruption at financial institutions often derives from the abuse of power, we can conclude that it is preferable to limit some possible profits which could be obtained with greater opacity if this means that a better balance of powers will be achieved in society instead.

For example, the power of the media is a great aid to transparency. On occasion, their work can be a nuisance or even harmful to the institution. Even so, these difficulties are preferable to the abuse inherent to false information which is not contrasted by other bodies.

The defencelessness of customers or shareholders is already a clichÈ, but that does not mean that it is no longer talked about. Some formulas have appeared to articulate the power of customers or shareholders, in the same way that the trade unions organised workers' power in the past. Even so, customers and shareholders are extremely weak powers in comparison with the strong power of the management of financial institutions.

Consequently, a balance of powers which corrects abuses of power, or at least makes them more difficult, is to be recommended. However, it is also important for an institution to be big enough to resist the pressures from these other powers. The temptation to give in is strong, especially when the other powers are particularly strong in certain circumstances.

For instance, the temptation to give in to journalists or politicians in exchange for obtaining certain favours or concealing certain information is always there. Sometimes it is a question of in-and-out blackmail, although it is normally a case of a little pressure being exercised. Giving in to the powerful is an old failing.

Sometimes the powerful party is not so much the financial institution as the television or a political party. In these situations, what is ethical is precisely to affirm one's own power in the face of the other's power. This is another reason for insisting that it is advisable for financial institutions to be strong.

VII. Conflicts of Power

However, conflicts between one power and another can degenerate into an open fight, or into a war. Not into what is so inappropriately called a „war" when alluding to the war over high-yield accounts or mortgages. Sometimes what happens is that the balance between powers is broken and a genuine struggle for power ensues, when the conflict leads to one power being completely subjugated to another, or even destroyed.

These conflicts may occur between a certain financial power and a social power, such as, for example, political power. Conflicts may also arise in competition between different financial institutions. Moreover, it would be naïve to think that these conflicts are rare exceptions. In fact, it seems that minor conflicts constantly occur and major conflicts happen all too often.

The ethical thing to do in the face of these conflicts is to try to keep violence to a minimum. Violence means imposing one's will on others, failing to respect other people's freedom and forcing them to behave according to one's own desires. Now, if freedom is an important good for man, taking away his freedom, or at least making him act against his will, is undoubtedly an evil, and a very serious evil, because it implies the loss of an important good. Consequently, violence is an evil (Hobbes 1987, p. 103). And consequently, anything that reduces the margin of violence is ethically positive.

In short, when conflicts occur in business, the ethical thing to do is to try to dispell them, or at least to try to channel these conflicts into negotiations or pacts. Violence generates more violence, as Clausewitz was very much aware of (1972, p. 40), and the process is only halted by the tiredness which comes with beating down the opponent's resistance. In other words, the management of a financial institution has to try to reduce conflicts to a minimum.

However, this is not always possible. If one has been subjected to violence, a defensive response - which could also imply violence - is ethically acceptable provided that it is in proportion. For example, even if the law and good lawyers allow a person to be put in jail in certain circumstances, this response is not always proportional. And vice versa. The use of violence which is legally sanctioned is not the ultimate ethical criterion on violence.

In any case, as far as conflicts are concerned, the voluntary nature of violence cannot be overlooked. This may seem paradoxical, but it expresses very normal conduct. Let us consider a boxing match, where both parties voluntarily fight in order to beat their opponent or to be beaten by him. Generally speaking, in all sports people voluntarily fight - oppose each other - to break the will of their opponents.

In the same way, in the world of business there is voluntary competition on the market to impose one's own will. In these cases, it is a question of imposing one's will on the competitor, which is in some way violence, albeit minor, because there was the will to do this at the outset. Generally speaking, the market assumes that this régime of competition was voluntarily desired by the majority of the players.

Generally speaking, voluntarily submitting oneself to rules which govern conflicts is a way of reducing the margins of violence. This is the usual situation in the majority of societies, where there are laws which govern conflicts and are interpreted by judges. The existence of these laws and judges makes it possible to keep violence within certain limits, and these limits constitute the institutional violence of the State.

Consequently, a financial institution's strategy should be directed at competing with others within the law, i.e. following the rules of the game which the competitors have voluntarily established. Anything which fuels conflicts outside these rules of the game is ethically an evil, because it increases violence.

However, in critical situations, when someone is frightened of being totally defeated, or, when someone aspires to demonstrate his superiority over the other powers once and for all, he may well use any means to do this.

A financial institution can easily run its business by trying to concentrate excessive risk, getting round legal limitations or blatantly overriding them, provided that the these risks and offences can be concealed by giving the accounts cosmetic treatment. It is part of a strategy in the power struggle, or, in other words, a way of resolving a conflict between one power and another, to discover who is the most powerful and who imposes their will on the other.

In any case, if we accept that in conflicts of power one party defends real goods (in other words, it is right), while the other party defends goods which are only apparent (because it is wrong), then what is ethically good is for the former to win, for those who defend real goods to impose their will on those who are looking the wrong goods. For example, it is preferable for those who defend freedom to impose their will on those who defend tyranny.

This means any power should not only aspire to seeking and defending real goods, but also to being strong enough to defend its own principles against pressure from others. Of course, it is difficult to know who is right and who is wrong. But, even in a situation of scepticism every power has to be strong, because all of them can be a threat if they suddenly arbitrarily decide they want to dominate.

VIII. Human Capital

Thus, power is a real good for a financial institution. Acquiring and protecting it is a central principle in management. And what makes a financial institution strong? Efficient management undoubtedly. But management is work performed by people. For this reason, it is usually said that the better a company's human capital, the stronger the company. In other words, the staff is an important part of the capital, the wealth and the power of a company. So it is reasonable to say that having capable staff is a good. And, thus, an important part of management is to adequately look after the people who work in the institution.

What is more, if what is ethically valuable is defined by respect and regard for people, then there can be no doubt that an institution which is ethically good is one that takes special care of its staff. Anything that improves people will be ethically good. And if making people stronger, more capable and more powerful is equivalent to improving them, then, if an institution's human capital increases, the ethical value of the institution will unquestionably be greater.

Etymologically the word „virtue“ means strength, capacity, power. While the Greek word „areté“ alluded to excellence, i.e. maximum good, the word „virtue“ refers to power. Machiavelli (1990) used the word in this sense alone to express people's excellence: the power to impose their will. Strictly speaking, Machiavelli's use of the word was not so far from the traditional use: only he saw power as the real good.

Now, if an institution concentrates on improving the capacity, or the virtue of its employees, then it is doing something which is not only valuable in economic terms, but also in ethical terms (Termes 1992, pp. 209-213). And this because it is managing and running the company according a fundamental ethical principle, which is to pay more attention to people than to things. In this sense, the current insistence in economic and business theory on human capital and human resources is a sign of great ethical progress (Schultz 1992).

It should just be pointed out that interpreting human capital or human resources from an exclusively economic point of view is insufficient from an ethical point of view. There can be no doubt that better health, better education, wider experience, greater knowledge, etc. enhances human capital. However, although these are important - or even extremely important - aspects of virtues, they are not the only virtues.

This is, above all, because the idea of human improvement when it only comes second to company profitability is minor ethics, because profits should not be man's primary aspiration. Consequently, improving people in order to make more money would be simply making use of virtues, and ultimately of people. But, even so, the insistence on human improvement and on the acquisition of virtues still has ethical value.

Thus, from the economic point of view, the emphasis is principally placed on selecting people who are very capable and virtuous, because this implies that one has a high level of human capital - staff who are highly-skilled, powerful. In economic terms, what is reasonable is to exclude all those whose capacities are not suitable for the business in hand. In other words, the people who work in a company are selected on the basis of certain virtues which are specially useful to the company. Secondly, from the economic point of view, it is worth encouraging these qualities as much as possible, i.e. with a view to the staff acquiring all the virtues which are useful to the financial business in all its force.

However, the ethical approach puts the emphasis on training, rather on than selection. And it does not put the emphasis on those virtues which are useful to the financial business alone, but on all virtues. Or, to put it another way, it underlines the virtues which are greater goods in themselves, and only then on the those virtues which are minor goods for man.

In other words, if we believe that everyone is equally valuable (or, to put it another way, have equal dignity), then selecting some people and not others has no direct ethical value. It has some indirect ethical value as regards the company as a whole and as regards society: that is to say that having people who have special capacities for a business means that these people will produce higher quality goods than other less skilled people. Thus, the service they give to society will also be better. What is more, because they have their own personalities, and certain characteristics, then their example will clearly influence the general behaviour of the company, and this implies that, from the ethical point of view, it will always be preferable to select the people with the greatest virtues.

It is not the same to look at a virtue from a strictly economic point of view as from an ethical point of view. In one case, the accent is placed on those virtues which are especially useful for the good economic performance of the company, while in the other the stress is on the best general virtues. The two aspects of virtue are different.

This explains why, on many occasions, what is ethically best is not the most profitable. Or, to be more explicit, why the ethical behaviour of some managers may ruin a company. They may have virtues which are very important in themselves, but they may lack the specific virtues which are useful for this business in particular. Moreover, the same could be said of any of the company's other employees.

Thus, if profitability is a necessary condition for a financial institution in a market economy - and thus has great ethical value, as it is a prerequisite for many other goods -, then we can conclude that the virtues necessary for financial business also constitute the condition necessary for the good economic performance of the institution. Consequently, they are ethically valuable, not only inasmuch as they improve man, but also insofar as they make it possible for the institution to be profitable.

In any case, a fundamental ethical obligation in managing and running a financial institution is staff training (starting with the managers themselves). This means devoting priority attention to helping the employees to acquire the maximum number of virtues. If the institution concentrates on them acquiring those virtues which are most useful to the financial business, then it will have made great ethical progress, since this improves people -or at least attempts to improve them - and secondly, because it helps the institution to be more profitable, with all the ethical advantages that this implies.

Of all possible virtues, a market economy necessarily demands the cultivation of freedom. An economy based on the creation of wealth, free exchange and man's freedom can grow, and the more freedom a person enjoys, the greater their power. Thus, personnel managers must foment the freedom of the employees as much as they can.

If a person does not act freely or spontaneously, if he does not have free initiative, if he lacks responsibility, if he does not take on risks, if he does not freely value different options - in short, if his freedom is limited -then his capacity is much more restricted. His power is limited, and his virtue weak. When a man's freedom is restricted, when the value of freedom is rejected, when there is no belief in his free intelligence, then this man is reduced to his animal state; his capacity is reduced to that of animals, and man as a simple animal is not a being with any special capacities.

Freedom is the primary and most elementary power belonging to man, and that is why it is important to help it to grow. Freedom is a peculiar power, because it is a power unto itself, a power in itself. This means that a free person is a person who determines his own power, a person who has control over his own power. This freedom is the first degree of virtue: what is generally called self-control. It is the capacity over one's own capacities: in this sense it is the virtue *par excellence*. It is so elementary, so basic, that it directs the growth of capacities themselves and determines how they are used at each moment in time. That is why virtue is said to be free, inasmuch as the acquisition of virtues is free.

IX. The Use of Power

What is decisive, in any case, is the use of power. In ethics the key is not so much power in itself but how this power is used. Strong power is the condition behind the existence of a financial institution. But this power may be used well or badly. Mismanagement of resources, just from an economic point of view, is already a misuse of this power. Making scant use of human resources is - even from the economic point of view alone - misuse of this power.

It is not easy to get the use of power right. Because it always refers - by definition - to the future and, consequently, to something which does not yet exist, and is full of surprises and unexpected occurrences. Both economics and ethics aim precisely at ordering and articulating the future. At imagining it. In other words, they both try to find good ways of using power.

What use can be made of financial power? The following list springs to mind: violent domination of others, (including hurting certain people), the simple possession of power (and the attempt to increase it), ostentation, pleasure(consumption), service to other people. There may be other uses, but these are the main ones.

1. Violent Domination

We mentioned the violent domination of other people earlier, when we were talking about the abuse of power. Power can effectively be used to control others, or even to hurt them. Hurting others is not alien to human desires. Rancour, resentment and vindicativeness are normal human passions, and are usually expressed in a desire to harm the people we believe to be the cause of our wrongs. Having power clearly makes it possible for our desires for revenge to materialise. This is obviously an extreme way of hurting others, but it cannot be excluded from the different forms of violence.

Personal enmities or old wrongs are often behind sophisticated strategies, ultimately aimed purely and simply at hurting somebody, by destroying their image, ruining their business, hindering their projects or even trying to get them fined or jailed.

Violence can be exercised with all sorts of social powers: a financial institution can try to restrict the freedom of political parties, the media, public institutions, companies, private individuals, etc.

Obviously, violent domination does not necessarily involve bloodshed, but rather imposing one's own will on another against his will, forcing someone to do something he does not want to do. And there are obviously many degrees of violent domination, from extreme physical coercion -which, in the world of business, leaving Maffia-style practices to one side, normally means the application of penal sanctions - to simple pressure which causes a person to alter his decision for fear of reprisals. As Aristotle said, it is the willingness of someone who is forced to throw treasure into the sea to prevent the ship from sinking: there is willingness, but it is very limited and is determined by the pressure - the power - of circumstances (1970, III-1).

Violent domination can be used against the employees of an institution. They may be pressurised to accept a lower wage rise, or some may be pressurised to go and work in another town, etc. The pressures to which workers may be subjected may be -and, unquestionably are - varied and sophisticated. The person with the greatest power can use it to make other people behave in a certain way. (It is also obvious that a trade union committee may have greater power than management, and so may also impose its criteria against management's will.)

Obviously this despotic domination may also be employed with shareholders and customers. As management hold greater power - largely thanks to the information they have - they can impose their will. Normally the way of using force on shareholders and customers is by deceiving them, by giving them false information -in the form of balance sheets which have been submitted to cosmetic treatment, or in the form of misleading publicity - which makes them act according to the will of the executives, and not according to their own principles, since their decision would be different if they were given the true information.

Over the past few years, an increasing number of accusations have been levelled at executives who have taken advantage of their power to the detriment of shareholders. Legally these accusations may be unfounded. However, ethically these claims are well-founded since they are levelled at those who had promised to act in the interests of the shareholders, and who did not do so. This may be because they granted loans which are very difficult to recover, but which suited their own personal interests, or because they accumulated unnecessary risks by taking part in businesses that were unprofitable for the company (albeit perhaps lucrative for them or for people close to them), etc. What is clear is that the shareholders have been manipulated, dominated against their own will.

Generally speaking, when there is no clear distinction between shareholders' equity and outside resources, between the assets belonging to the institution and those belonging to management, between what are customer deposits and what are not, when this type of distinction is not established, and ambiguity and confusion is deliberately sought, then this is a sign that the means are being set up to manipulate shareholders or customers.

Another more general way of dominating others is by deceiving them, by falsifying human relations, by leading another to believe that there is trust when there is not, or friendship when there is ill will, or that one agrees when that is not the case. This form of deceit is almost inherent to some people who assume that hypocrisy is the logical form relations take in the world of business. It is an easy way of using people and of controlling them. It is very easy for the people involved in personnel management to do this, and pretend to show confidence, loyalty, affection and sincerity, when very often nothing like this exists at all. In short, it is deceit and, consequently, violence.

Violent domination of other people is an immoral way of behaving: in other words, it is misuse of power, because it undervalues or scorns the freedom of other people. Not respecting the freedom of other people also involves a loss of power - throwing chances away - for the institution and for society as a whole. The richest source of human power is renounced.

2. The Simple Possession of Power

Another typical use of power is simply possessing it. Having power may seem a minor illusion, inasmuch as it is no more than a means, and consequently, simply possessing power seems rather absurd. However, the figure of the miser is too familiar to overlook. What is more, the cliché traditionally applied to banking is the accusation of avarice and greed. The miser is indeed the symbol of one who aspires, above all, to having a lot of money but without spending it. In other words, in more general terms, the miser is the one who wishes to possess great power, but not use it, or, to be more exact, to limit its use to possession and increase.

Simply accumulating power can of course be motivated by a strategy to dominate other people. But it may also be simply possession, and the motive, then, may be related to looking for security for the future. Or it may also be related to the desire to be superior to other people, not so much in order to dominate them, but simply to feel more powerful than they are. The taste for power, the vanity about one's own strength is not restricted to great strength or physical beauty, as in the case of muscular men or attractive women. Vanity comes in a multitude of forms and one of them is unquestionably the satisfaction deriving from one's economic power or wealth. Luxury is very often little more than the vain ostentation of this superior power in front of other people.

There is a positive side to possessing power, which was stressed earlier: this is the increase in freedom. The satisfaction of knowing that one is free leads one, logically enough, to try to increase this freedom, to try to be more independent of circumstances, to have more say in one's own future. Being freer is equivalent to dominating the future better. This desire to increase one's own freedom even gives one greater capacity to defend oneself better against violence from outside.

This use of power, i.e. mere possession, has a lot to do with the search for security for the future. The future is uncertain and could bring unpleasant surprises. In order to control the future as much as possible, the only possible weapon is maximum power. An illness, the ruin of a company, a change in the international economic situation, a slanderous campaign, the aggressiveness of politicians, the appearance of companies which are competing for the same market share, etc., are all surprises which could occur, and which mean that one needs to be prepared for them.

All of this is of special importance at a financial institution. An insurance company can never foresee with total accuracy the number of car accidents there will be or the seriousness of any natural disasters that might occur. However carefully risks are calculated, it is always impossible to make exact forecasts. For example, twenty years ago, nobody could have imagined the proportions of AIDS, in the same way that no one can exactly measure the damage which may derive from future changes in the climate.

Risk management is an essential task at financial institutions. Thus, the tendency to accumulate power, to possess as much power as possible is a constant temptation, precisely in order to acquire greater solvency. Thus, it is an attractive proposition to constantly invest profits to strengthen the institution, and to reduce expenses and dividends as much as possible.

However, there may unquestionably be a lack of measure in this simple possession of power, for one reason in particular: forgetting the present. Possessing power can be an important objective, not only for a financial institution, but, in general, for any person or society.

The problem is not in recognising that this possession of power is a good that has to be sought, but in the fact that it is not a primary good. That is the miser's mistake, when he forgets about the present and only thinks of the future. A financial institution may also easily make the same mistake of only thinking of the future, only analysing future risks and accumulating resources so as not to be caught out by unpleasant surprises. All of this is a basic condition for the good management of a financial institution. But this must never be at the expense of the present.

The miser's mistake is not that he protects himself against the insecurity of the future by accumulating great power, but that he does not spend this power in the present as well. The miser dresses poorly, lives in a miserable house, eats with extreme frugality and, of course, does not care in the slightest about the present needs of other people.

The immorality in the possession of power is in its lack of measure, and specifically in not measuring the relationship between the future and the present properly. Living entirely in the future is pure nihilism, because the future does not exist. Installing oneself in the future at the expense of the present is equivalent to renouncing life.

What is more, if this extreme possession of power is achieved to the detriment of the power of others, that is to say, if a financial institution obtains excessive wealth to the detriment of others' wealth, then this accumulation is not only negligent nihilism, but also an act of violence towards other people. Violence in the present: violence towards people who are living in the present, in circumstances which are occurring at the present time. This accumulation of wealth may be motivated by profound concern about the possible needs of people who will live in the future, but this is really false- or apparent -solidarity, and conceals indifference about present needs.

3. Pleasure - Consumption and Image

Obviously, consumption is another way of using power. When one has a lot of power, it is easy to misuse it, to waste it, to consume badly. In other words, contrary to what happens in the case of the miser, the lack of measure between the present and the future can occur as a result of excessive concern about the present and neglect for the future. Spending too much implies that one is too concerned about present needs. The „too" implies that insufficient attention is being paid to the future.

There can be too much concern about people's present needs, if this implies endangering the future of many other people. Then it would be a case of apparent -not real- solidarity. For example, if a Bank condones certain debts for a State where there is some poverty at the expense of risking the Bank's future, then an in justice may well be being committed, not only to the shareholders, employees and the bank's customers, but also to many other people - and States -which could well benefit from loans from this bank in the future (Smith 1989, pp. 137-173).

Of course, another cruder way of misusing power is simply the lack of austerity in the institution's personnel and general expenses. Meals, trips, hotels, offices, property, private aeroplanes, cars, and so on, and so forth, can also be out of proportion; satisfying the present desire of many executives often takes priority over the future interests of the institution (and, logically enough, over the interests of shareholders and customers).

Often inordinate pleasure is taken in image, whether this be the personal image of certain managers, or the image of the institution as a whole (González Urbaneja 1993, pp. 267-283). It is obvious that image is not just a personal whim, as it also obvious that it is not restricted to the present. Images are engraved on the memory, and from there they are extremely decisive for the future. A good image means power - great power. Thus, a significant part of a financial institution's power and wealth resides in its image (including the image of its managers).

However, the use of the power of image may also be disproportionate. Recognition, prestige, social esteem, and praise are very human desires, and like any other desire can easily grow out of proportion. There is a lack of proportion when the image given does not correspond with real power, when it is deceptive.

There are always some business cultures which give greater importance to publicity than others - doctrines which emphasise the importance of marketing and doctrines which regard the role of marketing as being exaggerated. But measure is always determined by the veracity of the image. If the image expresses a false reality, then this is violence, manipulation, misinforming the people who receive this image.

4. Service

Nonetheless, there is one use of power at the financial institution, which is the most elementary of all: serving customers and the society as a whole. Does this mean that we are suggesting that all bankers are really philanthropic charitable people who want to serve others ? No, of course not, although the opposite is not necessarily true either. It is simply a case of remembering that a financial institution will only be chosen by its customers if it really lends a service.

In a market economy, the only way one can survive under the pressure of competition is by offering a better service (Basáñez 1992). That is to say, all financial institutions are obliged to lend people a service. Whether this be for purely selfish motives, or with philanthropic intentions, the result is the same, as Adam Smith emphasised (1988, pp. 38-45). This is true of any company operating on the free market.

Thus, service is a very basic use of power, and a condition for all other uses. Serving customers' desires and preferences, paying maximum attention to their requirements and satisfying their needs. This use of power obviously has strong ethical significance (although it has economic significance too).

Consequently, if a financial institution acts efficiently, if it is well-managed -technically well-managed, then it already has great ethical goodness in its favour, because its efficiency shows that it is lending many people a service.

Now, what is the service that a financial institution lends people (its customers in particular and society in general)? What, precisely, is the wealth created by a financial institution which is specific to it and distinguishes it from other companies and institutions in general? What are the particular features which characterise the goods offered by a financial institution ?

X. Communication

In my opinion, there is one answer to all these questions, and that is communication. The good produced by a financial institution is communication. The wealth created is communication. The service provided is communication.

Thus, the particular ethical principle of a financial institution has to be to create communication, to establish communication networks which are useful to people so that they can communicate better with each other. In other words, the great power a financial institution enjoys should be used in one way in particular: to establish communication which is useful to people.

A financial institution does not make cars, or build houses or publish books. These types of wealth, these goods, these services are characteristic of other companies. The goods and services specific to a financial institution are communication and mediation. What is meant by „communication" in this context? The communication of goods. Between all types of people. And not only at the present time, but also throughout the future.

The specific task of a financial institution has always been said to imply intermediation, i.e. establishing mediation, building bridges between one person and another. It is true that market itself already distributes resources, according to supply and demand. But what happens is that, in a complex society, where there is a great diversity of goods, where the population is large, where the geographical, cultural and other differences are so numerous, and where investments are enormous, in a society which is so complex, diversified and ambitious, exchange has to be made easier, and organised and fomented, if it is to be successful.

A financial institution thus helps the markets to become more agile, richer and more efficient. To put it another way, it helps people to exchange their goods according to their most specific desires. How does a financial institution perform this task? In two ways: firstly, by converting goods into symbols, and, secondly, through credit. Let us briefly analyse these two aspects.

1. Symbols

First, symbolisation. It is obvious that the exchange of goods would be much more difficult if the goods had to be carried about for any exchange to take place. If houses, hospitals and factories had to be seen, if the managers and staff of each company had to meet face to face every time a company share were bought or sold, in short, if goods were not symbolised, then communication would bě extremely laborious, so much so that it would undergo a drastic decline (Garay 1994b, pp. 160-218).

Money is unquestionably the symbol *par excellence* of economic life. It makes it possible to transform all sorts of goods into something that can be quantified and compared with other goods. Thanks to money, goods can be quantified by means of a price, which accurately measures people's regard for these goods. And together with money, there are many ways of measuring the value of goods, which facilitate the task of exchange, such as shares, bonds, and so on.

Reducing goods to symbols is certainly one of the great human inventions (Shell 1985), because the possibilities of communication have been multiplied. Accounting is a way of symbolising goods in order to measure them accurately. Ultimately, balance sheets simply evaluate certain goods through theoretically appropriate symbols.

The symbolisation of goods make it possible to do something which would otherwise be unviable: namely to exchange non-existent goods. In other words, goods which will presumably be produced in the future, but which do not yet exist. The options and futures markets, for example, are only possible because of the existence of symbols.

Generally speaking, symbolisation makes it possible to establish links or communications with the future. Of course there is no sure way of telling what the future circumstances will be, but even so commitments can be established which bind the future. That is to say that goods can not only be distributed in the present situation which is known, but also in the future which can only be vaguely envisaged.

Now, all of this is possible thanks to financial institutions, which establish, control and spread these symbols. To some extent, it is the financial institutions which certify the significance of these symbols, and state what they mean in relation to each other. And they do this, simply because they have money and all types of assets, in general.

The role of the issuing bank is undoubtedly essential in this, as are its ethical responsibilities. It is the central bank's job, for example, to ensure that inflation does not destroy the significance of money, and that the value of the currency is appropriate to a country's real goods.

Financial symbols always have a real physical reference. The symbols do not have an abstract meaning, as if they really meant nothing. Figures on the books material good. Handling financial symbols as if they meant nothing is immoral, since it implies that the fact that they correspond to real goods is being forgotten, and is, thus, equivalent to acting without any ethical consideration.

What do financial symbols ultimately mean? Power, goods and wealth. They are securities, they express and mean something valuable. Certainly, they are symbols which often do not directly signify physical goods, but more abstract general wealth or power. In other words, a company's share certificates for instance do not only signify ownership of the company, but also more abstract general power, since these shares can be constantly exchanged for many other goods on the corresponding markets. But, even so, they mean real goods to real people. To put it graphically, financial symbols have a soul.

2. Credit

The other fundamental feature of the communication created by financial institutions is credit. This communication is based on credit. There are other forms of communication which also involve credit. For example, a person who receives information gives certain credit to the one who is giving him the information. Generally speaking, when communication is established on a symbolic basis, credit is required - in other words, confidence that the symbols represent what they are said to represent.

Credit so closely defines financial institutions that even banks - one of the most common types of financial institutions -are actually called credit institutions. Credit is particularly characteristic of financial institutions, because credit is not only established because of symbolisation, but also because of time.

In other words, financial communication is based on credit in two ways: on the one hand, credit must be given to the fact that the symbols mean what they express; and on the other, credit must be given to the fact that actions which are now symbolised will be carried out in the future. The second of these is perhaps the most characteristic of financial institutions, and is that which thus determines the principal good, the fundamental wealth these institutions create. Consequently, it must be the basic criterion which defines and guides the management and administration of a financial institution from the ethical point of view.

What is the exact meaning of credit? To believe. To give credit means to believe someone, and, more specifically, to believe someone who promises something for the future. To give credit means to trust someone's promise. To put it another way, it is communication based on a promise and confidence in that promise.

In finance, promises tend to be mutual, because they are exchanges, the market. Someone promises something which another believes, while this other also promises something which the „someone" also believes. Communication is based on the promise and the credit which is given to this promise.

In short, financial communication uses two types of symbols: first, the symbols which represent physical goods; and, second, a special symbol: the word given by each of the parties involved in the business. The word which has been given symbolises future actions.

So, someone gives their word as a symbol, as a token that they will carry out certain actions in the future. These future actions do not exist, and, consequently, only their word can be given. Normally the word takes material shape in a signature on a piece of paper where the contract -the commitment undertaken by the two parties - is explained. The written commitment is not more than a way of protecting oneself against the other party not keeping their promise, but strictly speaking it is secondary to communication.

Financial intermediation is characterised by constituting a long chain of commitments based on credit and expressed by symbols. If a single link in the chain is broken, the whole chain of the business has to be reconstructed. Thus, never can the importance of the veracity of the symbols and the fulfilment of promises be sufficiently insisted upon, even when we are only considering the economic efficiency of the financial business.

If any virtues were to be emphasised as being specific to financial activity, these would be veracity and loyalty. First, veracity: telling the truth, not deceiving, not manipulating symbols. Second, loyalty, or keeping one's word. Or, to put it another way, telling the truth but not through words alone, but also through actions. Keeping one's word is really no more than telling the truth by means of actions, using actions at some time in the future to affirm what one had affirmed -promised- in the past. Keeping one's word is being truthful over time.

Risk is an essential aspect of financial communication. On the one hand, because the future is symbolised in risk, and future circumstances can never be totally controlled, but are accompanied by surprises which may make this symbolism false. On the other hand, there is the risk that one of the parties may wilfully not keep the promise. One party may always go back on their word and try not to fulfil what has been promised. For this reason, financial management is generally characterised as risk management.

In this sense, the virtue of courage is essential to financial management. A characteristic of a good financier is correctly measuring risk. A faint-hearted person who does not take risks, and a foolhardy person who takes on more risks than he can handle, are people who lack courage. Courage is an aspect of strength, which consists of seeking future goods, in spite of the obstacles. Courage in its own particular way helps to get over obstacles in the form of pressure from other powers (such as the media or a political power), or to get round difficulties like, for example, non-performing loans or defaults of payments.

In sum, the management of financial institutions has its own ethical style. The line of the argument is simple: a financial institution uses its power correctly when it lends real service to its customers; this service is essentially efficient communication; this communication is characterised by symbolism and credit; thus, the conclusion is that *one should* ethically take special care of the purity of symbols and the fulfilment of promises.

Consequently, the ethical goods which should be pursued in the management and administration of a financial institution can be summarized as serving customers to the best of one's ability, providing real symbols and fulfilling promises. Or to express it in a negative fashion: deception is the usual type of corruption in financial institutions, particularly deception in symbols and in keeping to one's word.

XI. The Use of Information

Generally speaking, telling the truth means that information is reliable and appropriate at every level. For example, the information to shareholders, staff, customers, the public authorities and so on, should be reliable. True information is not only a weapon against corruption, but the primary ethical condition of a financial institution, because the first good it provides is communication.

All financial institutions have deception in common. Using information is the usual way of using power in finance, as communication necessarily requires the transmission of information as a necessary element. There are numerous forms of corruption in the world of finance connected to the use of information, and not only because the information given is false, but because the promise to only use information in a certain context is broken.

Normally when a person joins an institution, he undertakes to make certain use of the information which he will have at his disposal. This undertaking refers both to legal regulations and to the institution's internal rules, which include precise instructions. Ethics primarily materializes here: in keeping one's word about the use of information. The virtue which defines the correct use of information is discretion. The person who works at a financial institution needs to be discreet, i.e. to make correct use of the information at his disposal.

For example, the importance of not using privileged information to one's personal ends, unless the management of the institution give their express or written approval, is usually insisted upon. However, what these specific rules about the use of information are, will very much depend on the circumstances of the country, the markets, each particular institution, etc. Obviously, the great principles which govern the market (such as equality before the law) and materialize in different ways according to each historical circumstance will be common to these regulations. But, in any case, even if the laws change, the ethical obligation of not being deceitful will always be valid.

It should not be forgotten that this ethical obligation also materializes in obeying the law, when one has promised to do so. In other words, keeping one's word is particularly relevant in terms of abiding by legal regulations: One is being extremely deceitful when one does not keep to the law. Not only is one deceiving public institutions, the State, or the people who represent the public powers, but one is also generally deceiving the people, society as a whole, the people who form the society.

This statement may appear to be a naïve exaggeration in a society - like Spanish society - where there is a great distance between citizens and the public powers, with the corresponding mistrust one both sides. But it should be remembered that the laws governing the market are precisely the rules of the game that a society has made for itself to regulate economic activity. These rules have been made by the citizens as a whole, and, consequently, put them under an obligation inasmuch as they accepted them. If a person publicly declares that he is against these rules, no objection can be raised. But then this person would have to be asked not to operate on the market whose rules he does not share. However, if he explicitly or implicitly accepts these rules, then he *must* keep to them. If he does not do so, he is deceiving society as a whole.

XII. The Use of Time

Using power to serve other people involves the correct use of time. The financier miss a specialist in time, an architect of time, who knows how to distinguish times. In this, he is very similar to a politician. He deals with the future, but not in general like everybody does, since he always knows how to distinguish the different futures of people, companies, countries, markets, etc.

The financier is an expert in cycles and rhythms. He distinguishes between the youth, maturity and old age of companies and institutions. He measures years, weeks, days and generations. He finds the best moment for each transaction: not a moment earlier, not a moment later. In sum, he is very much aware of the fact that time is not homogeneous, and that the value of each moment is different. Time does not have the same value at each second, or for each person, or for each culture. Thus, the service he should provide requires the correct use of time. In other words, his activities must always be carried out at the opportune moment.

The reference to time is characteristic of the virtues of the financier. That is why we have already indicated that virtues are required of him such as loyalty, which is characterized by telling the truth - or behaving truthfully - at a different time from the time of the promise. Courage is also required of him;

this alludes to measuring risk, and, with it, the future. For this reason, the financier's overriding virtue is the virtue of prudence, which implies getting the temporal or historical circumstances right. It means knowing that what should not be done at a certain moment will have to be done some time later. Or vice versa.

Constancy is another virtue typical of the financier, and this is also related to the correct use of time. It requires maintaining a suitable rhythm, despite unforeseen obstacles and the surprises which always appear. Obstacles tend to hinder action or even bring it to a standstill, and greater constancy has to be employed at these moments to get over these difficulties. Changes, unforeseen circumstances and surprises are essential components of time, and constancy is the feature which governs action when these occur.

What is more, the financier also needs the virtue of patience. There is a strong temptation to go too fast, especially under the pressure of competition. Very frequently, going too fast means concentrating excessive risk, or abusing one's power to the detriment of people or institutions. Thus, knowing when to hurry, when to slow down, and how to resist impatience is a characteristic feature of every good financier.

Recovering patience is important today, and especially so in our society which is dominated by impatience. Our society proclaims the value of present pleasure and undervalues the future good, it tries to eliminate mediations and speed things up as much as possible. In this social environment - even if everybody else forgets -the financier must remember that the true creation of wealth is slow and laborious. Wealth can be acquired very quickly by taking it off other people, but creating real wealth requires a good deal of patience.

XIII. Summary

To conclude, perhaps we can summarize the exposé in a few brief points:

1) Financial activity deals with goods and services, and, consequently, is a totally ethical activity. Any decision, be it strategic, political or of any other description, always has an ethical basis.

2) Ethically speaking, profits are a necessary condition for a financial institution. Thus, efficiency and the pursuit of profitability are unrenounceable objectives in the management and administration of these institutions, from an ethical point of view.
3) From the ethical point of view, it is advisable for these financial institutions to be strong and powerful, as their efficiency depends on this.
4) The management of financial institutions requires the correct use of the power they have, from the ethical perspective. In particular, they should avoid any abuse of power, i.e. any violent domination of other people.
5) More specifically, the correct use of power involves the correct use of the information and the correct use of time.
6) The power financial institutions have should be used to create wealth. The wealth created by a financial institution is essentially communication. Thus, the management and administration of financial institutions should be directed towards the creation of networks which facilitate the exchange of goods between people.
7) The communication created by a financial institution is characterized by symbolization and credit. Thus, management and administration should be oriented primarily towards the accuracy of the symbols, which leads to veracious accounting.
8) Secondly, credit, which defines the communication of a financial institution, requires that the fulfilment of all the commitments acquired by the people who work at the institution at any level.
9) The characteristic features or virtues which should particularly define a manager and staff of a financial institution are: veracity, loyalty, courage, constancy, patience, austerity, discretion and, over and above all of these, prudence.

References

ARISTOTLE (1970): *Ética a Nicómaco*, Madrid: Instituto de Estudios Políticos.
BASÁÑEZ, F. (1992): „Una fundamentación antropológica de la economía de mercado desde la dimensión donal de la persona", in: F. FERNÁNDEZ (Ed.):

Estudios sobre la encíclica Centesimus Annus, Madrid: Unión Editorial, pp. 475-516.

CLAUSEWITZ, C. VON (1972): *De la guerra*, Barcelona: Mateu.

GARAY, J. DE (1994a): „Los códigos éticos de las empresas", in: A. LUCAS (Ed.): *Sociología para la empresa*, Madrid: McGraw-Hill.

GARAY, J. DE (1994b): *El juego: una ética para el mercado*, Madrid: Díaz de Santos.

GONZÁLEZ URBANEJA, F. (1993): *Banca y poder*, Madrid: Espasa-Calpe.

HAYEK, F. A. (1991): *Los fundamentos de la libertad*, Madrid: Unión Editorial.

HERNÁNDEZ PACHECO, J. (1991): *Elogio de la riqueza*, Barcelona: Tibidabo.

HOBBES, T. (1983): *Leviatán*, México D. F.: F.C.E.

KANT, I. (1983): *Fundamentación de la metafísica de las costumbres*, Madrid: Espasa-Calpe.

MACHIAVELLI, N. (1990): *El Príncipe*, Madrid: Alianza.

SCHULTZ, T. W. (1992): *Restablecimiento del equilibrio económico*, Barcelona: Gedisa.

SEN, A. (1989): Sobre Ética y economía, Madrid: Alianza.

SHELL, M. (1985): *Dinero, lenguaje y pensamiento*, México D.F.: F.C.E.

SMITH, A. (1988): *Investigación sobre la naturaleza y causas de la riqueza de las naciones*, Barcelona: Oikos-tau.

SMITH, R. (1989): *La banca universal*, Barcelona: Grijalbo.

TERMES, R. (1992): *Antropología del capitalismo*, Barcelona: Plaza y Janés.

Chapter 6

Ethics in Financial Institutions

RAFAEL TERMES

I will begin with a premise on which my subsequent reflections are based; that the management and administration of a financial institution is essentially an ethical task, whether one likes it or not. The premise is correct in its strictest sense; it would not be so, of course, in the ordinary sense when „ethical", meaning good or correct, is regarded as being the opposite of unethical, meaning bad or incorrect. In the ordinary sense, the management of a financial institution is not necessarily ethical; it can obviously be unethical.

I. Human Acts and Morality

But, speaking with propriety, every free act of man is a moral or ethical act, if we accept that ethical and moral are synonymous. Indeed, every human act can be qualified morally - or ethically - according to moral norms. If it follows the norm, then it is a good act; if it does not comply with the norm, then it is a bad act. And no one is likely to question the fact that the management of a financial institution, like any other type of enterprise, comprises a series of decisions which are human acts. Thus, the management of a financial institution may be carried out in a way that is ethically correct or ethically incorrect. If this were not the case, the research project instigated by the Fundación BBV would be meaningless.

Now, having established this, and to go on with my comments about ethics in financial institutions, it is worth considering, first, what acts in the management of financial institutions are significant or important, and, second, what moral norms serve to qualify these acts.

The first of these obliges us to define what we understand by financial institutions, which will lead us to the ends and means of this type of enterprise, and will also allow us to identify, not only the people who comprise the financial institution, but also those people who are related to it from the outside.

II. The Financial Institution

As regards its purpose, the financial enterprise initially is no different from any other mercantile company. The mercantile company justifies itself through the achievement of a double objective; in other words, by reaching a bifrontal objective, in the sense that the two sides of the objective have to be reached simultaneously. On the one hand, the company should increase economic value, that is to say, it should create wealth for all the people participating in the company. On the other hand, the company should lend a real service to the society in which it moves. If the company does not create wealth, then it cannot be justified in economic terms; if it does not provide a service, then it cannot be justified in moral terms. Both of these are necessary. Let us look at this a little more closely.

Lending a service, a real service, means a service which contributes to the common good. But this common good understood as the realization of „the whole man", i.e. his all-round realization, and the realization of „all men", meaning all the people who comprise society, because a society's „common good" only subsists in the lives of people. Society, although it is a reality, is not a „person"; it does not exist without the people who constitute it. That is why there are companies which, despite creating wealth, cannot be morally justified, because the type of activity in which they are involved causes material or spiritual harm to the people who form society. They do not lend a service so much as a counterservice.

However, at the same time as it is providing a service, the company should also create wealth, and increase its economic value, that is to say, generate income for the people who form the company and for those who are related to it. That is why there are companies which cannot be justified in economic terms, even if the nature of their business is irreproachable from the moral point of view, as they do not generate sufficient income to give satisfactory remuneration for the work done and the capital used.

So much for its purpose. As far as people are concerned, they gather in every mercantile institution and form the company, since the company is, first and foremost, a community of people, those who provide the capital and those who provide the work in order to achieve the objective they have proposed, with the management of the company as the driving force. In this sense, a financial institution is no different from any other. In a financial institution the distinction between shareholder, worker and employer, or manager, is only partially correct, since, on the one hand, there are some people who are both workers and shareholders and, on the other, there are managers who are also shareholders; however, there are also shareholders who do not act as managers of the company in which they have shares, and there are managers who do not have shares in the company which they manage.

But, besides being composed of people, the active and passive subjects of intracompany moral behaviour patterns, the company is related to other people in the environment in which it operates, people who are affected by the behaviour of the people inside the company. Customers and suppliers occupy a special place in this group. The same thing occurs in financial institutions where, because of the nature of the business itself - which we will come back to shortly -, customers are those who demand financial resources and suppliers are those supply financial resources. They are also called, respectively, asset customers and liability customers.

Starting from these general considerations, let us see how the pursuit of the bifrontal objective I have been referring to takes material shape in the financial institution.

III. The Objectives of the Financial Institution

As regards lending a service, the specific objective, which, generally speaking, is the primary activity of the financial enterprise in its broadest sense, is to act as an intermediary between those who, after satisfying their desires for consumption and real investment, have resources which could be channelled towards financial saving and those who need more resources to carry out their consumption and investment projects. In the light of this mission, financial institutions can be defined as companies involved in receiving money from third parties in the form of irregular deposits, with a view to lending it, at their own risk, to those who require financing, under the conditions of security and remuneration which can reasonably be expected to enable the institution to return the deposits and pay the interest agreed to the depositors, while generating profit for those who supplied the risk capital, which is the basic guarantee when capturing these deposits.

In order to effectively perform their function of intermediary between saving and investment, on the one hand, financial institutions must create the conditions to provide remuneration, security and liquidity for the deposits which enable them to foment financial saving, which, in turn, will be used to fund productive investment; and, on the other hand, they must establish the conditions of disposability, cost and maturity for the financing to be granted, so that the resources are allocated to those activities and projects which are most desirable in economic terms. A financial system can be regarded as efficient when it produces optimum capture and allocation of resources; the greater the freedom within which the financial system as a whole moves, the more resources will be captured and allocated.

The deposits the financial institutions receive are irregular because money is fungible and this allows the institutions to invest the resources they have received in deposit, at their own risk, although they are obliged to return what they have received - not physically, but the same amount and the same quality as they received. The conditions in which the financial institutions should invest these resources are those deriving from the conditions established with the depositors; in other words, all the investments should first be liquid enough so that the principal can be returned to the depositors when the deposit matures - which could be on sight - and, second, they should be profitable enough to remunerate these deposits at the agreed cost, while generating profits for those who provide the risk capital, which, as I said earlier, is the basis on which deposits are founded. It is obvious that a financial institution would not be able to attract deposits if it did not have funds to cover the final risk, i.e. if it did not have its own capital which ultimately guarantees the institution's solvency. This is essential and would still be so, even if there were no legal regulations demanding this; but, generally speaking, in every country, and specifically in Spain, a certain volume of shareholders' equity is a prerequisite for capturing resources. And it is equally obvious that, without the remuneration they expect, shareholders' equity and risk capital would not come forward and the enterprise would be impossible.

IV. The Responsibility of Administering External Funds

It can be deduced from the above that the managers of financial institutions are administrators of external funds. And this is the basis for the morality that can be demanded of the behaviour of these managers. Indeed, although sometimes the contrary is believed - and perhaps occurs -, the money the managers of financial institutions have at their disposal is not theirs to do what they like with; they must manage it in accordance with the interests of, firstly, the depositors, who have the right to receive the principal deposited, plus the agreed remuneration, and, secondly, the shareholders, who are the owners of the shareholders' equity, and who invested their funds to obtain a certain return. This return is generally obtained partly in the form of a dividend, and partly, in the form of profit put into reserves, which, if it is used correctly, will produce an increase in earnings per share; even considering movements provoked by factors external to the company, this will ultimately lead to the appreciation of the shares on the market; these two, i.e. the dividend and the appreciation of the share, together constitute the return expected by the shareholders.

The function of receiving and lending money is the principal activity of financial institutions, but, as I commented earlier, these institutions also provide other types of services, which are not directly related to lending, and are all those typical of the mercantile commission. The range of services, other than lending, offered by financial institutions is becoming more and more extensive. Research into customers' needs and the most efficient way of satisfying them has led to all sorts of services; some of them were provided by non-financial institutions in the past and others are completely new. Thus, it is in this field that innovation is most vigorous at the present time.

In exchange for the all-round service financial institutions provide for society they receive remuneration from the people using these services. If for their primary activity, i.e. lending, financial institutions obtain a spread between the interest rate they pay depositors and the interest rate they require from those to whom they grant a loan, for the services which are not directly related to lending - although they may involve risk for the institution - they receive remuneration which is called commission. Thus, the income of financial institutions is the sum of the net interest income, or difference between the interests they charge and the interest they pay, and the commissions for simply providing services. This sum constitutes gross revenues from which, first, the allocations needed to provision loan loss, and then operating expenses, are deducted in order to obtain income before tax.

V. Profits and Confidence

Everything that has been said refers to the service typically provided by financial institutions, although, as we have seen and as was to be expected, providing a service is intrinsically linked to the other side of what I have called the bifrontal objective, i.e. the generation of income for all of those who take part in the process in one way or another. At every mercantile company, the achievement of this side of the objective is ultimately manifested by obtaining earnings for the shareholders, since this will be the sign that remuneration for work has been paid, as have the cost of debt, i.e. the interest on deposits, and the tax, which is the income attributed to the State, with a view, it claims, to redistributing this fairly.

Now, at the bottom line of the income statement, the financial institution is affected in a very different way from any other company. For any mercantile company, obtaining profits is an inexcusable objective since, in the medium and long term, the company cannot survive without profits, and thus any other objective it sets for itself is unattainable. But this requirement is even stronger at the financial institution. The financial institution must always make profits, i.e. every year; and besides, these profits, when compared to the institution's own environment and background, must be favourably valued by the market. The reason for this statement is simple. A company in any other sector can subsist with sporadic losses if its return in the medium term is clear, but a financial institution cannot be unprofitable at any time, because it would lose the confidence of the market. And the confidence of the market is essential to the survival of a financial institution. It is often suggested that the raw material of a financial institution is money. This is not true. Financial institutions do not buy and sell money; they buy and sell the right to use money. The word usury comes from use, and is the word originally employed to describe what we now call interest, which is nothing more than the price of using money. But the right to use money involves returning it. And trusting that the money will be returned, as Jes's de Garay so rightly said, is a question of credit, of believing that the promise will be kept. Even it only happens one year, if the external sign, i.e. profit, that the company is going well is not there, confidence and public credit, is lost and the survival of the financial institution is threatened.

VI. What Type of Ethics?

So far we have looked at the typical activities of financial institutions, at the people who perform these tasks within the enterprise, and those who are in contact with the institution from the outside, are passive subjects of the actions of, in particular, those who manage these institutions. As I said at the beginning, in order to reflect on the morality of these actions, first we need to know what moral rules we are referring to, since the moral qualification for any one action may vary according to the rule we choose.

The emphasis that I have been placing on the person probably already indicates my preference for first person ethics, as compared to third person ethics. In first person ethics, when a person proposes to carry out an action - whatever the external objective he is trying to reach - he asks himself about the relation between this action and his own progress towards his own goal, i.e. what he wants to be, or to put it more clearly, who he wants to be, what sort of person he wants to be. In third person ethics, on the contrary, acts are mainly valued from the perspective of an external observer who judges other people's actions and decides which are good and which are bad, according to conventional norms, the validity of which must either be proved or simply accepted.

First person ethics is the ethics of virtues, which are the potentialities that guide a person towards plenitude or perfection according to the order of being, in accordance with a certain anthropology and view of life. In third person ethics, the question of a person's goal and of the virtues which lead to this are relegated to second place; what is required is that external behaviour, in contrast with what is happening inside the person, performs the acts which the norm sees as good and avoids those which the norm views as bad.

The great weakness of third person ethics is that, since it considers that man's goals are debatable and private, and should not affect how actions are judged morally, it is difficult - if not impossible - to find a constant universal norm on which to base moral behaviour. The different ways of getting round this difficulty are to be found in consensual, relativist, subjectivist and circumstantialist ethics, in which the moral goal determined by the perfection of the subject, is replaced by how to achieve certain personal or socially desirable objectives in each culture, time and circumstance. This stance gives rise to the consequentialist and proportionalist currents, where the morality of human acts in corporate management - but not only in this field - are determined by their consequences or by the expected proportion between the good and bad effects of the action to be undertaken, in view of the greater good or lesser evil which may be effectively possible in a certain situation.

It is obvious, at least to me, that these subjectivist and relativist ethics, which are based on the consensus of opinion and which change with time and circumstances, cannot guarantee the ethical functioning of financial institutions, or of any other company, nor can they provide a steady foundation for a harmonious society. In my view, the reason is that the consensus of opinions is reached, in practice, through a majority vote, which may be a method for living together in peace, but it is not a method of investigating truth. „The truth is the truth, even if everyone believes the contrary". And social ethics cannot be based on anything which is not the truth. Objective truth effectively exists and its norms are to be found in human nature itself; consequently, it is universally and permanently valid.

VII. Virtues Versus Codes

Consequently, I believe that the ethical functioning of financial institutions cannot be trusted to the imposition of codes of ethical conduct, based on the opinion of the majority or on the culture prevailing in each place at each moment in time. The only way in which companies can be ethical is for the people in the companies to be ethical, and not only in their private individual behaviour - which they should also be - but also in their professional, business, and social activity or in whatever way a person's behaviour is expressed in relation to others. I believe that this approach leads to the affirmation that ethical goodness in the management and administration of financial institutions will only be ensured if the people responsible for this management and administration practise all the moral virtues, specified or defined according to the characteristics of this type of institution, when they are carrying out their functions.

VIII. Respect for Freedom

Virtues are those qualities which enable people to direct their behaviour towards good. The first good I will mention is freedom because freedom - freedom of choice - is man's first good. Without freedom there is no true good, but freedom alone is only real freedom when one keeps to truth and good; freedom fails when error or evil is freely chosen, although it also proves that human freedom exists - complete but imperfect. Freedom of choice requires freedom from coercion, that is to say not externally forcing human conduct, not even to impose truth and good, although there may be the real possibility of man using his freedom for deception and evil. For this reason, the primary virtue in the management of financial institutions is the respect for people's freedom - the freedom of the people inside the company and of those who are in contact with the company from the outside. Any form of violence or physical or moral coercion directed at imposing obligations or conditions is in opposition to this virtue.

A specific aspect of this respect for people's freedom, with no form of coercion whatsoever, is the obligation towards both asset and liability customers, and the respect for those who simply demand services. The obligation is to inform them in a correct and intelligible manner of the conditions applicable to the different operations, so that the potential customer can compare these with conditions offered by other institutions and freely decide. This same respect towards people implies that when a customer is captive, because of the facilities the institution has granted him, or for any other reason, advantage is not taken of this circumstance to impose abusive conditions or conditions which are not in line with the market.

Another area where people's dignity should be respected is in the relations with the staff employed by the institution. In this relationship, not only does the economic side of actions have to be considered, but also the psychological and ethical effects these actions may have on others, without forgetting that the three components of the actions should be oriented towards the overall realization of the people in question. Once the essential responsibilities are covered through remuneration - appropriately negotiated for each personal situation rather than globally - a whole series of responsibilities arise: decent working conditions, professional training, promotion opportunities in staff careers, reasonable facilities for solving personal and family problems, etc.

This does not mean that labour relations should follow a „paternalistic" approach, which may offend people's dignity. Quite the contrary, the responsibilities inherent to each post should be demanded, so that, by exercising these responsibilities, people may feel that they are realizing themselves satisfactorily in a meaningful undertaking, and that they can gradually become integrated in business processes. This respect for people requires the strength to make decisions to exclude those who offend their own and other people's dignity by being disloyal to the company, by wrongfully appropriating the company's goods or for any other reason.

IX. The Correct Exercise of Power

In the management of financial institutions, the risk of violating people's freedom is a very real one because financial institutions have power, and the temptation to misuse it can be very strong. I do not believe that the power of financial institutions resides in their size. What is more, I do not even believe that size in itself is a good of financial institutions; the real good which may be related to size to some extent, whether it be to pursue it or pretermit it, is profitability or, to put it another way, the creation of wealth, the generation of income, as I commented earlier. The creation of added value to a level which, after covering payment for work and the cost of debt, i.e. of deposits, satisfies the shareholders, is a real good in all mercantile companies, since if this objective is not achieved then all the other objectives the company might propose - however good they might be in ethical terms - would be unattainable.

Financial institutions are powerful, no matter how big they are, because every one of them in their own sphere of action is in a position to grant individuals and companies financial resources to carry out their investment and consumption projects in the form of loans or capital. This power does not reside so much in the quantity of resources granted; small volumes if the institution is small, and large volumes if it is large. The power resides in the faculty of giving or denying, i.e. in granting to some and denying others, in a completely discretional manner; indeed, nobody can demand that a financial institutional grant them a loan on the basis of objective conditions. Thus, financial institutions can decide on people's welfare and, what is more important, because of the implicit multiplying effect, they can decide which companies will survive and expand, and which will be condemned to stagnation and disappearance. In principle, this power is neither good nor bad; it depends on how the financial institutions use it. If the power is used despotically, those who act in this fashion would deserve to be repudiated as Pius XI repudiated them, when in he said, in words that are obviously archaic today, their power becomes more despotic than any other when, as absolute money-lords, they govern credit and distribute it at their will; it could be said that they administer the life-blood of the entire economy, and thus they have in their hands the soul of economic life; no one can breathe against their will.

However, financial institutions can use their power rationally, and not despotically. One way, which is certainly the usual way, is not to grant credit at whim or to serve the more or less base interests of the managers themselves, but to grant it to those whose conditions indicate that they deserve it. But financial institutions can and should do more in this respect; instead of merely being at the service of the autonomous decisions of industrial and commercial firms to finance the projects undertaken by those responsible for the real economy, financial institutions can make the effort to appraise the projects themselves and evaluate whether the company proposing the project is in a position to carry it out; they can even draw up more suitable alternative projects and suggest that they be carried out, thus taking on a role which is more active than passive.

In this way, the financial institution can use its power to constructively distinguish between companies, going beyond - but not forgetting - the principle of solvency and the repayment capacity of the potential borrowers, allocating the saving to more efficient projects, to the service of competitive strategies which lead to greater economic growth. This discrimination between projects and entrepreneurs would naturally mean abandoning other less efficient investments and might perhaps imply the disappearance of those companies which, because of a lack of innovatory creativity, make with routine businesses in mature sectors. This type of action, based on the rational selection of sectors and activities, would undoubtedly work to the common good and would be a good way of using the power of financial institutions.

X. Liberality and Magnificence

As we see, financial power is exercised through the handling of money, i.e. on the one hand, granting or denying it to those who ask for it and, on the other, putting it, at the financial institution's initiative, to those uses which are believed to be most attractive at each moment in time. The virtues associated with the handling of money or wealth in general, are the virtue of liberality, a potential part of justice, which, according to Aristotle, consists of the moderate use of wealth; and magnificence, part of strength, whose objective is to tend towards the realization of great things, with proportionate spending; in other words, great things, not necessarily because of the quantity spent, but because of the magnificence proportionate to the work, since *great* and *small*, according to Aristotle, are relative concepts. The opposite vices to these virtues are, at one extreme, avarice and meanness and, at the other, squandering and wastefulness. I believe that these virtues which, according to traditional ethics, consist of in a happy medium, i.e. halfway between the vices at one extreme and another, give sufficient enlightenment about what the ethical behaviour of the managers of financial institutions should be when they are using the resources at their disposal. As we pointed out earlier, these resources are not their own, but belong to third parties - depositors and shareholders - towards whom they have a responsibility.

At one extreme, an avaricious or mean approach would be contrary to the ethics of financial institutions if, because of an excessive aversion to risk, which is inappropriate to financial institutions, it led the institution to stop investing in companies which produce wealth and create or maintain jobs, and to exclusively or excessively invest in risk-free monetary assets or, what is worse in social terms, in safe-haven assets such as precious metals, works of art or any other type of unproductive goods which, when they are later sold, are expected to bring speculative profits.

At the other extreme, it would be unethical to squander and waste resources on operations which are only economically and socially productive in terms of satisfying the managers' desires for luxury and ostentation, or of exaggerately promoting the image of the institution; or in terms of controlling the media or pressure groups, in order to protect oneself against potential attack or revelations about the unfavourable aspects of the company's performance; or, lastly, in the pursuit of other ends, which, although they are licit in themselves, cannot be pursued at the expense of the profitability owed to shareholders or the institution's solvency owed to depositors.

XI. Prudence

Achieving a balanced happy medium in the liberal and magnificent use of financial institutions' resources leads directly to the virtue of prudence - not for nothing the guide, measure and reason for all moral virtues - and unquestionably the virtue which should be bankers' characteristic virtue, if I may be allowed - from now on and for the purpose of simplification - to use word banker as a synonym for financial entrepreneur.

Economic prudence - together with individual, governmental, political and military prudence - is one of the five types of prudence contemplated in the works of Thomas Aquinas, although, according to Aristotle, this restricts the word economic to order in running the family business. This does not prevent him from saying that economic prudence refers to the use of wealth as an instrument and not as the ultimate end. And it is in this sense that we say that prudence in the administration of financial resources is the banker's virtue *par excellence*. The banker's ethics must fundamentally rest on prudence.

According to the systematics I have been employing, at one extreme there are two vices, first, imprudence, with its components of haste, lack of consideration and inconstancy; and second, negligence, which is the opposite of care and is shown when the relevant means are not selected. At the other extreme, the contrary of economic prudence is a more dangerous vice than these two, because it presents a certain apparent similarity with prudence; it is cunning, the kind of feigned interested behaviour which, together with deception and fraud, uses crooked means to reach its end.

I do not think it is necessary to insist too much on all these different ways of failing the virtue of prudence, because their very names clearly indicate what prudent behaviour should rule out. I would rather insist on the importance of practising this virtue positively. Someone recently referred to the Federal Reserve's Recommendations made to bankers in 1863. Nearly all of these recommendations are the reflection of the virtue of prudence or indicate the inadvisability of falling into the opposite vices. I will quote just a few of the sentences which confirm that prudence has always been regarded as the banker's characteristic virtue, even though in recent times, both in Spain and abroad, we have unfortunately witnessed examples of behaviour that is not only imprudent but also foolhardy.

Amongst other sentences, the 1863 Recommendations go like this: do not grant credit that is not guaranteed beyond all reasonable contingency. Only facilitate those transactions which are legitimate and prudent. Insist on all paper being paid for at maturity, whether you need the money or not. Never renew an operation simply because you do not know where to place the money to obtain the same return if the payment is made. Spread your credit instead of putting it all into a few hands. Large loans granted to a single firm or an individual, although they may on occasion be licit and necessary, are generally unwise and often unsafe. Every dollar a Bank lends in excess of its capital and reserves, it owes, and its managers are thus under the strictest obligation towards its depositors, and towards its shareholders, to keep its discounts permanently under control. Never give a discount if you have doubts about its advisability. If you have reason to distrust a customer's integrity, close his account. Aim for a banking business which is direct, honest and legitimate. Do not allow the prospect of large profits tempt you to do anything that is not permitted. The „splendid financiers" in the world of Banking are generally either charlatans or rogues.

Where the need to practise the virtue of prudence is most clearly evident is in the banker's relations with his liability customers. These customers are the bank's creditors and have placed their trust in the institution, inasmuch that they believe that the funds they have lent the bank will be returned to them. That is why banks, because of their responsibility towards their depositors - which is greater and prior to their responsibility towards their shareholders, which in itself is great -have a moral obligation to appropriately invest the resources obtained from customers and to ensure, as far as is humanly possible, that they will recover the the principal and effectively receive the interest and commission which are the basis for the remuneration of deposits and for the shareholders' return. Thus, those banks which are driven by a disproportionate desire for growth, infringe their ethical duties if they pay more for their deposits than the credit market tolerates at each moment in time, or if they grant loans in inferior conditions to those which are possible, since, in this way they are endangering their solvency and their survival, which constitute the guarantee for their depositors.

Obviously the vulneration of the moral norm is even more serious when venturesome or excessively risky operations are undertaken, not with a view to benefiting the bank as an institution but in order to benefit some of its managers, or to cover speculative operations created by them. Moreover, it is clear that the moral qualification for these types of actions does not depend on whether the outcome is successful or not; abusing management for one's own ends is equally censurable, even if it does not have apparently harmful consequences for the bank, such as bankruptcy or insolvency; although these are unfortunately the only consequences which, generally speaking, hit the headlines.

XII. Veracity

Another virtue, related to justice, that the banker must hold in great estime is veracity, which is the antithesis of lying or falsehood and pretence. According to the anthropological model to which I feel bound, the banker, like anyone else, should practise this virtue for its own sake, assimilating sincerity and loyalty in this. Moreover, veracity is particularly necessary for the banker, because veracity is essential to maintaining the confidence on which the existence of a financial institution depends. If, at any point in time, the market, or the society in general sees that a financial institution is falsifying information about its situation, being deceitful about the conditions it publishes or simulating results by means of accounting devices, confidence in the institution will be lost and its future will become problematic.

The virtue of veracity is particularly important in the banker's relations with shareholders. I said earlier that the institution's main obligation towards the suppliers of risk capital is to safeguard their wealth, which does not only imply that this must survive, but also that its value in real terms is protected. And when I say real, I am referring to two different things. Firstly, I mean that it is the bank's obligation to try to ensure that the book value of the assets is adjusted to inflation, making it clear whether the dividend distributed is greater or smaller than net profit adjusted to inflation. Secondly, I mean that the value which interests the shareholder is not so much the book value, even if this is adjusted to inflation, but the stock market value of their shares. Thus, it is the banker's duty to use all the correct means he has at his disposal to protect and, if possible, to increase the price of the company's shares. In other words, the policies on capital increases and dividends should be aimed at maximizing the market value of the shareholders' assets, within the stock market circumstances at each moment in time, which, naturally, cannot be controlled by the bank, and are, thus, not its responsibility.

In addition to the responsibility of safeguarding the shareholder's assets, the bank has the responsibility of facilitating the sale of these, should the shareholder so desire. In other words, it is responsible for providing sufficient liquidity for shares, through correct market treatment, which, naturally, does not mean artificially repurchasing the shares - which would be a reprehensible practice, inasmuch as it would lead to a fictitious price - but rather channelling new real purchasers towards the shares.

The complement to these two concerns - the integrity and liquidity of assets - resides in the responsibility of offering appropriate remuneration in terms of the dividend and dividend growth adjusted to capital increases, which are the two factors that lead the stock to appreciate. This responsibility is directly linked to the responsibility of making profits.

Now, at the service of these three responsibilities - integrity, liquidity and payment - is the virtue of veracity which has to be manifested in two ways, First, by carrying out operations which are real in terms of their content and results. This is the opposite of the practice of generating fictitious profits, through asset sales and repurchase operations or by using any other accounting devices to present unreal results. Second, the virtue of veracity means that shareholders must be truly, clearly and punctually informed about the institution's performance and its results, so that all the decisions the shareholders may wish to make are based on a knowledge of reality.

XIII. Austerity

We have looked at some of the virtues the managers of financial institutions should practise, as - I repeat - the human beings they are; the moral rectitude of what we could analogically call corporate behaviour depends on this. In this review we have so far mentioned some of the virtues grouped under prudence, justice and strength. We must now devote some time to the fourth cardinal virtue, temperance. If, as I said, prudence is the banker's essential virtue, temperance should be its accessory.

Etymologically, temperance means balance and moderation, characteristics which common sense tells us are common to all virtues, since each virtue tends towards its own good, which is desirable for the nature of man in the appropriate form. And it is precisely these notes of balance and moderation that people want to see in a banker, in the very different forms of austerity, sobriety, discretion, modesty and also mildness and clemency, qualities which, according to Seneca, should shine out in every good man. It is logical that people should want this, since balance and moderation in a banker's private behaviour gives outside observers a guarantee that the funds belonging to third parties which they have been entrusted with are being managed correctly. The truth is that, generally speaking, good bankers have always been austere people.

XIV. Conclusion

After running through the principal virtues which, in my opinion, should govern the behaviour of the people who form part of financial institutions, I will end where I started. The only way that the action of financial institutions can be qualified as ethically correct is for the people who constitute these institutions and, in particular their managers, to share and respect the „values“ - as some people like to say, rather ambiguously - or as I prefer to say, practise all the moral virtues. In my view, the concern about ethics in business in general and in the world of finance in particular, that has recently attracted the attention of wide responsible sectors of society, cannot be resolved by drawing up a code of behaviour for the sector or by recommending that each institution draw up its own. I am not saying that it is not a good idea to do so, but I am saying that it is by no means sufficient.

The reason I say this is that codes of conduct, inasmuch as they are a compilation of more or less casuistic norms, the bulk of which are negative, may lead to - or, in the best of cases, risk leading to - formal fulfilment and, in other cases, to ways of getting round these norms, so that, in practice, what is considered important is simply not to get caught when they are not being obeyed. That is why I believe that a handbook on „what can be done and what cannot be done“ cannot be the real solution for ethical concerns. The problem of ethical behaviour is not so much a problem of norms as a problem of man, who realizes or destroys himself through his works. Thus, the steps which lead to an improvement in business ethics include the moral training of man, a training based on the recuperation or affirmation of moral conscience, starting from the first principles of natural law and its consequences. For this reason, the principal and virtually only recommendation that can be given is that of all-round training, at all levels of the company, through education, and above all, through example.

The approach I have just put forward explains why I have not stopped to consider subjects which, on many occasions, are talked about by those who are concerned with ethical questions, such as the use of privileged information for own's personal benefit, manipulation to change the price of things, etc. Anyone who is determined to behave in a way which leads him to be a person, and to be worth more as a person, whether or not this behaviour means that he will have a greater or lesser number of things, will know exactly how he should behave in these cases, even if there is no code of behaviour at his company which sets this out. On the other hand, if moral conscience - the product of the culture of being rather than of the culture of having - is missing, then no matter how many norms of behaviour there are, nor how many sanctions are established for disobeying them, the norms will go to the wall every time there is an opportunity for appetites to be satisfied, by crooked means.

As it is not usual practice and would take us off the subject we are talking about, I am leaving out the theories on banking with 100 per cent matching, defended by Von Mises and his disciples of the Austrian school.

Chapter 7

Ethical Issues in Financial Markets: The American Experience

PATRICIA H. WERHANE

Most people, most institutions, and even most politicians and governmental officials are decent, well-meaning people. Ethical issues sometimes occur not because people are evil or even greedy, but because the way in which their view a situation belies its ethical import. The model of financial markets one adopts, that is, the way one thinks markets operate or should operate, affects one's perception of those markets and whether and how one focuses on its ethical issues. Part of this model or perception is derived from the political, ideological, and economic context, (in the cases I shall discuss, the United States), and part from individual mores, corporate culture, or more global perspectives. Often ethical dilemmas arise because of a narrow perception of what is at issue, or because one has failed to see clearly how one's model or point of view concerning financial markets may be incomplete, narrow, or even erroneous. Often, too, that perspective does not include a moral point of view. Managers, traders, CEOs, financial analysts, and bankers do not always think clearly about the normative implications of their decisions and actions-how they will affect (positively or negatively) the well-being other people and other institutions, nor how their actions may or may not treat people fairly, respect them and their rights as human beings. This „moral muteness" in turn can have dilatory economic as well as moral effects. By illuminating these models one can sometimes begin to clear up these problems.

In what follows, focusing specifically on United States financial markets, I shall use illustrations to exemplify some ethical issues in financial markets, issues that face individuals, corporations, and some that are caused by the political system itself. The issues I shall deal with are: insider trading and the maximization of value for individuals, mergers and the maximization of value for shareholders, institutional investing, the recent savings and loan crisis, and bond trading and the role of political constraints. In each instance I shall show how a particular approach one adopts or presupposes in framing an issue impacts on its ethical substance and implications. In each instance I shall show how another, more inclusive framework, might better serve to alleviate the ethical dilemmas that arise in each case. I shall conclude with an example from banking that illustrates how moral leadership can have a positive impact on a community while being profitable as well.

An inclusive framework for thinking about financial markets is a framework that takes into account the moral point of view. What might be involved in taking a moral point or an „ethical perspective“ in dealing with financial markets? It is tempting here to appeal to one or more of the major streams of moral philosophy, Aristotelian virtue ethics, utilitarianism, and/or deontology, rights theory or theories of justice. A fruitful approach is to see what can be learned from these theories that is helpful in practical decision-making and moral judgments.

One way to evaluate the morality of an action is from a utilitarian perspective, judging an action in terms of its foreseeable outcomes, that is, in terms of what harmful or beneficial results could be expected to accrue. From this point of view, whatever one's motives or intentions are, we judge human action morally in terms of its utility, the positive or negative utility of an action itself to produce benefits or reduce suffering. The best sorts of actions are ones that maximizes human interests, best satisfy desires or pleasures, or minimize harms including benefits or harms to life, health, well-being, human dignity, autonomy, or mere pleasure. One measures harms and benefits in terms of their qualitative and quantitative merit, long-term and short-term results, and immediate or latent satisfaction. The best outcome is that which maximizes interests, leading to a net of benefits over harms for the most people, or minimally, reduces harms, all things considered. This harm may be to an economic system, to an industry or institution, or a more specific harm to some individual or individuals.

A second approach to moral reasoning is the appeal to more general standards that are not simply an evaluation of utilities nor merely reflect law, codes, of societal mores. Some actions are judged to be wrong not merely because of their positive or negative outcomes, but because they violate standards for acceptable behavior or moral rules. For example, most of us would agree that we should keep promises, avoid deception, respect basic rights of everyone equally, such as the rights to life, freedom, and privacy, treat people fairly, as well as avoid causing harm. These rules are standards of common-sense morality that reasonable people would agree should hold for everyone, the standards of openness, truth-telling, promise-keeping, equal rights, fairness, and absence of suffering. Reasonable people advocate and defend these standards (and there may be others) because it is in their long-term interest and in the interests of all of us if these rules are followed, and it is usually not in our long-term interests if these rules are habitually violated. Moral rules set the criteria for acceptable behavior by specifying how we expect others to act without making an exception for ourselves.[1]

Because they are general standards, moral rules help us to evaluate laws, codes, and social practices. But where do moral rules come from? There are a number of tempting explanations. Perhaps moral rules are God-given or part of human nature. But proving that that is the case involves us in religious debates that would take us far afield. Another way to derive moral rules is through a thought experiment. Imagine that you and your family and colleagues are on a spaceship heading for a distant planet you are going to populate. You are not sure how long the journey will take nor what the conditions will be when you arrive. During the journey you and the other passengers must set up the guidelines for behavior and standards for law and justice that will regulate the new colony. Since you do not know in advance what your status will be on the new planet, you are likely to choose guidelines that will give fair opportunities for all settlers including yourself and future generations. Under those conditions, you are likely to set out rules that specify equal rights to life and basic liberties, protect contracts and promises, punish lying, stealing, cheating, and murder, and provide equal opportunity for everyone to achieve their freedom and well-being. Assuming that the spaceship travelers are reasonable people, the guidelines or rules you develop will be those agreed upon by all members of the party. One can think of

1 See ADAM SMITH: *Lectures on Jurisprudence*, ed. R. L. MEEK, D. D. RAPHAEL, and P. G. STEIN (Oxford: Oxford University Press, 1978), especially A (i.ii. 12-14); and BERNARD GERT: *Morality* (New York: Oxford University Press, 1988), especially Chapters 1-5. See also, JEFFREY DOERING and PATRICIA WERHANE: „Conflicts of Interest“, in: *Ethical Issues in Scientific Research*, forthcoming.

moral rules, then, as those rules reasonable people, in ignorance of their own circumstances or future, would agree are the best standards for their own behavior and the behavior of others.

These ways of looking at the world, a moral point of view, is further buttressed by the obvious fact, sometimes ignored in traditional ethical theory, that all decisions, choices, activities, judgments, and evaluations are done within a community. The way one sees the world, acts, makes judgments, evaluates, and comets to conclusions is at least in part learned from and shared with the community (e.g., the family, company, culture, community, nation) in which individuals and institutions are imbedded. Because we are part of a community, another way to think about ethical issues is by way of virtues. Virtues are traits of character that make one a good person, that make a company a good company, or a country a fine nation. They are those traits that enable an individual or institution to function well and be worthy of admiration in the community. Social practices define virtues and virtues are the basis for a well-functioning community. So part of moral judgment is a judgment of character-of individuals and of companies.

Keeping these qualifications in mind, an outline form a framework for moral decision-making might include the following:

A) Moral decisions are normative decisions. They have to do with what one *should* do, all things considered, not necessarily with what, in fact, any of us do in a particular instance.
B) Moral decisions have to do with relationships between individuals or between individuals and institutions. So any moral evaluation must take into account the various stakeholders who are affected. Depending on the particular circumstance, stakeholders include the company at issue, its employees and managers, its shareholders, its clients and customers, its suppliers, and the community in which it functions.
C) Because a moral decision is a normative decision involving human relationships, a moral decision should be impartial. That is, it sets a precedent for what one thinks should be rules applying to everyone in a particular set of contexts. It should be the kind of decision one would be proud to defend in public to peers as well as to the industry or constituents one represent, both for its practicality and because it is the kind of decision one would expect others to make in a similar context[2].

2 See BERNARD GERT: *Morality* (New York: Oxford University Press, 1988), especially Chapters 1 and 4. Gert would not formulate the framework in the

D) Moral decisions are also contextual. So a moral decision must take account the peculiar circumstances of the situation at hand, the personality and social history of the participants, the context of the decision, its institutional and regulatory framework, and the historical and cultural precedents that preceded that situation and decision.
E) Any acceptable decision must meet what I would call „moral minimums, that is, those negative „bottom lines“ beyond which ordinarily one would agree that no action should be undertaken. These moral minimums are derived from traditional ethical theory. They include:

a) A decision and subsequent action should not improve one's situation, if it worsens the situation of others, unless each party to the interaction is fully informed and in an equally competitive situation. In any case, one should avoid an action that increases harms.
b) A decision should not be unfair either to individuals, groups of individuals, or to those who would be affected by similar decisions.
c) An action should not violate basic moral rules, those rules that reasonable people agree are necessary for decent human existence such as keeping promises and contracts, avoiding deception, respecting rights, and preventing suffering.
d) An action or set of activities that involves one in dealing with persons, institutions or communities of questionable character often gives the perception of impropriety, it abets questionable, and should be avoided whenever possible.

I. Short-Termism

It is impossible in a paper of this length to review all the legal dimensions of financial markets and how each issue is related to the more general political, ideological, and economic background that is peculiar to the United States. However, I do want to set the stage with a brief discussion of „short-

---

way I do, but his work has influenced my analysis as has the work of RONALD GREEN, particularly his essay, „The First Formulation of the Categorical Imperative as Literally a ‚Legislative' Metaphor“, *History of Philosophy Quarterly*, 3 (1991).

termism," a phenomenon peculiar to the United States financial markets. When I was invited to give this paper the United States was in a economic recession. Much of this recession was blamed on „short-termism," the habit of American corporations, traders, raiders, and investors to think in terms of quarterly earnings reports, and the attempt by corporations to please short-term investors and Wall Street rather than focus their goals to the long term. The model or ideal was of course, Japan, whose markets function and judge returns on investment from corporations in 10 to 20 year blocks.

As I finish this paper, Japan is in economic disarray and the United States is enjoying a competitive boom. According to a recent *New York Times* article, despite it is estimated that 2 million manufacturing jobs have been lost each year for the last 10 years, the net decline over that period for factory jobs was only a total of 1 million jobs. More importantly, during this same period we have added 18 million new jobs including 2 million during this past year of drastic downsizing. Accompanying this net job increase of almost 20% is the fact that American workers are now (since 1990) the most productive in the world, surpassing German and Japanese workers. The development of new global markets in developing countries should further improve this trend[3].

Perhaps the problem was not so much our short-termism, but a failure to be clear about what it is that U. S. financial markets are and do. Short-termism illustrates a failure to take into account stakeholders other than short-term investors. In the discussions that follow we will see how such a failure can be redressed. Second, the United States is good at new ventures, entrepreneurship, technological development, and service industries. But we are weaker in financial policy, industrial and technological planning, and thinking long-term both nationally and globally about the economy in the 21st and 22nd centuries. This is not merely because of our short-term thinking on Wall Street. Rather it derives from a fear or mistrust of government, a fear that developed over 200 years ago when the country was founded. This mistrust of government involvement in business, in regulation or in government financing precludes some innovative developments in economic policies which might, in fact, help business. In what follows we will see how confused regulations or the lack of them has led to some moral difficulties in financial markets. Third, along with a distrust of government, U. S. investors, managers, and shareholders have an overindulgent faith in free mar-

3 Sylvia Nasar: „The American Economy, Back on Top", *New York Times*, Section Three, pp. 1-6, March 17, 1994.

kets including financial markets as the best regulators of behavior. Using insider trading and mergers as examples, I shall argue that markets are dependent variables, the outcome of exemplary or questionable business behavior. So what one does or what a company does contributes to and creates the market that allegedly regulates its activities.

II. Insider Trading

Foster Winans was a reporter for the *Wall Street Journal* and author of the influential and widely read column, „Heard on the Street." Despite a *Journal* policy requiring all employees to treat information „gleaned" during the course of employment as company property and therefore confidential if nonpublic, Winans became involved in a scheme in which he provided securities-related information that was to appear in his column to friends who traded on that advance information. By Winans telling them information a day before it appeared in his „Heard" column and trading on it, Winans' group was able to earn more than $690,000 in just over one year (1983 through early 1984)[4].

The question is, what did Winans do wrong? In the United States (and in some other countries as well) insider trading in the stock market is characterized as the buying or selling of shares of stock on the basis of material information known only to the trader or to a few persons. In discussions of insider trading it is commonly assumed that the privileged information, if known to others, would affect their trading decisions as well. The present guidelines of the Securities and Exchange Commission (SEC) prohibit most forms of insider trading. Yet a number of economists and philosophers of late defend this kind of activity both as a viable and useful practice in a free market and as a practice that is not immoral. The arguments in its defense are persuasive. They include the following.

Insider trading is difficult to define and impossible to pinpoint in most instances. While clearly, trading by an employee on secret corporate infor-

---

4 *CARPENTER, et al. (Felix and Winans) v. United States*: „Slip Opinion," no. 86-422 decided Nov. 16, 1987. The scheme was eventually uncovered, and the men were charged with misappropriation of information under sections 10(b) and 10b-5 of the SEC Act, mail and wire fraud, and lesser violations.

mation not yet made public is an obvious case of insider trading, not all cases are so clear-cut. If one overhears privileged information, if one receives a recommendation from one's broker, or if one comes in contact with that information involuntarily, and uses such information, is this insider trading? Moreover, even under ideal circumstances it is impossible either to disseminate information to all interested parties equally and fairly, or alternately, to preserve absolute secrecy. For example, in issuing a new stock or deciding on a stock split, a number of parties in the transaction from brokers to printers learn about that information in advance just because of their participation in making this activity a reality. There are always shareholders and other interested parties who claim they did not receive information of such an activity or did not receive it at the same time as other shareholders even when the information was disseminated to everyone at the same time. Thus it is, at best, difficult to stop insider trading, to judge whether a certain kind of knowledge is „inside“ or privileged, or to evaluate each time whether or not a trade was based on „inside“ information. These are not good reasons to defend insider trading as economically or morally desirable, but it illustrates the difficulties of defining and controlling the phenomenon.

Second, if insider trading was decriminalized or not prohibited by SEC regulations, it is contended, insider trading would not be unfair because anyone could engage in it without impunity. The market would function more efficiently since the best-informed and those most able to gain information would be allowed to exercise their trading options and the stock in question would closely coincide with its company's value. Moreover, those who become privy to inside information, even if they take advantage of that information before it becomes public, are trading on probabilities, not on certainties, since they are trading before the activity actually takes place. They are taking a gamble, and if they are wrong the market itself will „punish“ them. It is even argued that brokers who do not use inside information for their clients advantage are cheating their clients.

Looking at insider trading from the macro perspective of efficient markets it would appear that it actually makes the market more efficient by allowing the quick adjustment of stock price to its present market value. So economists like Henry Manne argue that insider trading is beneficial to outsiders. Whether it is more beneficial than its absence is a question Manne admits he cannot answer. But Manne defends insider trading because, he argues, it reduces the factor of chance in trading both for insiders and outsiders. When shares are traded on information rather than on rumor or whim, the market reflects more accurately the actual economic status of that company or set of companies, because of insider trading stock prices go up or down according to real, factual information. Outsiders benefit from this because stock prices more closely represent the worth of their company than shares not affected by insider trading. Insider trading, then, actually improves the fairness of the market, according to this argument, by reflecting in stock prices the fiscal realities of affected corporations thereby benefiting all traders of the stocks[5]. The market itself would regulate the alleged excesses of insider trading. I use the term „alleged" excesses because according to this line of reasoning, if the market is functioning properly, whatever gains or losses are created as a result of open competition are a natural outcome of that competition. They are not excesses at all, and eventually the market will adjust the so-called unfair gains of speculators.

But let us look at insider trading from another perspective. Insider information, e.g., information about a merger, acquisition, new stock issue, layoffs, etc., information known only to a few, is the property of those engaged in the activity in question, and they should have the right to regulate its dissemination. Employees of that company or others who have that inside information and trade on it, then, bring into question their fiduciary responsibility to their shareholders[6].

There are more serious difficulties. Suppose I am a shareholder of a company that is to be purchased by another, but that information is not yet public. Suddenly I notice that there is more than the usual amount of trading activity of that stock, and the price in fact rises. Sometimes this is reported by the media, the *Wall Street Journal*, in particular, watches and reports on these sorts of trades. Had I been privy to that information I could have bought more of this stock earlier on. Similarly, a stockbroker and her clients will benefit by the information the market gives when a stock rises as a signal that this company is about to be purchased. But had they been privy to that information they could benefit more, and more equally, with those who had that information.

---

5 MANNE: *Insider Trading and the Stock Market* (New York: The Free Press, 1966), especially Chapters X and XI, and DERYL MARTIN and JEFFREY H. PETERSON: „Insider Trading Revisited", *Journal of Business Ethics*, 10 (1991), pp. 57-61.

6 See JENNIFER MOORE: „What is Really Unethical About Insider Trading?", *Journal of Business Ethics*, 9 (1990), pp. 171-182, and PATRICIA H. WERHANE: „The Ethics of Insider Trading", *Journal of Business Ethics*, 8 (1989), pp. 841-846.

Insider trading, then, is unfair because it benefits some individual traders more than others, as all trading does, but it benefits insiders more, and more quickly. It also punishes insiders more quickly if their speculations are erroneous. But this is also a problem for outsiders. Insider trading might run up a stock on erroneous speculation that the company is undervalued. Such speculation and the resulting erroneous valuation of that stock would actually make the market less efficient. Thus even from a macro perspective if this so-called „insider" information were public knowledge the market would function more efficiently as it does when insiders trade, since all traders would have access to equally available information[7].

Insider trading is a phenomenon that occurs daily in the United States despite laws to the contrary. Most traders think the law is flawed and trade accordingly. This is because, I think, their model of markets does not take into account the affect of insider trading on traders not privy to this information or on companies who need to protect certain information. It appears that trading is evaluated only in terms of its long-term overall outcomes without considering how individual trades affect insider trading and the price of a particular stock on any particular occasion. In a country where „short-term" is valued over „long-term" this is a strange anomaly. But even from a macro perspective such a Manne's insider trading turns out to be less efficient that trading without that information and, more importantly, interferes with fair competition between traders or between traders and investors, so it fails the test for meeting minimum moral standards.

III. Mergers and Acquisitions

The Dayton Hudson Corporation (DHC) described itself as „a growth company focusing exclusively on retailing." Headquartered in Minneapolis, the company operated 475 stores in 34 states at the end of 1986, employing some 120,000 people nationwide (full-time and part-time). In that year it had pretax earnings of $494.2 million on sales of $9,259.1 million. In its 1986 Annual Report, DHC stated that its performance objectives were to „earn an after-tax return on beginning shareholders' equity (ROE) of 18%," to

7 See PATRICIA H. WERHANE: „The Indefensibility of Insider Trading", *Journal of Business Ethics*, 9 (1990).

„sustain an annual growth in earnings per share (EPS) of 15%..." Though DHC remained a profitable company, 1986 was a disappointing year. Revenues increased by 12% and passed the $9 billion mark, but net earnings per share dropped by 9%.

In July of 1987 the Dart Group Corporation began to purchase DHC stock with an eye to taking over that company. Dart, which had owned a drug store chain, was not an ideal company. Dart's „history" as a retailer was not without blemishes. The company was famous for breaking up the corporations it acquired, spinning of the less desirable assets. It was not well-known for treating its employees well, it had shown no interest in community relationships, and the notion of social responsibility was not a term commonly cited in its annual reports.

When the news of Dart's buyout attempt became evident to DHC, its management began a concerted effort to prevent the takeover, urging its shareholders to vote against the buyout, urging the community to protest, and lobbying the Minnesota legislature to pass protective legislation. Luckily for DHC the legislature did pass anti-takeover legislation and with shareholder backing DHC was able to prevent the buyout[8].

In the United States the 1980s was the decade of „merger mania." The term „merger" technically means the joining of two equal companies. This almost never is the case, in most instances one company is acquired by another, the acquiring company being in control. Also under the heading of mergers and acquisitions one usually classifies leveraged buyouts, wherein a third party (often an investment banker) buys the stock in a company or a group of companies and thereby takes them „private" and out of the public domain of the stock market. Some LBOs are management buyouts (MBOs) whereby the management of a company buys back the stock and takes it private. In almost all cases of mergers, acquisitions and LBOs the purchase is made possible by the sale of high yield, unrated „junk bonds" to finance the purchase. In what follows I shall use the expression „merger and acquisition" to refer to all these activities.

Like the discussion of insider trading, how one approaches the issue of mergers affects how one perceives its ethical issues in this phenomenon. One approach considers the phenomenon of mergers in the aggregate to analyze how, in general, these activities affect the economy. A prevalent justification for present unregulated market of mergers and acquisitions is based on

8 See ROBERT G. KENNEDY: „Case Study ‚Dayton Hudson Corporation'" (Washington D. C. Council on Foundations, 1990).

an economic theory called the theory of the „market for corporate control" (hereafter abbreviated MCC). Derived from a neoclassical economic model, the theory, in brief, argues, that the market functions efficiently. Market activities including mergers, acquisitions, and leveraged buy-outs, should be unregulated, since an efficient market will both control excesses and generate economic value[9]. The reason a company becomes a target for acquisition is because its stock price is undervalued, so that someone or some other company is willing to pay more for that stock than its present market value.

According to this thesis there is „a high positive correlation between corporate managerial efficiency and the market price of shares of that company."[10] An undervalued stock is evidence of changing market conditions, need for corporate restructuring, weak management, an ineffective board of directors, less than optimal uses of company resources, or some other failure to maximize value in that company[11].

A takeover of that undervalued company raises its stock price, because in almost every case target shareholders are paid a premium for their shares. A subsequent takeover allows the acquiring company to institute more efficient use of resources as a result of the merger, to provide more effective management, and/or to disengage that company from its board and stockholders. So the market is a catalyst for more efficient use of corporate and capital resources and thus generates economic growth.

Therefore, there is a good economic reason for every market transaction, and in the long run at least, there are no good reasons for regulating or otherwise restricting mergers and acquisitions. The market will „weed out" unsuccessful mergers, and mergers and acquisitions maximize the aggregate economic good by (1) making management more efficient, (2) benefiting target shareholders, (3) developing more efficient use of target resources, and (4) restructuring corporate assets. I shall return to that point in the next section.

---

9 See, for example, HENRY MANNE: „Mergers and the Market for Corporate Control", *Journal of Political Economy*, 73 (1965), pp. 110-120, MICHAEL JENSEN and W. H. MECKLING: „Theory of the Firm: Managerial Behavior, Agency Costs and Ownership Structure", *Journal of Financial Economics*, 3 (1976), pp. 305-360.

10 O. MANNE, „Mergers...," p. 112.

11 MICHAEL JENSEN: „The Takeover Controversy", in: JOHN COFFEE, LOUIS LOWENSTEIN, and S. ROSE-ACKERMAN (Eds.): *Knights, Raiders, and Targets* (New York: Oxford University Press, 1988), pp. 314-354.

The theory of the market for corporate control espouses the value of increasing aggregate economic growth through maximizing the efficiency of business resources (including management) and thereby maximizing and/or increasing shareholder wealth. These are unquestionably positive values and proper goals for a market system. The question is, does the phenomenon of merger activity always achieve these goals? What is interesting in the Dayton Hudson Case is that management was keen to avoid the takeover even if it meant not maximizing their short-term financial interests or the interests of their shareholders. It became DHC's and the long-term interests of the shareholders and other stakeholders to preserve Dayton Hudson intact. Thus values *other* than short-term shareholder return became the basis of the decision.

The theory of MCC is based on a neoclassical model of the market, a model that is also implicit in defenses of insider trading. This model or sometimes talks as if, the market is an independent as well as an efficient regulator of economic behavior. The market cannot prevent failures in specific instances, but in the aggregate it will adjust those failures. In the long run, the market will adjust inefficiencies, poor management, a weak board, and externalities to reach an efficient equilibrium. If this is the case, is this a „black box" theory of the firm? Does this imply that how an individual manager behaves or what an individual corporation does makes little difference in the overall aggregate of market behavior, because the market will adjust „abnormal" behavior? This, too, is an ethical issue, because it raises the question of when and how a manager is responsible and thus liable for her actions[12]. The implicit belief is that mergers and acquisitions as well as insider trading, even when driven by self-interests, will be restrained by the „invisible hand" of an efficient market. So a poor acquisition is merely one complication but not an oddity or an aberration in the market. This is an exaggerated picture of how a free market could function, but I think it accounts for talk about the market *as if* it worked in this independent yet forceful way. Insider trading and/or any kind of acquisition should not be regulated, because in the aggregate and in the long run the market allegedly will control

12 This emphasis that probably derives originally from a misreading of the so-called „father of modern free enterprise", the 18th century economist and philosopher, Adam Smith. Specifically a misreading of Smith's notion of the Invisible Hand. See ADAM SMITH: *The Wealth of Nations*, ed. R. H. CAMPBELL, A. S. SKINNER, and W. B. TODD (Indianapolis: Liberty Classics 1776; 1981) IV.ii.9.

the excesses of self-interested economic activities and poor merger decisions[13].

Defenders of MCC will, of course, reject this picture of the market. What they argue is that the security price accurately reflects corporate financial value and even takes into account future potential earnings, investor analyses, and market trading[14]. Michael Jensen and W. H. Meckling, argue that defining the firm as a nexus of contractual relationships precludes a „black box" theory of the firm. How management defines and carries out these relationships determines the direction and value of the firm[15]. At the same time Jensen and Meckling claim that we can treat a firm as a black box for many purposes, particularly as its stock functions in the market[16]. Thus, they appear to argue both that how a manager behaves matters, because, for example, an inefficient manager will create an undervalued company, while an efficient manager will improve that company, and does not matter, because the market will control inefficiencies and self-interests through takeovers and create aggregate economic good. What happens within the alleged black box is reflected in its market price. When that price indicates an undervalued company the market „regulates" that situation, because this low price signals to the financial world that that company needs new management control and is a good target for takeover.

What I want to suggest is that the market is more complex. Ordinarily one assumes that how a manager behaves or how a corporation behaves affects the market price of that company's stock. Similarly, the behavior of individual and institutional stock analysts and traders makes a difference in how the stock market behaves, not just how it behaves in reaction to such trading, but how it will behave in the future[17]. The way in which a market regulates, its „character and personality," is determined by the institutional framework in which the market functions and by the aggregate input from economic actors: managers, corporations, investment bankers, traders for

---

13 See PATRICIA H. WERHANE: „Mergers, Acquisitions, and the Market for Corporate Control", *Public Affairs Quarterly*, 4 (1990), pp. 81-96.

14 JENSEN, „Takeover Controversy," p. 320.

15 JENSEN and MECKLING, p. 310-311.

16 MICHAEL JENSEN and W. H. MECKLING: „Rights and Production Functions: An Application to Labor-Managed Firms and Codetermination", *Journal of Business*, 52 (1979), p. 494.

17 EDWARD S. HERMAN and LOUIS LOWENSTEIN: „The Efficiency Effects of Hostile Takeovers", in: COFFEE, LOWENSTEIN, and ROSE-ACKERMAN, pp. 211-224.

large funds, or even, the government. There is no „market" apart from those activities that create and sustain it and the institutional framework in which it operates.

An example of the complex nonlinear interrelationship between economic actions and the market is exemplified in the Dayton Hudson case. In the process of preventing the takeover, Dayton Hudson management became aware of its own shortcomings, and within three years the stock price of Dayton Hudson rose 30 points. Its management activities created wealth for a company and influenced the market for its company's stock. However, without the intervention of the Minnesota legislature and strong community support, it is unlikely that the Dart takeover could have been prevented. So it is not always the case that the market by itself can always regulate possible abuses.

There are, then, a number of difficulties with the theory that justifies the nonregulation and proliferation of mergers and acquisitions. First, not all acquisitions increase aggregate wealth. According to some statistics, only about 50% of mergers are financially successful[18]. Second, the market is an imperfect regulator of economic behavior and depends on the input of investors, traders, management, boards and other stakeholders for its efficiency or lack thereof. So even a partial black box theory of the firm distorts how individual and corporate economic activities create and change the market, and implies management exoneration for actions to which it contributes. Third, one needs to sort out whether management responsibility is to (a) the short-term or long- term interests of shareholders or (b) the short-term or long-term interests of all its stakeholders. Dayton Hudson's management saw themselves as committed to the long-term interests of all their stakeholders, and this commitment justified their short-term activities to prevent a takeover. Dayton Hudson's management placed the interests of its employees, its customers, and the community on a par with those of its stockholders.

Even if the market is efficient so that mergers and acquisitions increase the aggregate economic good or alleviate economic loss, one may ask, is this the only good? What about rights of stakeholders other than target shareholders and top management? Does the value of the aggregate economic good override harms or injustices created as a result of a merger or acquisi-

18 E. B. MAGNHEIM and D. C. MUELLER: „Are Acquiring-Firm Shareholders Better Off After an Acquisition?", in: COFFEE, LOWENSTEIN, and ROSE-ACKERMAN, p. 171-193.

tion in every case? A second approach to the question of mergers studies and evaluates each merger or buyout separately to see how each affects various stakeholders involved in the activity. This more piecemeal analysis argues that economic efficiency is not the only justification for a merger, and mergers or acquisitions that create harms to stakeholders need to be carefully scrutinised. Assuming for the sake of the argument that a corporation is a nexus of contractual relationships, one of which being a fiduciary duty to its shareholders, a stakeholder approach argues that a corporation affects and is affected by a number of parties. A corporation has complex interrelationships and thus duties toward a number of stakeholders: with its employees, its customers, agents working on behalf of the corporation, e.g., lawyers, advertising agencies, and the like, and even to the community and the environment. Indeed and obviously, a corporation cannot function without these stakeholders, and each has equally valuable, although sometimes competing, claims. By focusing merely on the shareholder of common stock as the net benefactor or loser in an acquisition, the MCC ignores both the benefits accrued by agents during merger activity, and it also ignores possible harms to other stakeholders that result from a merger.

Important and often neglected stakeholders are those managers and employees who are not directly responsible for, nor directly benefit from an acquisition or takeover. The rumor of a possible merger or acquisition, even an unsubstantiated one, often has a dilatory effect on productivity, absenteeism, team work, loyalty, etc. of middle managers and other employees both in the acquiring and in the target companies. In any merger or acquisition personnel are shuffled, the organizational structure is changed, lines of responsibility are altered, etc[19]. Dayton Hudson tried to take these interests into account during the takeover attempt, but it is clear that employees, while well-informed in this case, were rightfully upset.

A second stakeholder is the corporation and corporate culture. Ordinarily a corporate culture is disrupted, if not radically altered, when a company is taken over. Sometimes, too, the culture of an acquiring company is changed by an acquisition. Some studies have suggested that corporations which have experienced stability over a long period of time both exhibit the best eco-

19 PRICE PRITCHETT: After the Merger: Managing the Shockwaves (Homewood, IL: Dow Jones-Irwin, 1985), and PATRICIA H. WERHANE: „Two Ethical Issues in Mergers and Acquisitions", *Journal of Business Ethics*, 7 (1988), pp. 39-43.

nomic performance and have a strong value system in place[20]. Evidence of Dart's previous management philosophy demonstrated that Dayton Hudson would have become a radically different company under Heft's leadership. At the same time, mergers often create the climate for competitive challenge and thus improved economic excellence. The threatened takeover surely put Dayton Hudson's management on notice and their performance improved markedly after the takeover was thwarted.

A third stakeholder is the consumer, and along with the consumer an almost forgotten stakeholder, the public. How consumers are affected in a merger or acquisition is seldom studied[21]. Mergers, by creating a debt-driven company, sometimes damage long-term investments in research and development, research that is crucial for the long-term self-interest of the company and to keep a competitive edge in global markets.

A fourth stakeholder is the community. Dayton Hudson, unlike some other companies, had made an explicit commitment not only to its customers but also to the Minnesota community, a commitment it has carried out in a variety of community activities and contributions. Their commitments to these stakeholders allowed the company to appeal to the community and to the Minnesota legislature, and appeal that was responded to as part of a reciprocal recognition of Dayton Hudson's previous acts of social responsibility.

This piecemeal stakeholder analysis is not developed to neglect shareholders. It is just that they are not the *only* stakeholders. A stakeholder analysis does not merely consider the aggregate benefit of a merger to the aggre-

---

20 R. EDWARD FREEMAN and DANIEL GILBERT, JR.: *Corporate Strategy and the Search for Ethics* (Englewood Cliffs, N.J.: Prentice-Hall Inc., 1988), THOMAS PETERS and R. Waterman: *In Search for Excellence* (New York: Harper & Row, 1982), and THE BUSINESS ROUNDTABLE: *Corporate Ethics: A Prime Business Asset* (New York: The Business Roundtable, 1988).

21 It has been suggested, too, that sometimes research and development, and thus new consumer products, are curtailed when an acquiring company takes on a heavy debt load as a result of a buyout. A forthcoming National Science Foundation study of LBOs suggests that research and development has been substantially reduced after a leveraged buyout, although some of the data on research and development investment questions this conclusion. See „An Assessment of the Impact of Recent Leveraged Buyouts and Other Restructurings on Industrial Research and Development Expenditures", National Science Foundation, 1989, and HERMAN and LOWENSTEIN, *op. cit.*, and JENSEN, „Takeover Controversy."

gate collection of shareholders, but wonders about the benefits or costs of a merger to *each* kind of stakeholder. For example, even if shareholders of the acquired company profit from a merger or an LBO, what is seldom asked is whether they have profited more by keeping that same company in tact, retaining their shares, and enacting the same „reforms" to be carried out when the company is taken over or goes private. While the answer to this question is always speculative, what is worrisome is that the question is almost never even debated. The Dayton Hudson shareholders may have concluded that the company's management was not maximizing stakeholder wealth before the Dart offer. Yet many of them were Minnesota residents who also resented Dart's threat, and they became crucial „players" in preventing this takeover attempt.

A sixth stakeholder is the corporate bondholder. Evidence suggests that bondholders suffer losses as a result of a merger or acquisition even if they hold bonds in the acquired company. There has been a long-standing precedent in the financial world that bonds were a low-risk and ultimately safe investment of prudent conservative people. Yet the recent rash of mergers broke precedent, and traditional corporate bondholders became literally holders of junk. When such investors are treated in this manner and such implicit expectations are violated- the market, which operates on the basis of trust, takes on another, not altogether honorable personality.

The issue in this discussion is not merely that stakeholders are sometimes harmed or even benefited as a result of a merger. It is that questions of stakeholder rights, benefits, and harms are not always raised, nor are these stakeholder issues taken into account in the analysis of the viability of most mergers. Interestingly in the Dayton Hudson Case it was because of these stakeholders that the antitakeover tactics were developed. Management was sure that employees, customers, and the community would suffer under Dart management, and these concerns were primary in their justification of fighting the takeover. In many takeover attempts or planned mergers only the top management is privy to the negotiations, and what is occurring is kept secret to prevent stock fluctuations, competing offers, and other market changes. Little information is disseminated to any employee, and even shareholders are usually kept in the dark. Such secrecy seems necessary so that the merger or takeover can take place with the smallest amount of fiscal damage, but the result is the dissemination of ungrounded rumors which creates fear and thus unrest or even psychological trauma for almost every employee. Dayton Hudson, on the other hand, kept its employees fully informed about details of the threatened takeover. They also informed the public immediately so that stockholders and Minnesota citizens as well as employees became partners in stopping Dart. This deliberate openness and communication demonstrated respect for the rights of stakeholders to be informed about the future of Dayton Hudson. It was also a propitious move in stopping Dart since it united the press and the legislature against Dart. It prevented further harm to the company and strengthened employee and community trust.

Stakeholder analysis and appeals to moral minimums, then, gives one tools to measure the affects of merger activities more accurately than some finance theories. As the Dayton Hudson Case demonstrates, various stakeholders are essential constituents of a well-functioning company. From a stakeholder perspective, the market for corporate control theory neither takes into account fully responsibilities to acquiring or acquired shareholders or bondholders, nor measures the effects, either economic nor in terms of harms to, or conflicting rights of, other stakeholders affected by a merger or acquisition.

IV. Institutional Investing

Lens, Inc. is a small activist-oriented institutional investment firm led by Robert Monks, its founder. In late 1990 Lens began pressuring Sears, Roebuck and Company, a corporation whose stock was part of Lens' investment portfolio, to focus on its core business rather than attempt to combine a financial supermarket with a department store. After almost two years of pressure, Sears announced that it would concentrate on its retail business and sell Coldwell Banker, its real estate operations, as well as 20% of Dean Witter and Allstate, its principal financial holdings. Lens claimed that its efforts generated more than $1 billion in shareholder value because the price of Sears stock rose sharply over the two years. But the rise in the stock price generally followed the rise in the S&P 500 during the same period. Only two points [of that stock price rise] are clearly from Lens's efforts: the company's stock substantially lagged the S&P 500 before the campaign began, and the stock rose almost $4 on the day Sears announced it was selling its financial businesses[22].

Institutional investors have become increasingly important in the United States. The majority of voting shares of publicly traded stock is now owned by institutional investors: private, municipal, and state pension funds, employee stock option plans, mutual funds and other large institutions who invest vast sums of money for their institution, their clients, or employees. A single institutional investor can own and vote large blocks of stock of any company, and thus influence its direction and decision-making. An active institutional investor can give its investor-shareholders a substantive voice in corporate policy, and this new phenomenon has changed the traditional 20th century „hands off" shareholder-manager relationship. As an owner or shareholder, having a voice in what happens to the company in which one owns shares would appear to restore the classic tradition of owner control that characterized early management arrangements of the 18th and 19th centuries. Indeed, from that perspective, shareholders, as owners of a corporation, have responsibility for its direction, and institutional investor activism is a feasible method for the exercise of that responsibility.

However, this way of looking at investor activism may be an oversimplification of what is at issue, and institutional investor activism raises a number of ethical issues. Because institutional investors can create change in organizations they have an enormous responsibility to do so with due diligence. Institutional investors are not always experts in corporate management, finance, marketing, or other areas in which they offer advice. Because of this lack of expertise, many CEOs and board of directors question the value of investor activism and view this kind of activity as unnecessary meddling. Institutional investors play the role of outside directors, and like outside directors they are viewed both as external consultants and as pariahs by internal directors and managers.

Professionally, institutional investors represent their clients, and their primary aim is to maximize the return on clients' investments either in the short-term or in the long term. If an institutional investor veers from that goal that can only occur with the permission of her clients since such activism is paid for out of clients' investment money. From a utilitarian perspective in the Lens case it is not clear that Lens maximized the return for its clients. Because institutional investor activism is costly to clients, if it

22 ROBERT C. POZEN: „Institutional Investors: The Reluctant Activists", *Harvard Business Review*, January-February 1994, pp 142-3.

does not increase the stock price or return on investment, then it is a at best a questionable procedure given the professional role of the institutional investor. Did Robert Monks at Lens attack Sears in an attempt to raise its stock price for his clients, or was his interest in Sears motivated by other of his own financial interests?[23] The kind of precedent he set should be examined carefully to be sore it is a desirable one.

The professional role of investors as agents for their clients is often brought into question in other contexts.

Recently John Kaweske, the successful manager of Invesco Funds and a leader in the mutual fund business was fired. Apparently Mr. Kaweske, while employed at Invesco, purchased valuable securities for his own account, securities in companies about which he had intimate knowledge and on whose boards he sat, and then invested in that stock for his clients. There is an intimation, not proven, that selling the stock to his clients helped raise its price. Kaweske was fired for failing to report he was a director of some of these companies, a violation of Invesco's code of conduct[24].

Because mutual fund managers, investment banks, financial firms, and other traders are not prohibited by law in the United States from trading both for their clients and for their own accounts, aggressive trading for one's own account often takes precedence over client interests. In these cases investor-traders have a conflict of interest between taking care of their own accounts and its financial rewards and their representation of clients' interest. Such conflicts of interest such as the Kaweske case naturally arise when one is trading the same stocks for one's own account and for clients. In some industries such as in law firms and in government agencies, one is prohibited from owning stock in a company one represents or in some way connected to one's professional capacity. However, no such prohibitions exist for traders, investors or investment bankers. Interestingly, the SEC, is now just beginning to take a careful look at this set of issues, and some regulation on trader investing is likely to be forthcoming.

From an impartial perspective the practice of trading the same securities both for oneself and for one's clients raises questions. Merely disclosing trading practices is not enough, in each instance, to preclude placing one's personal financial interests before one's professional obligations to clients. Conflicts of interest such as these between clients and their traders or in-

---

23 POZEN, *op. cit.*

24 SARA CALIAN and SUZANNE MCGEE: „Kaweske Gained from Stock Pick long before his Funds", *Wall Street Journal*, January 17, 1994, pp. C1-C10.

vestment counselors should be avoided. The best way to avoid such difficulties is to eliminate the conflict by separating investor-client activities such as underwriting, trading and activism from trading for one's own account or other activities that are in one's own financial interest.

V. Banking Issues: The United States Savings and Loan Crisis

Recently in the United States thousands of Savings and Loan institutions (S&Ls) went bankrupt, closing their doors at a cost of more than $50 billion dollars to the government who guarantees savings up to $100,000 at S&Ls. In assessing the responsibility for the recent Savings and Loan crisis in the United States most experts construe three kinds of thesis. First, the plight of the thrift industry is a result of government regulation of the thrift industry which virtually remained unchanged until 1980, and the subsequent deregulation of the industry during the 1980s. During the period from 1934 to 1980 S&Ls were by and large small financial institutions who lend money for home mortgages. After deregulation these institutions were free to loan money for a variety of real estate and other projects. Moreover, despite deregulation, the government guaranteed savings at these institutions up to $100,000 per account. Second, during this period there was a changing banking industry in which savings and loan institutions became obsolete because banks and the U. S. government became involved in mortgage lending. Third, market conditions created new money markets, junk bonds, and volatile rising interest rates, that were responsible for pressures on S&Ls to make risky loans[25].

However, one seldom cites the management and boards of directors of savings and loan companies orchestrated the direction of these institutions, the kinds of loans that were chosen, and extended amortization of asset losses, responsibilities that were almost solely their's after the series of deregulatory measures taken in the early 1980s. Were they merely pawns in the system, which allowed S&L operators to loan money to a variety of individuals and projects? What we have done in this case is blame government,

---

25 See, for example, G. CHRISTIAN HILL: „A Never Ending Story", *Stanford Law and Policy*, 2 (1990), pp. 21-36.

Congress, regulations, and the market for the Thrift crisis, letting off Boards of directors and managers of thrifts, and forgetting that Congress is made up of people, regulations are created and enforced by individuals and groups of individuals.

Let us assume, optimistically, that one can restructure regulatory mechanisms consistently so as to encourage responsibility in savings and loan management. We are still left with the issue of individual managerial fiscal and moral responsibility. For whether or not the present regulatory mechanisms are kept in place or are subject to change, managers and boards of thrifts are ultimately responsible not merely for protecting their depositors, but also for the viability of their institution and the protection of its assets[26].

As I suggested in connection with institutional investing, a condition for taking moral responsibility is get at a distance from one's own point of view or the point of view of one's colleagues, one's constituents, and/or the institutional or regulatory framework in which one is operating. If one can take a critical approach to issues and decisions, without displacing them from their proper historical and social context and keeping in mind the variety of stakeholders in each situation, one can often develop moral imagination and cultivate the habit of moral leadership. This does not mean that the decisions one makes will always be accepted by all parties, but that the aim is a decision and a plan of action that is most likely acceptable, all things considered. Any decision requires not merely working one's way through a particular situation, but also appealing to, or setting precedents for, other decisions. Such reasoning helps the manager to step back, evaluate a particular situation, and work her way out of dilemmas some of which are created out of conflicts arising from the very ingredients of business in which that manager or director flourishes. Whether a decision-maker means to or not, business decisions are made in a public arena. Thus even apparently unimportant decisions set precedents, precedents that other managers and other institutions follow. To give an obvious example, the bailout of some thrifts has set a precedent for further bailouts. These activities created models for other similar actions, precedents were set, and it is difficult to change that.

Keeping these qualifications in mind, in outline form a framework for moral decision-making in the savings and loan industry might include the following. First, no decision, e.g., no loan, should be acted upon if it harms

---

26 See PATRICIA H. WERHANE: „The Savings and Loan Crisis", *Stanford Law and Policy*, 2 (1990).

the affected stakeholders, e.g., one's clients, depositors, a municipality, a corporation, unless each party to the interaction is fully informed and in an equally competitive situation. Second, a decision should not be unfair either to individuals, groups of individuals, or to those who would be affected by similar decisions. For example, abrupt regulatory changes are sometimes unfair to institutions who have operated by another set of rules. Third, an action should not violate basic moral rules, e.g., the rights of all the stakeholders, such as the rights of depositors not to be deceived about their investments and savings.

In practice, to take into account all of these factors is admittedly tedious and difficult. But, I return to the idea of an impartial perspective, Sometimes, when you can step out of your role as a regulator or Congressperson or manager, or even as a member of the public, you expand your horizon and can get another, more dispassionate, perspective on a particular crisis which provides a window to a new solution. The municipal underwriting affair is one such concrete example.

VI. Municipal Bond Trading

Let us consider a more difficult set of cases that involve entrapment in a system of political pressures, a set of scenarios that *Business Week* has recently called „Institutional Back-Scratching on the Street." When a state or local government in the United States needs to raise money, particularly for projects such as schools, highways, or hospitals, it often issues municipal bonds or „munis." The actual bond issues are handled by underwriters, typically investment banking firms who issue and sell the bonds to their clients and other interested investors. Municipal bonds are desirable investments because they are tax exempt in most states, their yield is high, most these bonds are rated as to their value and likelihood of maturing (e.g., by letters such as „B", „A," „AA", etc.), many are insured, and there is an extremely low default rate, even on low-rated uninsured bonds[27]. The problem is as follows. According to *Business Week*,

For decades, Wall Street investment bankers and state and local politicians have enjoyed a mutually beneficial relationship. Politicians dispense more than $1 billion in taxpayer dollars a year to the Street in fees to un-

---

27 See SUSAN E. KUHN: „Munis: the Last of the Tax Havens", *Fortune: 1991 Investor's Guide*, pp. 189-192.

derwrite municipal-bond issues. The Street, in turn, sends politicians millions in campaign contributions[28].

Two examples:

The US Attorney's office and the SEC are looking into whether Merrill Lynch & Co. bestowed financial favours on a tiny Clementon (N.J.) brokerage form to win $2.0 billion worth of New Jersey Municipal-bond business. At issue is whether the firm, Armacon Securities, helped Merrill get business through Armacon's part owners, Joseph C. Salema, who happened to be the NJ Governor James Florio's chief of staff. All parties deny any wrongdoing or that they are targets of the investigations. Salem had said his Armacon stake is in a blind trust[29].

Last September just as a $210 million Chicago Cook County bond issue was about to hit the market, underwriters and attorneys on the deal got a message from County Board President Richard J. Phelan's chief fund raiser... On stationery emblazoned with „Citizens for Phelan" a Democratic fund-raising committee asked bond advisers for $1500 contributions to three Phelan political allies....". „Citizens for Phelan" has already collected over $400,000 from bond professionals who work on Cook County deals including $91,500 from Goldman Sachs and its employees. That is almost 25% of Phelan's entire $1.75 million campaign war chest[30]. Holland and Light, pp. 46-7, 1993]

What is wrong with this *quid pro quo* arrangement? It is not illegal, and in fact municipal bond underwriting is unregulated. Nevertheless, there is an obvious possible conflict of interest on the part of politicians. Contributions to these politicians leads to the strong likelihood that there will be favoritism to donors rather than competitive bidding based on the merit of the underwriting contracts. The *quid pro quo* arrangement, then, reinforces questionable political behavior. Moreover, some underwriters also act as financial advisors to municipalities where they underwrite the issue-another possible conflict of interest.

Third, this system is costly to taxpayers, because municipalities do not always get the best price for the underwriting fees. For municipal bond in-

28 Leah Nathans Spiro, Larry Light, Chuck Hawkins, and Geoffrey Smith: „Back-Scratching on the Street," *Business Week*, May 24, 1993, pp. 122.

29 *Ibid*, p. 122.

30 *Ibid*.

vestors insufficient disclosure is coupled with the fact that there is no public market for trading; so one does not always pay the best price for the bonds. From the underwriter's perspective, one is involved in giving political contributions that are not always voluntary nor to a party of one's choice. These firms are „held hostage to the system," doing what almost no underwriter would think was the „right thing." Thus almost every stakeholder except politicians suffers as a result of this practice.

Municipal bond underwriting is an interesting phenomenon, because almost all underwriters are involved in some payoff scheme. In fact, however, most underwriters do not approve of these procedures, they recognize the improprieties, but they feel trapped. If an underwriter does not contribute, the company is unlikely to get the underwriting. So it appears that companies are trapped not because they are unethical but because of the political system of contributions and payoffs. How should underwriters deal with this sort of situation?

In October 1993, 17 of the largest Wall Street underwriting firms instituted a voluntary ban on campaign contributions and announced guidelines for putting this into effect. Under the sponsorship of the SEC Chairperson Arthur Levitt they agreed to put an end to contributions to state and local campaigns by their firms, by their political action committees, employees, and senior management. Any exceptions require disclosure of contributions and no contribution can be made to a political candidate or official with whom one is doing business. To date 42 of the largest underwriting firms have subscribed to the voluntary ban, and the Municipal Securities Rulemaking Board, a self-regulatory organization, is developing a rule that prohibits municipal bond companies from doing underwriting for two years if they violate the ban[31]. This move took creativity and moral imagination. It was risky, because one was not sure of the extent of the buy-in by all underwriting firms, and, like most decisions, it is not a perfect solution. Small firms, particularly those who live in small communities where part of being a good citizen is making political contributions are questioning the decision. But it is a way to stop the political entrapment and corruption, perhaps the only way except excessive regulation.

---

31 See JONATHAN FUREBRINGER: „Bond Firms Disclose Guides for Banning Political Gifts", *New York Times*, December 9, 1993, pp. D1, D18, and MERCEDES M. CARDONA: „Political Gifts Ban Considered", *Pensions and Investments*, November 1, 1993, pp. 2, 58.

VII. Moral Leadership

Engaging in a moral dialogue, being morally imaginative, treating all stakeholders fairly, and taking into account moral minimums is risky, one may fail--fair morally and/or fail financially. I want now to conclude by describing a positive example of such risk-taking, the development of the South Shore Bank of Chicago.

The South Shore Bank is located in the South Shore area of Chicago covering a neighborhood population of about 80,000. Before the 1960s the neighborhood was made up of lower-middle class and middle class apartments and houses and one 4-block square section of mansions. The neighborhood was primarily Jewish, and there was a tradition of staying in the neighborhood moving up to more affluent areas as one's economic status improved. In the 1960s as you all know there was a mass migration of blacks into the Northern cities and a subsequent „white flight" from certain neighborhoods, including South Shore. By 1970 the population of South Shore was primarily black and poor and it was predicted that within 5 years the neighborhood would become one of the worst slums in Chicago. The South Shore Bank, whose deposits had been steadily falling to $42 million, was for sale, and in 1973 a group of entrepreneurs led by Ronald Grzywinski borrowed enough money to buy the institution for under $4 million. Today, still located in South Shore, this bank has assets of almost $180 million, it is profitable, although not wildly so, and its net loan losses in 1991 were .12%, the lowest for any bank of its size. Yet until recently most of its loans were to the South Shore neighborhood. (Two years ago it moved into a second low-income neighborhood in Chicago: the Austin neighborhood, and it has also opened a bank and a program in rural Arkansas.) How is this possible?

What the bank did was to focus its attention on housing and to loan money to people willing to rehab buildings in South Shore. It also set up a series of subsidiaries, one of which concentrates on real estate development, another on minority business enterprises, a nonprofit institution that works with state and federal programs to rehab and develop housing for low income residences, and a subsidiary that serves as a consulting firm for these other projects. It has raised money through what it calls Development Deposits, encouraging wealthy people from other neighborhoods to open accounts at South Shore. Today South Shore, still primarily black except in the mansion area which is 40/60, is a viable place to live. Drugs and gangs are virtually absent, and more than 3/4 of the residences and apartments are restored and inhabited.

It took imagination and leadership, moral imagination and moral leadership, to engage in a project that no other Chicago bank at that time would engage in, in a neighbourhood that leading sociologists had written off, particularly when the project is neither a government project nor a charity but is a for-profit and a profitable enterprise, and to see the low-risk element in this kind of venture. The South Shore Bank team had to rethink the traditional banking model which, for the most part, was fiscally conservative. For its part, South Shore Bank officers do not claim to be Mother Theresas. Rather, they argue, they lent money to people and enterprises that were less risky than many Third World recipients of Big Bank loans[32]. From a moral point of view South Shore Bank developed its stakeholders: its customers and the community, it respected their interests and in the process became very successful.

Finally, why should one try to become a moral leader? Why take the „high road" when making money in financial markets is so easy? This is highly speculative, I would suggest that sometimes, just sometimes, if one sets a standard and one is a leader, positive changes will occur that benefit more stakeholders and benefit them more in the long-term. Sometimes, then, if one takes the risk of leadership, one sets a positive precedent, and changes occur that are morally appropriate and financially successful as well.

---

32 See RICHARD TAUB: *Community Capitalism* (Boston: Harvard Business School Press, 1988) for a detailed analysis of the South Shore Bank and its development.

Chapter 8

Comment on Patricia H. Werhane

K. ALEC CHRYSTAL

The traditional role of a discussant of an academic paper in the Anglo-Saxon world seems to be to criticise. This role raises its own ethical dilemmas. Especially in the context in which the primary author has done a great deal of work, without which the discussant would have no role at all. Indeed, in the present context criticism would be inappropriate for two reasons. Firstly, the author is an established expert in the field of business ethics, while the discussant is not. Secondly, there is almost nothing in the paper with which I could greatly disagree. However, I think it fair to comment that Professor Werhane stays on safe ground by focusing mainly on the identification of ethical dilemmas and less on the more difficult solutions. In the absence of disagreements it is, nonetheless, incumbent upon me to say something. So I thought that it might be helpful to add some observations from a British perspective.

Some of these observations are motivated by the issues Professor Werhane raises, while others are additional.

I. Short-Termism

I was very surprised to find Professor Werhane referring to short-termism as a uniquely American phenomenon. Before reading her paper I thought it was a uniquely British phenomenon! Could it be that this is a more wide-spread issue than either of us realises. Certainly it has been hotly debated in Britain over the last few years. Indeed, only within the last two weeks there have been statements from both the Government and the opposition Labour Party supporting the view that pressure from financial markets for high dividends has harmed long term investment. The evidence from Britain is hardly supportive of this view. Many of the most actively traded companies are also the biggest investors in research and development. Names which spring to mind include three of the world's top drug companies, Glaxo, Wellcome and SmithKlein-Beacham as well as Rolls Royce, ICI, British Aerospace and GEC. The puzzle in Britain is, rather, why when we have so many successful big companies are we so lacking in successful small and medium size companies? The blame is more likely to lie in the shortage of entrepeneurship rather than in the short-termism of the financial markets.

One reason for this is that the country's brightest students have traditionally sought careers in the City or the professions (law, accountancy and civil service) rather than in manufacturing industry or commerce. This has meant a „class“ difference between the financiers of the City and the industrialists of the North of England. The mutual mistrust which this has engendered goes back at least to the early years after the industrial revolution-early 1800s. A polite word for this mistrust seems to be short-termism.

II. Insider Trading

Insider trading has been around for a long time. In 1672 the English government (Scotland was still independent) stopped payment on its paper debt. A securities trader operating at the sign of the Grasshopper (a sign which can been seen today outside the Lombard Street offices of Banque Paribas) had advanced warning of this „Stop of the Exchequer“ from a friend in government and managed to sell his holdings, and those of his main clients, before the market collapsed. The fact that the event has been reported in the history books suggests that his contemporaries were not too pleased with his behaviour.

An interesting footnote to these events is that, not surprisingly, no-one would lend to the government for a long time after that. A wheeler-dealer named William Paterson, who had failed to launch many schemes before, came up with a plan to launch a new bank. This bank was to raise a loan for the government in exchange for special privileges. These privileges included a monopoly of government banking, a monopoly of joint stock banking and later a monopoly of the note issue. So successful was this scheme, that we are celebrating the 300th anniversary of this institution, the Bank of England, this very month.

Coming up to date, a new regime is just coming into force in the London financial markets. The Appendix to these comments sets out the detail of the new legislation and SFA (Securities and Futures Authority) rule book as communicated to the employees of a major London merchant bank. Also included are a set of legal interpretations by a prominent firm of City lawyers, also distributed to the same employees. Clearly, insider trading is being taken very seriously.

The most difficult part of this legislation relates to analysts. The job of analysts is to study companies and to use the product of study to form a view of companies likely performance and then to advise clients on which stocks to buy. However, under the new law „...an analyst will be an insider under the new law if, through his own research, he arrives at a price sensitive conclusion about a particular company - even though he has no connection with that company and does not have any inside information in the traditional sense. If he passes on his views before making them public, the recipient of his advice will also be an insider. Fortunately, an analyst who bases his price sensitive conclusion on public information can treat his conclusion itself as public... The analyst whose conclusion is based on a mix of published and unpublished information may be in a more difficult position - even where the unpublished information is not in itself significant.“

One cannot help but wonder whether the regulators have gone too far. Why would anyone hire an equity analyst if all they can use is published information? Analysts and the portfolio managers they advise are supposed to have specialist knowledge based upon, among other things a direct knowledge of the companies in the sector they are monitoring. Is such intimate knowledge to be a thing of the past? If so we should all return to picking stocks with a dart board.

III. The Market for Corporate Control

My main trouble with the discussion of the Market for Corporate Control (MCC) is that in England we know MCC as the Marylebone Cricket

Club. Apart from this, I found this the most interesting part of Professor Werhane's paper. It was very thorough and I learned a great deal from it.

There are two points in this section of her paper that I would like to expand a little. First, she sights a statistic that „only about 50% of mergers are financially successful" (p15) as evidence against the let „let it rip" school of MCC. In fact her statistic suggest that the MCC is, indeed, highly efficient. This number is consistent with takeovers being concluded at or close to the true market value of the underlying assets. Hence, on average about half do well and half do badly. This would be true of the normal population of firms. However, she omits to say that the previous owners of the target firm have on average walked away with a 30% profit on their shares, compared to the pre-bid price. Hence, the takeover has eliminated a pre-existing inefficiency rather than creating a new one.

May second point relates to the Dayton Hudson example which is quoted with approval. It may well be that this case worked out for the best. However, subsequent cases will suffer from a problem that economists call „incentive compatibility". If Minnesota were to create a general climate in which all similar takeovers would be prevented by state regulators, then other Minnesota firms would rest on their laurels and presume themselves to be safe from takeover. Dayton Hudson shook themselves up because they thought they might not be safe. But this could only happen once. If they had known in advance that they were safe, they could have carried on with their old inefficiencies, creating losses for many stakeholders. Hence, just because this case worked out does not mean that the threat of takeover should be reduced or even eliminated.

The final two points I wish to make relate to hot topics in the U.K. which have not been mentioned so far.

IV. Corporate Greed

The biggest ethical issue around today in Britain relates to the enormous salaries of senior managers at a time when workers are being laid off and the companies they run are not doing especially well. Indeed, in many cases the payout is a reward for being fired! This issue has been further complicated by privatisations. Many mangers of newly privatised utilities have taken the opportunity to award themselves massive pay rises, while carrying on the same job in a protected industry.

The following are quotes from London Newspapers in the last week alone (but relating to a longer period).

> „John Clark, chief executive of BET, received a pay rise from £708,000 to £924,000 last year. The average wage at BET rose last year from £8,200 to £8,400."
> „Dr Ernest Mario, ousted in March 1993 as chief executive of Glaxo, left with payments estimated at more than £3million - the largest payout in British history."
> „Bob Horton, sacked as BP boss in 1992, walked away with £1.5 million."
> „Jim Maxmin, who left Laura Ashley after a dispute, was paid £1.2 million for loss of office."

And there are many more. Clearly these figures raise serious ethical issues about corporate governance. It is also a problem which has become globalised along with the globalisation of financial markets. Executives claim it is an international executive market and they have to be paid at international levels. This may be true, but it does not make the facts any easier to swallow.

V. Best Advice

My final point relates to the area of financial advice to retail customers. Britain was plagued in the 1980s with sales advice which was motivated by the commissions received by salesman, rather than by the interest of customers. In excess of 1 million people were persuaded to opt out of company pension plans and invest in private pension schemes in the late 1980s. In almost all cases this was a crazy thing to do because, as a result, they lost their employers pension contribution, dramatically lowering their long term pension. A similar story could be told about endowment policy linked mortgages. In both cases, the advice has been motivated by the commission received by the salesman.

The puzzle in this story is why the regulators dragged their feet so long before forcing a full revelation of commissions. This comes into force in 1995. However, since 1986, we have had in operation a Financial Services Act which was supposed to protect the consumer. The regulators failed to act sufficiently strongly because the insurance industry lobbied too hard. „Insurance is sold not bought“ they used to say. Now we know why!

In conclusion, I would like to thank Professor Werhane for her thought provoking paper. I learned a great deal from it and I am sure that it will be agreed generally that she has made an important contribution to our understanding of these serious but neglected issues.

Chapter 9

Comment on Patricia H. Werhane

A. CRAIG MCKINLAY

I found this paper by Professor Werhane to be a thought provoking piece. It certainly lead me to think about a number of issues which I previously had not considered. It seems that financial ethics as a field is still in its infancy. I believe that projects such as this research conference will play an important role in its development.

In terms of the specifics of my discussion, I will address three topics considered by the author. First I will make a few comments on ethics and insider trading. Then I will comment on the author's analysis of the ethics of mergers and acquisitions, and finally I will comment on ethics relating to institutional investors.

In my discussion I will attempt to bring an economics and finance perspective to the table. If I were to define an underlying theme to my discussion, I would claim that the divergence of rational economic behaviour and ethical behaviour is not as large as it may first appear. Also, I would argue that as the field of financial ethics moves forward, additional empirical work will be valuable to verify or reject theories.

I. Insider Trading

Insider trading perhaps represents the cleanest example of an apparent divergence between ethical behaviour and rational economic behaviour. As the author reports most economic analysis of the role of insider trading argues that the prohibition of insider trading leads to prices being less informative and as a consequence the capital allocation process in general will not be efficient. Hence society as a whole would be better off in the presence of insider trading.

The author argues, I believe correctly, that such a view is flawed because the analysis does not fully incorporate all the effects. Indeed, some recent research illustrates with a richer model that on economic grounds it may be desirable to regulate insider trading. The divergence between ethics and economic efficiency is eliminated and the prohibition of insider trading can be justified on economic grounds as it is Pareto improving. Lawrence Ausubel has a 1990 article in *The American Economic Review* titled „Insider Trading in a Rational Expectations Economy“ which provides such a model. In his model the fact that outsiders expect insiders to take advantage of them in trading leads to the outsiders committing less capital. The reduced investment from outsiders can more than offset the gains to the insider from inside trading. I think the idea of reduced investment represents a more realistic form of „punishment“ to insiders than does the possibility of trading on wrong information that the author discusses. The bottom line is that ethical behaviour and rational economic behaviour may not be as inconsistent as some would argue.

Let me add to the authors comments on the American experience with insider trading. In the United States there have been at least three main approaches to minimize the volume of insider trading. One approach has been for the Securities and Exchange Commission (SEC) to actively pursue insider trading cases using existing laws. This serves as an after the fact deterrent. A second approach has been for the SEC to impose stringent reporting requirements for publicly traded firms. This helps to minimize the existence of inside information. A third approach is for the exchanges to monitor the trading process and identify and investigate times of unusual price or volume behaviour. For example the New York Stock Exchange has a „Stock Watch“ unit which flags unusual activity. When unusual activity is noted trading can be halted until an explanation is obtained. In aggregate the approaches in the US implicitly suggest that the control of insider trading is an important ingredient for a successful stock market. It would be interesting to investigate if there is any correlation between the degree of insider trading and the importance of the stock market as a source of capital across countries. In general, such cross-country investigations could be fruitful.

As a side bar to the reporting requirements, it is interesting to note that the NYSE is requesting the SEC to waive some of the stringent requirements for foreign firms which are listed on the exchange. Apparently these requirements are a major impediment to the listing of more foreign corporations. The NYSE believes that foreign listings represent an area for potential growth in terms of trading volume. So this is a case where regulation may be unnecessary and costly.

Although most would agree that insider trading is unethical, the extent to which it is a real problem in the US is debatable. Meulbroek (1992) in an article published in the Journal of Finance studies stock price effects of insider trading for cases prosecuted by the Securities and Exchange Commission. She finds that market prices adjust quickly on what are identified as insider trading days. This finding suggests that the potential damage from insider trading is reduced by the fact that the market seems able to recognize informed trading.

II. Mergers and Acquisitions

Mergers and acquisitions give rise to an interesting ethical question which the author puts forward. She persuasively argues that the ethics of the acquisition decision are questionable given that normally only the interests of the stockholders are considered. The interests of the firm's other stakeholders are largely ignored. These other stakeholders include the employees, the customers, the community, and the debtholders of the firm. She then argues that the extent of unethical behaviour can be reduced through legislation restricting acquisitions.

The argument is illustrated by an example. The example is the attempted takeover of Dayton Hudson, a US discount retail chain, by the Dart Group, a competing retail conglomerate. This case, which occurred in 1987, involved the management of Dayton Hudson strongly opposing the acquisition and persuading the Minnesota legislature to intervene. The author concludes that „without the intervention of the Minnesota legislature and strong community support, it is unlikely that the Dart takeover could have been prevented.“ And she goes on to say „So it is not always the case that the market by itself can always regulate possible abuses.“

In reading professor Werhane's analysis a number of questions come to mind. First, taking as given that the management decisions should be in the joint interest of all the stakeholders, how do we measure the interests of the stakeholders beyond the stockholders? How does one separate target management acting in their own interests from acting in the interest of the non-owner stakeholders? What is the appropriate cost-benefit tradeoff between the stockholders and the other stakeholders? How effective is legislation in restricting takeovers? I do not believe these questions have easy or clear cut answers. If one wants to play the role of the devil's advocate, one can put a different spin on the case of the attempted acquisition of Dayton Hudson by Dart Group than the author does. Let me elaborate.

In order to address the issues presented by the author and the questions outlined above, I did some background research on the Dayton Hudson case and the financial performance of its common equity. Briefly, based on articles from the Wall Street Journal, this is how the case played itself out during 1987. On June 22 the Journal reported that Dayton Hudson confirmed that the Dart Group had a stake in it and was interested in acquiring it. Also reported was a company request to the Governor of Minnesota to call a special session of the legislature to toughen the state's anti-takeover law. Stories in the Journal on June 23 and 24 reported that Dart had made on official offer for Dayton Hudson and that the management's request for more legislation was likely to be successful.

On June 26 the Journal reported that the Minnesota Legislature had indeed passed a stronger anti-takeover bill. The bill, among other things, gave the shareholders the right to decide if a given shareholder could vote more than 20% of the company's shares and restricted the acquirer's ability to sell the target's assets after a takeover. The article also correctly speculated that Dart's attempt to acquire Dayton Hudson may not yet be dead. One month later on July 27 Dayton Hudson made public a letter from Dart indicating its intention to acquire Dayton Hudson .

Over the next several months, Dart's interest in Dayton Hudson remained strong with another formal offer reported in the Journal on September 18. On October 15 it was reported that Dayton Hudson had rejected a sweetened deal under heavy criticism from its major shareholders. A few days later with the market crash of October 19, 1987 the potential for a merger came to a quick end. The Journal reported on October 21 that Dart dropped its effort to acquire Dayton Hudson due to uncertainty of financing.

In addition to tracing the history of the deal, I analyzed the value of the common equity of Dayton Hudson. I considered two time periods: May 18, 1987 through December 31, 1987 on a daily basis and December 31, 1986 through December 31,1993 on a monthly basis. The daily results are presented in Figure 1 and the monthly results are reported in Figure 2. For comparison the figures also include the value of a $1 investment in an equally weighted portfolio of the equity of two of Dayton Hudson's competitors, K. Mart and Wal-Mart, and the value of a $ 1 investment in a value weighted market basket of stocks (the CRSP value-weighted index).

FIGURE 1

Growth of $1 Investments

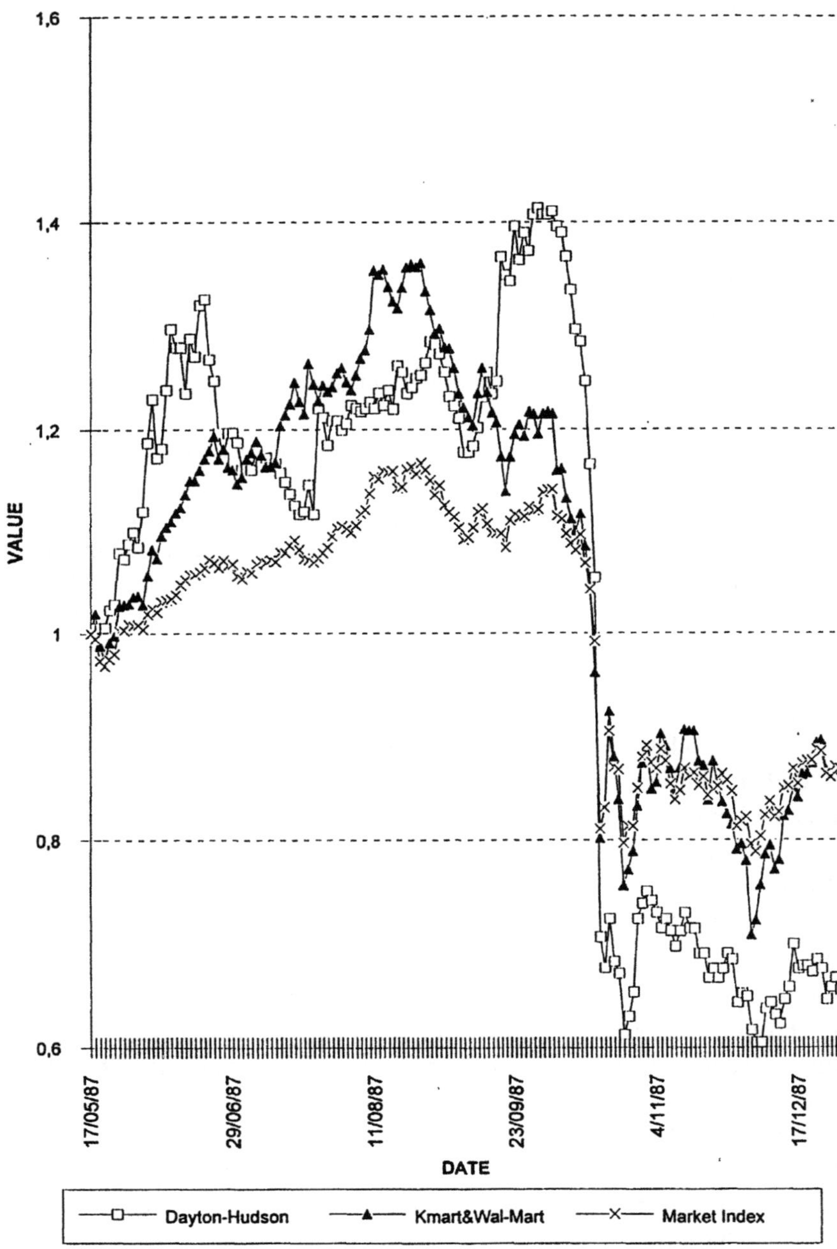

FIGURE 2

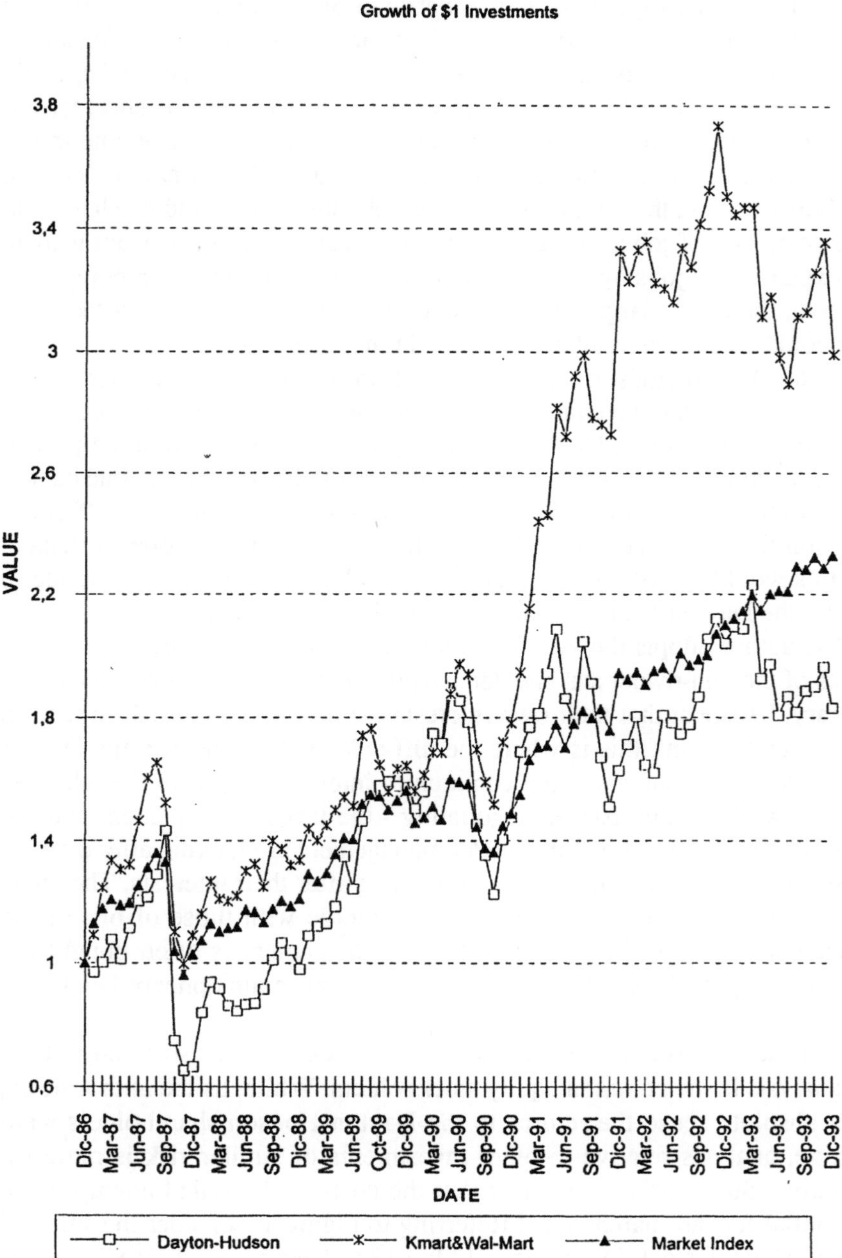
Growth of $1 Investments
VALUE
3,8
3,4
3
2,6
2,2
1,8
1,4
1
0,6
DATE
Dic-86
Mar-87
Jun-87
Sep-87
Dic-87
Mar-88
Jun-88
Sep-88
Dic-88
Mar-89
Jun-89
Oct-89
Dic-89
Mar-90
Jun-90
Sep-90
Dic-90
Mar-91
Jun-91
Sep-91
Dic-91
Mar-92
Jun-92
Sep-92
Dic-92
Mar-93
Jun-93
Sep-93
Dic-93
Dayton-Hudson
Kmart&Wal-Mart
Market Index

Drawing on this information now I will address the previously posed questions. Measuring the costs or benefits of an acquisition offer for non-owner stakeholders of the target firm is invariably subjective. This subjectivity, I believe, is partially responsible for the apparent lack of specific consideration of their interests. Consider the employees. In the short term it seems clear that if they lose their job they are worse off. But beyond that it is difficult to say much. Indeed, relating to the author's distinction between the short term and the long term, it is possible that there could be short term costs (e.g. loss of jobs) but larger long term gains (e.g. significant growth and expansion of jobs by a restructured firm). From an purely economic perspective, there is a danger that focusing on employee interests in the short term could actually hurt all stakeholders in the long term.

In the Dayton Hudson case, since the firm is still an ongoing concern, it seems plausible that the employees gained from the fact that the takeover attempt failed. However, Dayton Hudson, prior to the takeover attempt, had closed or sold five divisions which did lead to job losses. Hence, one cannot rule out the possibility that the employees might have been better off under the control of Dart. Although Dart's prior record may lead one to suspect that this would not be the case, the firm did claim that it would continue to operate the Dayton Hudson stores without eliminating employees.

The author adopts the view that target management are acting in the interests of the non-owner stakeholders. While I cannot present evidence to the contrary, I suspect that their own interests are not being ignored. In fact, to some extent, I think this is where the difficulty with respect to the lack of consideration of employee and community interests arises. In the takeover process, we have two parties negotiating - the target management and the bidder management. I think the bidder management are looking after their interests and the target management are looking after their interests. The interests of others go unattended unless the coincide with those of one of the management groups. The fact that target management is often bought out with golden parachutes is not consistent with their main concern being employees and community interests.

The one group of stakeholders for which we can provide some cost - benefit analysis is the common equity stockholders. While, as the author notes, in an absolute sense the returns to the Dayton Hudson shareholders were positive, analysis relative to other investments of similar risk is more informative. Such analysis suggests that the costs of the failed attempt were substantial for the shareholders. Referring to Figure 1, consider the value of Dayton Hudson stock for the period May 17 to December 31, 1987. For the overall period the value of Dayton Hudson declined by 35%. In contrast, the value of a portfolio of Dayton Hudson's competitors K.mart and Wal-Mart declined by only 13%. Over this period, the decline of the Standard and Poor's 500 stock index was also much smaller at 13%. Clearly in terms of the short term value of their holdings, the Dayton Hudson shareholders did not fare well.

Even if one takes a long term view, the common stock of Dayton Hudson appears to be a laggard. Consider the returns for Dayton Hudson and competing investments for the seven year period from the end of 1986 through the end of 1993. These results are presented in Figure 2. Over this period Dayton Hudson appreciated at an annualized rate of 9.0%, whereas the K.mart and Wal-Mart portfolio appreciated at an annualized rate of 17.0% and the S&P index appreciated at a rate of 12.8%. I believe there is a lack of support for the view that the equity holders of Dayton Hudson were not harmed by the failure of the acquisition.

Lastly I address the effectiveness of legislation as a tool for blocking undesirable takeover attempts. While I am sure there are many cases which support its effectiveness, I do not believe that Dayton Hudson represents such a case. As previously noted, the Minnesota legislature passed an anti-takeover bill which was reported on June 26. Yet Dart's pursuit of Dayton Hudson actively continued into the fall of 1987.

The *Wall Street Journal* on September 18 reported that Robert Haft, Dart's president, did not view Minnesota's law as a deterrent. Returning to Figure 2, the markets seem to confirm that investors still thought the takeover may succeed after the law was passed. The passing of the legislation did initially have a large impact on the value of Dayton Hudson's stock, with the value declining close to 20% from mid June until mid July. But then as Dart persisted, the price of Dayton Hudson increased to new highs throughout July, August, September, and October.

What brought an end to the takeover attempt was an exogenous economic event, the stock market crash of October 19, 1987. When the US market declined over 20% that day, it became apparent that Dart could no longer obtain financing for the takeover. Indeed, over the October crash, the value of Dayton Hudson dropped by 52%, reflecting not only the crash itself, but the elimination of the premium that existed in anticipation of Dart's takeover.

What do we learn from this analysis of the Dayton Hudson case? What I take away from it is that detailed investigation will often reveal questions about commonly drawn conclusions. In particular for this case a number of quibbles with the author's conclusions are possible. For example:

1. I believe that the evidence supporting the argument that the nonowner stakeholders of Dayton Hudson were better off without the merger is weak.
2. In my view there is evidence supporting the view that the Dayton Hudson shareholders were worse off. Also the Dart owners suffered large financial losses. (See *The Wall Street Journal*, October 21,1987).
3. I believe that the key factor in the acquisition not going ahead was not the new Minnesota legislation but an unusual and unexpected economic event, the Market crash of October 1987.

I make no claims that my differing conclusions from this case are completely general. Indeed, 1 think that an examination of other cases would illustrate great difficulty in arriving at general conclusions.

III. Institutional Investing

The author provides an interesting analysis of institutional investing. She asks whether institutional investor activism on a general level is in some sense unethical. I think not. I believe that the dominant effect of such activism is to provide checks and balances for corporate management which otherwise may go largely unmonitored. Perhaps more examples of nonowner stakeholders being damaged by such activism would be helpful.

The discussion of the case of the fund manager being fired for trading on his own account ahead of the fund he manages in my view provides a good example of how a well functioning free market can induce ethical behaviour. Invesco fired Kaweske, not because any regulation required it, but because the firm felt keeping him employed would be costly in terms of their reputation and future business. Since this case surfaced the mutual fund industry has, independent of any government action, taken the initiative of establishing guidelines for ethical trading by fund managers. (See „Fund Industry To Unveil Rules On Personal Trades“, *The Wall Street Journal*, May 9, 1994, page C1.)

IV. Concluding Remarks

In summary I would like to again commend Professor Werhane for writing such an interesting paper. It is my hope that papers such as this will stimulate more work in this area.

References

AUSUBEL, LAWRENCE W. (1990): „Insider Trading In a Rational Expectations Economy", *American Economic Review*, Vol. 80, No. 5, pp. 1022-1041.

MEULBROEK, LISA K. (1992): „An Empirical Analysis of Insider Trading", *Journal of Finance*, Vol. 47, No. 5, pp. 1661-1700.

Chapter 10

The Ethics of Banking
On the Ethical Economy of the Credit and Capital Market, of Speculation and Insider Trading in the German Experience

PETER KOSLOWSKI

A developed money, credit and capital market which provides the economy with the financial resources necessary for economic transactions and growth is a generally acclaimed hallmark of economic development. Banks play a vital role as the intermediary institutions in the money, credit and capital market. They mediate the money supply in the money market between the central bank and the economy. They mediate credit between the demand for credit and the supply of savings, and they finally function as mediator between industry's demand for capital and secured loans and the supply of capital from industry, financial immediaries and private individuals. Banks are therefore the intermediators par excellence. In a system of universal banking as the German banking system, banks are, however, not only intermediaries for investment but also judges of investors and of alternative investment uses of capital as well as of the creditworthiness of their customers in the credit market. They are not only mediating, but constantly evaluating risks and creditworthiness. Banks furthermore act as investors for their own account in the stock exchange and give advice to institutional and private investors for their investment in the capital market. Their roles as evaluators and judges in the credit market and as investors and consultants to other investors in the capital market cause that they are influential factors in the economic process far beyond their function as mediators between savings and investments.

Where there is a lot of influence and power there must be a lot of responsibility and moral consciousness since power is in itself a moral or ethical phenomenon. All powerful action must be morally responsible and defendable. It seems therefore a matter of course to demand an ethical code for banking and the stock of exchange. When we look at the present discussion in German economic science we find little literature on the ethics of banking.[1] The reason for this is the separation of economic and ethical analysis brought about by general equilibrium analysis in neoclassical economics. In general equilibrium, the economic good, i.e. efficiency is defined independently from the ethical good, i.e. justice. Due to the assumption of general equilibrium theory that preferences are what they are (revealed preference theorem) and are coordinated to allocative efficiency solely by economic, not by ethical, adaptation (*tatonnement*) there is no space for ethical considerations concerning the justice of the preferences, of the original distribution of endowments and of the outcoming allocation of factors, goods and services. Since the stock exchange is generally considered to be a perfect market approaching conditions of perfect competition there seems to be no need for an ethics of the stock exchange. Here, more than in any other market, it is thought that general equilibrium is reached without recourse to ethics. The paper will demonstrate that this is not the case. The credit and capital markets are more in need of a business ethics than other markets due to the abstract and intangible character of their business, financing, and due to the fungible and space independent character of their merchandise, money.

There has been a more elaborate discussion on the ethics of banking and the capital market in Germany in the 1920ies in the natural right tradition which went beyond the confines of positive economics and included ethical argument in the economic analysis. This approach of an economics including ethical considerations to banking and the stock exchange responded to the Great Inflation and Depression and the stock exchange crashes of the years between the two World Wars[2] just as today the interest in the ethical analysis of banking and financial market responds to the insider trading and speculation problems of the 1980ies. In the following, elements of the discussion from the 1920ies will be used and applied to current problems.

1 Cf. ANDREAS (1992); JACOB (1990); JACOB (1992).

2 Central is NELL-BREUNING (1928).

A. General Ethics and Ethical Economy: the Theoretical Foundations

I. General Ethics

1. Virtues, Goods, and Duties

Ethical theory analyses and gives prescriptive propositions on the attitudes, preferential acts and rules of coordination of actions. It aims at clarifying and improving the habits of the individuals, their preferences and the rules by which they coordinate their actions with those of the others.[3] Since Stoic ethics, ethical theory aims at the theory of virtues, the theory of goods and the theory of duties. Virtues are about the attitudes and *habitus* of the acting persons. Goods are about what values the acting persons do or should estimate and prefer at the external goods that carry these value qualities. Duties describe the obligations to stick to the rules that reasonably govern the interaction with others. Virtues, goods and duties form the basic concepts or categories of general ethics. The „ethics of banking", therefore, analyses, criticizes and formulates the virtues, the preferences for goods and values, and the duties of the persons working in financial institutions.

2. Individual Ethics, Personal Ethics, and Institutional Ethics

Ethics can furthermore be distinguished on another dimension according to the addressee of ethical reasoning. The question whether the individual in his or her relationship with him- or herself, whether the relationship with the personal other in personal interaction, or whether the relationship of all with each other, the institutional setting of actions, is concerned renders a different type of ethical analysis, i. e. individual, personal or institutional ethics. The „ethics of banking" can mean the ethical analysis of the institutional setting of banking and financial markets, of the rules of banking, or the ethical analysis of the individual's actions within the set of rules and institutions of banking. The ethics of banking comprises as well the analysis of banking institutions and rules of action, the social or institutional ethics of banking, as the analysis of the individual and personal ethics of banking, the analysis

3 KOSLOWSKI (1988).

of the individual banker's action and attitudes towards him- or herself and the analysis of the banker's personal interaction with others, his coworkers or clients. In the following, all three aspects, the individual, personal and institutional ethics of banking shall be examined. The ethics of banking investigates into the norms of banking, into the virtues, goods, and duties of the banker in his or her relationship to him- or herself, in his or her relationship to others and into the virtues, goods, and duties of the banking industry that guide the definition of its institutions and informal and formal rules. Ethics explains, criticizes and tries to improve the ethical rules that govern the financial industry.

3. Morals and Mores

Ethics is the analysis of the morals (*Sittlichkeit*) and mores (*Sitte*), of the universalizable and unconditional rules of morality and of the historical and changeable, conditional role expectations of customs and conventions. Since ethical rules of morality and cultural customs are not the only normative rules and means of social coordination in society, ethics must also analyse the relationships of the ethical order to the other normative orders of the economy in general and of banking in particular, i. e. to the rules of law and of positive economics.

4. The Ethical as the Totality of Normative Aspects Versus the Ethical as Justice

Ethical analysis can furthermore be distinguished along another dimension as the analysis of the totality of the aspects of the good which includes all aspects of normative analysis. Ethical analysis in the wide sense embraces the economic analysis of the efficient, the aesthetic analysis of the beautiful, the political analysis of the common good, and the ethical analysis of the ethical in the narrow sense as just or fair conduct towards others. In the wide sense, the ethical includes all dimensions of the good and judges institutions and actions according to the criterion whether they fulfil all these aspects. To be ethical or just is the state or virtue of an institution or a person in which all aspects of the good and of virtue are realized. Justice (*iustitia*) as the state of the virtuous person includes all the other cardinal virtues, the virtues of prudence/ wisdom (*prudentia/sapientia*), temperence (*temperantia*), and bravery (*fortitudo*).

In a more narrow sense, justice is defined as the ethical as far as it concerns human exchange relationships. It is then just one of the four cardinal virtues. Justice in the narrow sense is the virtue of giving each what he or she is due to receive, *suum cuique tribuere*. Justice as the cardinal virtue of actions in human exchange related to things is the pivotal economic virtue. As the unshakeable attitude and duty to render each his or her own it demands proper conduct and just exchange with others. „The particular character of justice in the narrow sense is, in difference to the other virtues, to order the conduct and exchange related to things which humankind exerts with each other. Justice means, as the name suggests, a certain equilibration."[4]

This ambiguity of the term justice being at the same time one virtue amongst others, the virtue of proper conduct and just exchange, and the totality of all virtues, the character of the righteous human being, has been familiar to ethics from Plato and the Bible until Thomas Aquinas. In his *Republic*, Plato emphasizes that justice is, at the same time, the whole of virtue integrating all other virtues like prudence, wisdom, temperance, and the particular virtue of exchange with others, the virtue of giving each what is due to him. Fair banking and justice in the financial markets requires primarily justice in exchange. Since the attitude of justice in exchange, however, follows from a firm will and habit to act justly it is improved if the people acting in the banking industry follow the general virtue of human excellence or justice in the wide sense.

The Platonic wide concept of justice reminds us that the ethical or moral is not one aspect besides others but is the highest and most encompassing criterion under which we judge social institutions and action.

5. The Definition of Obligations in Institutions Arises from the Nature of the Matter

When the ethical is the most comprehensive understanding of the good the question of the ethics and morality of banking does not primarily contribute an additional moral aspect to the economic, sociological, and political aspects of the topic of banking; rather, it must be understood as the inte-

4 THOMAS AQUINAS, *Summa theologiae* II-II q. 57 a.1re.

grating and moral evaluation of the totality of arguments. Morality is not one aspect among others of an action or institution, but a way to appreciate the perspectives and arguments of the sciences, to order and evaluate them, and to render them meaningful for human action. Ethics tries to do justice to the nature of the matter, to all traits of the matter.[5] The question of the ethics of banking must be which institutional setting of banking is justifiable since it does justice to the nature of banking and the function it fulfills in society. Which conditions of banking make it fulfill its functions in the economy in the proper and just way?

It is the principle of ethics in the tradition of natural right theory, particularly since the Baroque period, that the moral obligation arises from the nature of the object.[6] The ethics of banking can be justified only by the nature of the object, that is, the proper function of banking, the proper conduct and fair exchange that corresponds to this function, and the contributions banking makes to the furthering of human self-realization in the economy. Ethics amounts to appropriateness to the matter and cannot consist in the abstract opposition of a moral ought as against economic arguments. As the distinction between descriptive and prescriptive propositions was never fully maintained and an economic natural right of efficiency always prevailed in economics, the question of the ethics of banking need not fear the naturalistic fallacy because it is not clear whether this fallacy is not in itself a fallacy. The moral inquiry is not opposed to economic theory but must take up the latter and ask whether all aspects of the matter are done justice to.

---

5 This ontological theory of the just and ethical has been worked out most completely in the study of law as the „ontological foundation of law". It is here transferred to ethics. Since ethics is the introduction to the law or the natural law to the positive law this tranfer from law to ethics is well founded. Cf. MAIHOFER (1965) and KOSLOWSKI (1982a).

6 Compare LUIS DE MOLINA: *De justitia et jure* (On Justice, Natural Right and Law), Moguntiae (Madrid) 1602, vol. 1 disput. 4 n.2: „obligatio juris naturalis oritur a natura objecti" (the obligation of natural right arises from the nature of the object); n.3: „Obligatio oritur a natura rei" (the obligation arises from the nature of the matter). Molina was born in Cuenca in 1535 and died in Madrid in 1600. Cf. DÍEZ-ALEGRÍA (1951) and WEBER (1959).

II. Ethical Economy

1. Ethical Economy as Synthesis of Justice and Efficiency in Rational Economic Choice and in Pricing

Ethical economy is the theory of the synthesis of the economic criterion of efficiency and the ethical criterion of justice in exchange and pricing. It takes from economics the microeconomic theory of rational action and from general ethics the theory of justice as the virtue and duty in exchange relationships. The allocative or efficiency criterion is only one aspect of the good and must be supplemented by the fairness criterion*within* the analysis of economic action and exchange.

In the ethics related to production and personal exchange, in general economic ethics as well as in the business ethics of banking, the ethical principle of justice demands in addition to the criterion of efficiency that economic action be not only efficient but that it be also a) proper conduct and b) fair exchange. The efficient *and* fair solution must be realized in the market place. Proper conduct means doing justice to the nature of the matter of the economy and, in our case, to the matter of the financial institutions. Fair exchange demands that the just price and mutually beneficial exchange is realized.[7]

a) Justice as Proper Conduct

The basic prescription of economic ethics is that decision makers act properly to the nature of the matter, i.e. appropriate to the functions of the economy. Economic ethics in their negative formulation demand the cessation of unethical practice such as unfair competition, bribery and corruption. Positively formulated, they demand: act appropriately for the economy. Obey economically proper conduct. The purpose of the economy is to allow the individuals in an economy self-realization and to secure the satisfaction of effective consumer demand. This purpose can only be fulfilled by realizing the efficient allocation of all resources and by doing justice to the matter and to the persons of the economy. Efficient allocation requires the absence of unethical practices by individuals and does not come into being automatically in spite of the wide-spread use of unethical practice.

The demand for proper conduct does not only mean obeying the economy's rules and regulations but refers also to the contents of the intentions

7 See KOSLOWSKI (1989) and KOSLOWSKI (1991).

and plans of people in business. A decision maker in an economy must be oriented towards the purpose of the economy. He must bring into his intentions the purpose of the economy, which is the satisfaction of effective demand and the enablement of the self-development of as many people as possible. The economic decision maker must make the purpose of the economy his own purpose. He must not consider personal profit as the sole content of his intentions, because profit is only one of the means and incentives by which the market economy tries to achieve the goal of an efficient system of allocation and of a good society.

b) Justice as Fairness in Exchange

Regarding the price system and trade, the demand for proper conduct of business turns into the following rule: „In a price system, always act correctly in accordance with the objective goal of the price system", i.e., „When trading, give everybody what he is entitled to according to the undistorted rules of the price system". Proper conduct of the price system demands that everybody receives what he is entitled to according to the rules of coordination by market price. Fair trade is a distinct case of a general fairness principle: „To each his own" (*suum cuique tribuere*). According to the natural right tradition from the Roman *Corpus iuris* up to Thomas Aquinas, fairness is the permanent attitude, supported by will and directed by prudence, to give each his own, especially his rights.

In terms of trading and exchange this principle means: if everybody receives that which he is entitled to, then everybody receives the value equivalent of his goods or services. He receives equivalent money for his goods or services or, on the other hand, equivalent goods for his money. The exchanging of equivalents represents the equilibration of services rendered and renumerations paid. Economic interactions must be made so that nobody is being taken advantage of and everybody receives what he deserves.

Therefore, fair trade includes the fair setting of prices. Fair prices are especially in demand in situations where great leeway for prices exists and where the entrepreneur not only adjusts his quantities to a given market price but where he sets prices, i.e. where oligopolistic or monopolistic market power exists.

Proper conduct and fair price in trade and exchange are defined by four criteria:

1) The actually agreed upon and finally realized price must correspond with the prevailing price, i.e. in the market economy with the market price.

2) The goods exchanged must be genuine and not fake or of bad quality. One must not sell „bogus wheat" instead of real wheat.
3) The exchange must be of benefit to both parties, i.e. not to the disadvantage in net wealth of any of the involved parties.
4) The exchange should represent a fair equalization of interests. The gains of the trade should not be accumulated on one side only.

The demand for fairness or justice in exchange is inevitable, for every free contract needs and creates creative leeway for all contract partners. Prices and contracts do not emerge „by themselves" from the mechanics of the price system. Adapting individual prices to the market price is one of the crucial aspects of fair exchange and trade. In a market economy, harmonizing market prices and individual prices is an ethical problem of price fairness, too.

The theory of ethical economy assumes that the ethical motivation and selective criteria of ethics are of higher rank and obligation then the economic motivation and selective criteria. They overlie the economic motive and goal of efficiency and utility maximization. In normal business there is no conflict between ethics and economics provided that the economic institutions are just. Thus, in normal business, ethics usually need not be emphasized. It is just a matter of course. In a perfectly competitive market, the market price is the just price which the traders must follow. Realizing the market price means realizing the just price. In other, imperfect markets, the prevailing market price has the presumption for itself to be just. There are, however, situations under which the market price is not just since the conditions of its formation violate higher ethical norms like human rights or vital interests of the population etc. Under these circumstances, the theory of ethical economy must demand a change of market conditions on the institutional level and an ethical consideration of fair exchange by the individual and his or her adaptation of the individual price to the just price on the level of his personal business with others.

c) Overdeterminedness of Economic Decisions

Ethics and economics codetermine the conditions of ethico-economic rationality of production and consumption decisions. They are normally not mutually exclusive or contradicting each other but complementary. To use the term „overdetermination" from Freud's interpretation of dreams[8], one could say that human action is „overdetermined" by ethical, economic, and

8 FREUD (1900), vol 2, p. 306ff.

aesthetic determining factors which are usually not in conflict with each other but in coexistence and complementarity.

It must also be emphasized that ethics as well as economics are under normal conditions not an order of the ought or compulsion (*Sollensordnung*) but an order of intention and affirmation (*Wollensordnung*). It is only in situations of conflict between economic utility or profit maximization and ethical demands of justice that the ethical is felt as a constraint on the pursuit of economic action since it then overrules economic self-interest. The aim of economic ethics must be to form economic institutions in which the ethical rules are felt as motives and ethics is considered to be an order of wanting, not of compulsion.

d) Economic Ethics as Inducement to Economic Law

Economic ethics is the inducement to economic law. It prepares and tests new law and it persuades to comply with existing law. Ethics demands and furthers the attention for the principles of fair and efficient business, the *attentio* to the rules and attitudes, and it requires and strengthens the intention and inclination to follow these principles, the *intentio* to realize good business and management. Economic ethics aims at the right intention or *intentio recta* of business.

The right intention plays as vital a role in business as in all professions. The acting person must have the intention to use his or her knowledge and expertise in the proper way since the professional has better knowledge than the non-professional about the possible misuses of his expertise. The stock exchange broker or banker can use his or her knowledge to stabilize or destabilize a currency or a market. „Everything depends on the right economic intention and attitude.“[9] This intention is, however, not controllable or enforcable from the outside and by the law. The law can only aim at the external behaviour, not at the inner motives. Since the inner motives matter ethics matters, and since the law aims only at external behaviour ethics cannot be substituted by the law. According to H. Kantorowicz, the law is the totality of social rules that prescribe external behaviour and are seen as justiciable (*gerichtsfähig*). Justiciable are rules that are apt to be applied by an organ of the judiciary in due process.[10] Business ethics formulates norms

9 BRAUER (1925), p. 190: „Es kommt alles auf die Wirtschaftsgesinnung an.“ Brauer's sentence is also quoted as motto in NELL-BREUNING (1928), p. 1.

10 KANTOROWICZ (1963), p. 90.

that are able to shape the inner motives and it includes norms that are not justiciable and therefore transcend the law.

Business ethics forms an order of obligation, of internal and nonjusticiable obligations, that lies between the rules of economic efficiency, the rules of the economic game, and the rules of economic law. Not everything that is not justiciable is allowed or at the free disposal of the acting persons. The law formulates only an ethical minimum which must be supplemented by ethically sound practices and attitudes in the economy. Plato writes in his *Laws*[11] that the laws are of two kinds: the law in the proper sense and the proemium or introduction to the law. The former is a tyrannical prescription, the latter, the introduction to the law formed by the ethical rules, is made up by propositions of persuasion that try to persuade to the free acceptance of and compliance with the rules and virtues.[12] To the different kinds of rules correspond three different kinds of sanctions. The economic, the ethical and the judicial norms carry economic, ethical and judicial sanctions. The violation of the economic rules is sanctioned by financial losses, the violation of ethical rules moral and cultural is sanctioned by bad conscience and loss of reputation, and the violation of laws by legal punishment.

2. Ethical Economy as a Positive Theory of Social Coordination

The sequence of economic, ethical and legal rules and sanctions leads to the second part of ethical economy which is formed by the positive theory of social coordination.[13] Ethical economy as an ethico-economic theory of social coordination analyses the coordination of self-interested action, particularly in markets, by means of economic, ethical, and legal motivation, rules, and sanctions. The question is here under which conditions the social coordination of the pursuit of self-interest by markets succeeds and where it breaks down. Ethical economy gives the conditions under which economy failure occurs in situations of prisoners' dilemma, under which conditions this economy failure can be corrected by ethics, and under which conditions ethics failure occurs and is compensated by law and religion. Applied to the capital market or stock exchange, ethical economy analyses under which

11 PLATO, *Leges* 722e.

12 Cf. KOSLOWSKI (1982), pp. 42-46.

13 KOSLOWSKI (1988), pp. 20-45.

conditions business ethics can correct unethical practices like insider trading, under which conditions the business ethics of financial markets, in turn, breaks down and must then be corrected by criminal law.

B. Applications of the Theory of Ethical Economy to the Markets for Credit, Capital, and Corporate Control

I. The Ethical Economy of the Credit Market

Banks are suppliers of services for payment transactions and of credits in the market for these goods in which banks as suppliers and individuals and firms as consumers interact. Banking should be described in terms of the market for credit and payment transaction services, not in terms of a quasi-governmental office of granting credits. In the German tradition, banking and supplying credit has been too often formulated in terms of quasi-governmental administration and granting of credit to petitioners („Kreditgewährung") although there remains an element of trust and belief in the customer in allowing credit to him or her that is much weaker in other markets.

It is also the economic connection between the credit market and the capital market that makes it advisable to formulate banking in terms of the market for credit. According to the portfolio theory of investment, the investor allocates his or her savings to investments of different risks. The differentiation between investing one's savings in a bank account with the possibility of instant withdrawal, between investing in a bank account with fixed period of exclusion of withdrawal (*Festgeld*), between investing in secured loans (*Gläubigereffekten*), and between investing in securities in the capital market depends on the investor's attitude towards risk and preference for availability in time or liquidity of his or her invested money.[14] The suppliers of savings optimize their portfolio between the different investments of their savings either in the credit market in short term and long term bank accounts or in secured loans (*Gläubigereffekten*) and in the capital market in shares (*Teilhabereffekten*).[15]

---

14 Cf. FRIEDMAN (1987).

15 There are different definitions of and demarkations between the credit and the capital market. In the German discussion, the capital market is defined as the

Banks compete therefore for the financial assets or savings of their deposit customers not only with each other in order to acquire these assets as deposits in bank accounts but also with the alternative uses of savings in secured loans (*Renten*) and shares (*Aktien*).

1. The Tasks of Banks and of the Credit Market

a) The Tasks of Banks for the Customer as Creditor

The deposit customers hand in their money to banks and thus invest in different kinds of bank accounts for three reasons. They invest money in current accounts for facilitating their payment transactions and for safekeeping their cash under conditions of liquidity at every instant of time, and they invest their savings in interest bearing bank accounts with fixed periods of exclusion of withdrawal as the part of their portfolio that bears low risk and yields low profit. The deposit customer expects the bank to reduce or even bear his risks in payment transactions, in the safekeeping of liquid money and in financial investments.

The first duty of banks towards their customers who give them money stems, therefore, from the nature of the matter of banking, from the nature of the banks's very business of reducing risks for their depositing customers. Their first duty towards their deposit customers is reliability and safety in the management of the customer accounts, and the first virtue of the banker reliability and awareness of risk.

The tasks of banks in their relationship to the deposit customers can be summarized as follows:

(1) Banks facilitate and coordinate payment transactions,
(2) offer the safekeeping of liquid money under conditions of continued liquidity, and

---

market for long run financial means or credit of long terms, thus TUCHTFELDT (1978), p. 433. In the Anglo-American discussion, the capital market is, following the portfolio theory of investment, the market for risk bearing financial investments, thus FRIEDMAN (1987), pp. 320f. The secured loans are in the latter definition part of the market for credits, in the former part of the market for capital. Since secured loans are long term investment for the issuer and bear some risk of price although not of loss or bankruptcy they lie between bank credits and shares in stock. In this paper, the secured loans will not be considered. The definition of the capital market that is followed is the one of the market for risk bearing investment in the portfolio theory of investment.

(3) offer opportunities for capital investment that is risk free and profit bearing.

b) The Tasks of Banks for the Customer as Debtor

On the side of their debtors, banks face quite different expectations. The private and industrial debtor expects his bank to provide him or her with inexpensive financial means even for risky uses. On the market for credits to industrial clients, the banks compete again with the capital market and the alternative possibilities of the firms to finance their investments. Firms can raise capital by issuing bonds or shares in the capital market or by self-financing, by turning their profits into equity. Banks compete for debtors and profitable loans as well with each other as with the capital market and the self-financing of firms.

The first duty of banks towards their customers who demand credit stems, therefore, from the nature of the matter of giving loans, from the nature of the banks' very business of providing financial resources for the risky enterprises of their credit customers. The first duty of banks towards their credit customers is objectivity and reasonable courage in lending out money to good investment projects. The first virtue of the banker towards his credit customers is objectivity and reasonable courage towards risk.

c) The Task of the Bank as Intermediary Between Creditors and Debtors

It is obvious that the duties and virtues of the assets side of the bank's balance sheet and those of the liabilities side are not harmonious but conflict with each other. In its actions and attitudes towards its deposit customers, the bank must be risk adverse and careful, towards its industrial credit customers it must be risk loving and courageous. The bank must therefore find a way to equilibrate the different duties and virtues of risk reduction and risk taking. It must mediate between the expectations of their deposit customers to avoid risk and the expectations of their credit customers to bear risk with them.

The tension between the two role expectations and virtues of banking and the need to mediate them reflects on the level of the ethics of banking the bank's task to mediate between the supply of and demand for financial assets, between saving and investment, or more precisely, between the supply of funds for low risk investment and the demand for funds for high risk investment. It is obvious from this analysis that banks cannot simply mediate the supply of funds for low risk investment and the demand for funds for high risk investment since the supply and demand for financial funds are not congruent and compatible. They become compatible only when banks pool the low risk funds of their deposits and transform them into normal and high risk funds for their credits. Banks must pool risk on the side of their creditors (depositors) and on the side of their debtors (loan takers).

d) Intermediation as Transformation of Time Periods and Risk-Taking

This pooling of risks is at the same time a pooling of time horizons of investment. The transformation of funds provided for low risk investment uses and under very differing time horizons into high risk investment of diverse time periods require that banks perform a twofold function of transformation:

In oder to transform deposits into credits, banks must

(1) transform deposits of diverse and partly short-term periods of depositing into short- and long-term credits, and they must

(2) transform the different attitudes towards risk by pooling risk on both sides of their balance sheet. They must pool the different attitudes toward risk among their creditors and among their debtors and with each other.[16]

In the modern market economy, it is rational to complement fully owned capital or equity by outside capital, i.e. credits, since one would miss too many business opportunities if one relied on one's own long-term savings only. In this respect too, credits have the function of transforming the time distance between payments. The differential between the compensation for the transformation of time periods paid by the borrower to the bank as lender and paid by the bank as borrower to its deposit customers as the bank's lender constitutes the profit of the bank. Banks deal with the differential between two payment promises: on the one hand, they borrow from deposit customers and promise to pay back the deposits, while, on the other hand, they lend to their debtors who promise to pay back the credits to the bank.

From these functions of banking, form the nature of the matter, the possible ethically sensitive areas and the corresponding ethical duties and virtues of banking can be derived. The obligations of the people working in the banking industry can be founded on the nature of their task within the

16 See also LUHMANN (1994), p. 191.

economy. Their reason is given by the critical interpretation or hermeneutics of the functions and institutional purpose of banks. It will turn out that many ethical duties of banking coincide with the legal duties formulated by banking laws and regulations. The laws of banking can, however, formulate only legal duties, not duties of intention and virtues of action. It cannot oblige to make the intention of the law one's own intention and can only define the moral minimum of compliance to the rule of law, but not the compliance to its intention.

2. The Duties of Banking Arising from the Nature of its Tasks

a) Duties of Banking Arising from the Task of Facilitating Payment Transactions and Safekeeping Liquid Funds

The function of facilitating payment transactions is, in itself, not very ethically sensitive, but it is still open to ethical questions. Bank clients in Germany often complain that the transactions of deposits often are delayed, whereas withdrawls are booked immediately from their accounts (*Wertstellungspraxis*). By doing so the banks save deposit interest and earn interest on additional interest on short term overdraft facility of those customers whose accounts are in debit. Consequently banks earn money in addition to the fees charged for the transaction and the interest they gain by working with the money in the deposit. In the case of those customers being in debit, the opportunity costs for the customers include even the interest paid on their debit balance which they would have saved by a faster booking.

When German consumer groups tested the time it takes to transfer money they often found that the payment transactions were not faster today than during the time of the Fugger bank in the 16th century. Especially slow and costly are transactions with foreign countries. These delays are not caused by real problems of transportation or communications. Due to modern electronic communication systems the international industry of finance manages to transfer huge amounts of money back and forth across the globe in virtually no time. Therefore the practice of delayed payment transactions cannot be explained by technical problems but are a means for the credit institutes to earn additional profit.

There is also a problem of justice in exchange since customers being in debit on their deposit accounts pay debit interest on the amounts of transfers that would diminish their debit whereas those whose accounts are in credit loose only the much smaller interest on credit. The practice is therefore more harmful to the poor and to those in debit. It is not neutral in terms of distribution. The practice of the banks does not fulfill the criterion of justice in exchange.

Since customers deposit part of their savings in current accounts to have liquid financial means it is one of the major duties of banks to make sure that it is liquid at all moments of time.[17] The legal precaution of the liquidity reserve aims at securing the bank's liquidity. There are, however, situations conceivable in which the legal reserves are not sufficient. The bank has, therefore, the duty to fulfill the legal obligations and to overfulfill the reserve limit when the nature of its business, e. g. extraordinarily high withdrawal of cash by its customers, requires to do so. The duty of the business ethics of banking transcends the ethical minimum of the legal duty.

This observation can also be extended to the money market. The money supply of the economy is created in the cooperation between the central bank and the commercial banks. The ethics of banking obliges the commercial banks to cooperate with the central bank to secure the proper money supply and to avoid inflation by an oversupply of money and deflation by an insufficient supply of money. Here again, banks cannot only stick to the minimum prescribed in the legal regulations. They must make the common good of price stability as well their self-interest or particular good and support the central bank or, if necessary, criticize it.

b) Duties Arising from the Task of Transforming Deposits into Credits

It is the duty of banks to respond, on the side of their deposit customers, to the function of reducing risk for their customers who invest in deposit accounts and at the same to respond, on the side of their credit customers, to the function of providing capital for risky enterprises. The bank must find an equilibration between the two contradictory role expectations stemming from these functions, and this equilibrium between its different functions must enter the definition of its business practices, of its attitudes and virtues, rules and duties.

Proper conduct of banking requires a synthesis of risk aversion and readiness to take over risks, of sober control and openness for venture capital investments. There might be a inherent danger in universal banking that this synthesis is taken to much in favour of the deposit customers' interest in

17 MESSNER (1955), p. 431, calls the liquidity principle the first principle of the ethics of banking.

risk free investment since they are the donors of capital to the bank. Particularly the big banks have often been accused of denying credits to enterpreneurs who, although they are trustworthy persons and are offering promising projects, cannot supply the usually required securities. Big banks, therefore, have the duty to control the tendency inherent in any bureaucratic institution to follow immobile general rules that do not do justice to the single case. The branches of big banks are in danger to follow the regulations of the headquater in a rigid and unimaginative manner and to neglect by this the personal credit to the promising entrepreneur who would be supported with credit by the personal private bank. The big banks tend to pay not enough attention to the unsecured personal credit. This is an obstacle for venture capital and sometimes prevents promising projects.[18]

On the other hand, not to stick to the technical rules of banking can be unethical, too. Quite often, the business ethics of banking does not require the introduction of new rules but the implementation and enforcement of existing ones, demands to assure that the rules - and often very simple rules - are taken serious. One example is the latest German financial crash of the *Schneider*-bankruptcy in the real estate business. In this case, banks made the mistake of refraining form very simple monitoring procedures. They did not look into the land register (*Grundbuch*) to check the register of the mortgages nor did they go to the buildings they gave credits for to make sure that the size claimed in the request for financing did in fact correspond to their actual size.[19] The simple rule of seeing each object at the spot with ones own eyes had been disregarded - partly due to the danger inherent in repeated business: one does not tend to check each object one finances as carefully as at the first business occasion when one has been conducting business with a person for a long time.

The evaluation of investment projects lies within the free decision of the credit institute and is therefore, like any other free decision, also subject to moral responsibility. Banks have unavoidably the discretionary power to decide whether a project that depends on outside capital is creditworthy or not. In its decicion-making-process, the bank must apply criteria of economic efficiency and ethical justice in exchange and pricing which are only partly formalized. However, the results can never be completely anticipated by experiment or scientific method. The assessment of the future outcomes of investments implies discretionary freedom.

---

18 See ENGEL (1993), p. 112.

19 See Cover-story of SPIEGEL-magazine: *Der Spiegel* (1994), pp. 22-30.

Banks have to treat every applicant for credit in a fair way, i .e. they must treat equal situations equally and unequal situations unequally. They must adhere to the principle of equality of rules and to the principle of objectivity and universality. The interest rates of all customer credits must follow the market rate of interest. Favouritism in the evaluation of creditworthiness must be ruled out as well as special favours in consulting customers or unjustified reductions or agios in credit costs.

The same principle of just price and just interest rates holds true for the bank's relationships with the holders of the current and deposit accounts. Here, market price and market interest rate must be followed in the individual prices and interest rates. Banking ethics requires that the banks neither practice favouritism towards the wealthy nor undue austerity or indulgence towards the less wealthy or poor customers.

The duty of impartiality[20] and objectivity is emphasized by the fact that banks often have a natural monopoly in local contexts where the market is not large enough to support many competing local branches of different banks. These local monopolies of banks in small towns or villages are problematic from the point of view of competition and consumer choice. They have, however, some justification since they may handle personal credit more efficiently then anonymous banks due to their personal knowledge of their customers and the local community.

Banks have to balance their credit decisions between benevolence and strictness. On the one hand, they have to be willing to take certain risks in order to facilitate innovation while on the other hand they necessarily have to make sure that they are not investing in unsound projects. The credit institutes do not lend their own money but the deposits of their customers. In the dialectic combination of creative entrepreneurial imagination and the sense of reality, objectivity and thriftiness lies the duty and virtue of efficient and fair banking.

Banks are often criticized for basing their decisions about credit for entrepreneurial projects on the aspects of profitability and security only. Criteria transcending economic efficiency in the narrow sense like considerations of the environmental effects of investments or of the common good are said not to be taken into account sufficiently. Banks usually reply that the profitability of credits given to private and industrial customers, their profitability for the bank, and, therefore, for the maximization of the shareholder value of the bank's shares are the control principle of banking and

20 Cf. BRADY (1993).

cannot be watered down by the intrusion of other principles into the objective function of the bank.

Two objections can be made to this claim. First, there is a growing number of shareholders and customers who prefer banks whose objective function is wider although they do not loose sight of the need to make profit. Many bank customers want their bank to include some ethical considerations in their credit decisions. The emergence of „Ethics or Green Fonds" or alternative banks like „Die Öko-Bank" in Germany or „The Cooperative Bank" in England give testimony to that demand. It might become profitable for commercial banks to widen and deepen their criteria for credit decisions in order to attract more demanding customers.

The second objection to the „profitability only" objective is a logical one. If positive profit is the necessary condition for the continued business of a firm and a bank it does not follow that positive profit is the sufficient condition for the bank's operation also. Nothing hinders a bank to deepen the control principle of profitability by additional principles which should, however, not decrease profits in the long run since this would indicate shortcomings in the bank's operations.

II. The Ethical Economy of the Capital Market

What is proper conduct in the capital market and what does justice in exchange and in pricing mean in the stock exchange? The question of proper conduct in the capital market is debated heatedly at the problem of insider trading which receives great attention in the debate about the business ethics of the capital market. There are, however, other aspects of proper conduct in the capital market like the ethics of the selection of stocks for investment, the ethics of the investor, and the ethics of the corporations listed in the stock exchange concerning their behaviour towards their shareholders and the stock market. There are also questions of an ethics of the intermediaries in the stock markets like brokers and bankers transcending the insider trading problem.

1. Insider trading as a Focus of the Ethical Questions of the Capital Market

The ethics of all these three groups of participants in the stock exchange, investors as suppliers of capital, corporate finance as demand for capital and the financial intermediaries as brokers between supply and demand is touched upon in the problem of insider trading, so that the pros and cons for insider trading go to the core of an ethical economy of the capital market. The German discussion on insider trading is controversial among economists. The fronts in this discussion follow the line separating economists and legal scholars. Whereas economists usually favour insider trading with the argument that insider trading increases the allocative efficiency of the stock market[21], legal scholars argue in favour of its prohibition with arguments of justice, of equal justice towards all shareholders, and of legal safety and stability in the stock exchange.[22]

This opposition between the points of view of economists and legal scholars in the assessment of insider trading indicates the underlying difference of normative criteria between the two disciplines. Whereas economists tend to concentrate on the aspect of the allocative function of the stock market, legal scholars favour a perspective that takes several normative criteria into account. In its attempt to synthesize the criteria of efficiency and justice, the theory of ethical economy finds itself here closer to the legal than to the purely economic approach, since the former is more open to the integration of numerous criteria.

The judgment from the perspective of ethical economy is of a higher order than the economic one, since it aims at integrating the two aspects of the good, the efficient and the just, into its reasoning. Applied to the capital market and the question of insider trading, the question of ethical economy is whether insider trading is efficient *and* just or fair, not whether it is efficient only. When the legal point of view is added to the one of ethical economy, the criteria of the legal safety and calculability of the rules and of the justiciability in cases of offences against the rules of the stock exchange enter the picture. The law is defined by its ability to foster certainty of expectations and legal safety as well as to render conflicts justiciable.

The question of the ethical economy of the capital market and of the admissibility of insider trading is twofold. It is first the question of the insti-

---

21 Cf. ENGEL (1991) and SCHNEIDER (1993).

22 Cf. GRUNEWALD (1990) and HOPT (1991).

tutional ethics and economics of the institution „capital market", which is part of the ethics and economics of the larger cultural sphere and the societal subsystem or concrete order of life „market economy". It is, thereby, a question of economic law, too. The ethical economy of insider trading is secondly a question of the personal ethics of those working within the rules of the game „stock exchange".

The system of obligations arises from the nature of the matter in three respects. The obligation is derived from the purpose or teleology of the institution, from the idea of justice, and from the prerequisites of legal safety. The purpose of the sphere of culture and law in question, the idea of justice, especially of formal justice in the sense of the principle of equality, and the demands of certainty in the definition of law and in jurisdiction define the obligation of ethics and of law. According to Radbruch, the idea of law arises from the purpose or teleology of the sphere to be ruled, from the principle of formal justice and from the principle of safe legal procedure.[23]

2. The Nature and Function of Stock Market Speculation: Uncertainty Bearing

Applied to the question of the ethics and legislation of the capital market, one must judge the problem of insider trading from the criterion of the purpose or teleology of the institution „capital market", from the criterion of formal justice or equal right of all participants in the capital market, and from the criterion of legal safety and stability.

The teleology or function of the institution of the capital market within the order of the economy is the following. The capital market fulfills two tasks in which it resembles the credit market. Like the latter, the capital market functions as the transfer process, in which savings are transferred into investment, and as the transformation process, in which investment of different terms of time periods are transformed into investments of long term ownership titles or securities. The transfer of savings and the transformation of time periods are accomplished in the capital market for shares not by the financial intermediaries of banks but by the securitization of the loans, by their marketability in the stock exchange, and by the existence of speculative trading of securities. The function banks fulfill in the credit market is exercised in the stock exchange by other institutions, namely by

23 RADBRUCH (1973), p. 114.

the control of the issuing of new shares effected by the stock exchange administration or by government[24], by the marketability of shares and securitized loans, and by professional and amateur speculation about future prices of stock.

Investing in shares in the capital market is - compared to deposits in banks - an investment of higher risk. The stock market serves as the means to allocate investive funds to companies according to price differentials reflecting the expected risk and profit of the companies taking part in the stock exchange as they are seen by the market participants. The prices of shares reflect the assessment of return and risk.

Shareholders are investors bearing as owners the full risk for their invested capital. Given full publicity about the past and present record and the future strategy of the corporation, the price of its shares is formed in the market according to the assessment of the past and present performance and of the future expected return and risk.

In an ideal market, each share would have a fixed market price. Hardly any trading would take place, since the price would be the same for everyone at every period of time. In reality, however, there are huge trading volumes in the existing modern capital markets. According to Friedman, the annual trading volume on the New York Stock Exchange, for example, is normally nearly one half of the total value of listed existing shares.[25] Friedman explains this huge trading of shares by the different risk assessments of investors but does not mention the differentials in the intended duration of investment and the contingently changing decisions to desinvest shares. Shares are permanent or at least long-run investment. The ownership title they define remains constant, but their actual owners change in time. The periods of holding shares can be transformed at low transaction costs compared to other ownership patterns. The transformation is made possible by the marketability of shares in the stock exchange. That shares be marketable requires in turn that the supply of a given share find a demand for that same share at any given moment in time, even if the originally intended time periods of investment in this share do not coincide between the buyer and seller.

---

24 In Germany, the so called „anchoring principle" (Verankerungsprinzip) is effective. The law states that issuing bonds or shares in German Marks (DM) can only be effected by an issuing bank whose headquarters is in Germany. For the effect of this principle on decreasing international competition in the German capital market cf. BREUER (1990), p. 101.

25 FRIEDMAN (1987), p. 323.

The transformation of different periods of investment is done by trading. The supply and demand for shares, their marketability, are enormously increased by a group that, in the division of labour, professionally trades stock, the group of professional speculators.

Professional speculation creates trading volume by adding supply and demand of shares in the stock exchange that exceed the volume that would exist in the absence of speculation, when investment in shares is effected for returns from permanent investment only. Speculation is that sort of economic activity that tries to gain profit from differentials between present and future prices of stock. The speculator speculating à la hausse („bull") assumes that the future price of a share will be higher than its present. Speculation à la baisse („bear") speculates that the price will be lower. The bullish speculator tries to make profit by buying shares today and selling them in the future. His investment decision does not concentrate on the expected return from dividends but on the differential between future and present stock value of the share. The division of labour in the stock market between those concentrating on the returns and capital value of the stock, the investors in the proper sense, and those concentrating on the differentials of fluctuations of stock value in time, the speculators, makes sure that the investment in shares can be liquidated at any given moment of time.[26] The speculation in shares increases the marketability of shares and, thereby, the transformability of time periods of capital investment in the stock market. Professional stock market speculation decreases the risk not to be able to transform the periods of investment and desinvestment in shares and thereby renders an important service to the economy.

Speculation bears part of the uncertainty about future random changes of investment periods and increases the investor's independence on the time horizon of the other investors, of their time schedule for their investment or desinvestment in stocks. The profits from speculation are the price that the non-speculative investors must pay to the speculators for their provision of the additional trading of stocks. Professional speculation - besides having other more problematic aspects - is the intelligent gambling for profit that produces the side effect that the trading of stock is increased and the transformation of investment periods facilitated. Speculation on the spot market for stocks resembles the speculation in futures in its effect on the increase in the trading of stock.

---

26 Cf. RÖPKE (1926), p. 708.

The speculation in the forward market for commodities, currency or stock enables the hedging of prices for those commodities and stocks whose producers or investors do not want to speculate but to calculate with predictable prices for future goods. Speculation in futures serves as an insurance on future prices for the non-speculators. In the same manner, the increase in trading by speculation in stocks in the spot market is an insurance for those who want to be free in their decisions about the time period of their investment in shares. The spot market speculation in stock assures the non-speculative investors that they will be able to find demand for their shares whenever they want to desinvest them. In the forward market, the division of labour between the speculating and the hedging market participants stems from the fact that some people must speculate so that others can calculate with ascertained or certain future prices.[27] In the spot market for stocks, the effect of speculation is not the complete insurance of future prices but the assurance that the time periods of investment in stocks will be transformable in the future by selling or buying in the stock market.

The assurance of time transformability of shares through speculation in the stock market is only economically advantageous if speculation is not interested in price fluctuations of stock and, therefore, does not increase in the fluctuations of stock prices over time. In case the professional speculation increases the price fluctuations because it makes profit out of them, the negative effect of increased price fluctuations through speculation can outweigh the welfare gains from increased marketability of shares. Economic theory distinguishes between speculation in stocks with a negative and a positive elasticity of demand for shares on expectations of stock prices. Speculation with negative elasticity of expectations describes the speculative investment in stocks that acts contrarily to the expectations of the market and, therefore, sells shares when the market expects higher future prices and buys when the market expects lower future prices. This sort of speculation decreases the fluctuations of prices of stock by contracyclical investment behaviour. Speculation with a positive elasticity of demand for stock, in turn, buys and sells stock in accord with the prevalent expectations of the market, acting cyclically with the majority of the participants in the market.

---

27 Cf. NELL-BREUNING (1928), p. 129: Professional speculation fulfills „das Entlastungsbedürfnis derjenigen Wirtschaftskreise, ‚die nicht spekulieren wollen, sondern nur kalkulieren möchten‘ (Terhalle)“ (the favour demand of those participants in the market who donot want to speculate but would like to calculate only).

It thus increases the fluctuations of prices and results in negative welfare effects.

Speculation is, however, most profitable when its price anticipations are correct and when it acts contra-cyclically under negative elasticity of demand for stock on market expectations. It is not very profitable when it follows the market expectations with positive elasticity, and it is not profitable at all when it is wrong in its prediction about future prices. There is, therefore, a built-in tendency in speculation, brought in by the profit motive, to anticipate future price-changes of stock correctly, and there is a motive to speculate in such a way that stock market fluctuations are suppressed by the higher profitability of contra-cyclical speculation.

The thesis that speculation in the spot market for stocks absorbs uncertainty about future transformability of periods of investment contends that it is the function of speculation in the stock market to reduce an uncertainty of the market participants that cannot be made up for by other means. The risk of return and bankruptcy can be calculated approximately by the market, the uncertainty about future periods for which investors want to hold their investment cannot be calculated by means of the calculus of probability.[28] It can only be speculated about it.

The part of pure speculation about the uncertain and random path of stock prices being independent of returns and the part of genuine long run investment in shares as the risk bearing of owning partners should, therefore, be analytically distinguished. In actual stock market behaviour, however, the speculators can only speculate by being investors in stock also. Stock market speculation is ethically admissible since it fulfills an objective function in the economy: the reduction of uncertainty about marketability of shares in the stock exchange. Profits from speculation are payments for this service rendered to the public in the stock exchange and are justified by the economic surplus created by speculation.

That the contribution to the common good by reducing uncertainty justifies professional speculation means in turn that speculation which does not reduce an otherwise, i.e. by other means than speculation, irreducible uncertainty is not economically and ethically justifiable. Speculation is justified as the absorption of uncertainty where there is no other way to handle it. Where uncertainty can be reduced by less costly means than speculation, this means should be used. Where speculation does not really reduce uncertainty, it is not justified.

---

28 See for the distinction between risk and uncertainty KNIGHT (1921).

3. Insider Trading as Pseudo-Speculation and Agiotage

The problem of insider trading in the stock exchange is the case in which there is no real uncertainty, since the facts of the insider information are already known, and in which uncertainty can be reduced by less costly means, i.e. by the publication of the insider information to the public. The insider produces no real good and renders no service to the stock market participants that could not be produced by the simple publication of the insider fact by the corporation affected. The insiders' speculation is a sort of pseudo-speculation, since the speculating insider does not bear uncertainty but a pseudo-uncertainty about the facts of his insider information. The insider still bears some risk - the takeover could fail to take place in the end although the insider was told so, the effects of the journalist's recommendation for a share could be less strong than he or she anticipated etc. The insider's risk is, however, much lower than that of the other speculators acting in the same market.

Profits from professional speculation are the remuneration for the productive effect of absorbing uncertainty. Where the speculator's effort is not productive, since he or she bears only pseudo-uncertainty, it does not carry the legitimization to earn profit. The insider speculator absorbing only pseudo-uncertainty is not entitled to the profit arising from his or her insider trading. In analogy to gambling, the inside speculator plays with marked cards by reducing the element of chance and uncertainty inherent in speculation only for himself and not for all players. The inside speculator is playing the game with less uncertainty than his or her co-speculators, and the profit he or she derives from playing the game with marked cards does not correspond to his or her economic performance and productive contribution.

a) Arbitrage, Speculation, Agiotage

The productive result of insider trading speculation is neither arbitrage nor true speculation but agiotage. Arbitrage is the productive effort to earn profit from equilibrating price differences in space. The arbitrageur makes profit by lowering the price differential between different places at the same time. When the level of the interest rates for credits is low in Tokyo and high in Rome at the same date, it is profitable arbitrage to borrow money at low interest in Tokyo and to lend it at high interest rate in Rome. The arbitrageur reduces the differential between the prices at different places and equilibrates price levels between two places by removing an oversupply in one trading place and reducing a shortage - in our case a shortage of credit -

in the other. Arbitrage creates welfare effects by equilibrating prices between different markets at one moment of time, speculation is the equilibration of prices at the same market place between different moments of time. Speculation is, so to say, arbitrage between points of time, not between points of space. Both, arbitrage and speculation, render the service of equilibrating prices to the economy.

From arbitrage and speculation, agiotage must be distinguished. Agiotage designates the activity of making profit by raising a mere surcharge (*agio*) on a given good or service without adding value to it. The price difference between the shares bought and the shares sold is just the surcharge or agio levered by the agiotageur. The insider is an agiotageur who, although he or she buys at time t and sells at time t+1, adds no value to the goods traded, i.e. shares, since the information on which he or she bases the profit was already there at time t. The distinction between arbitrage in space and arbitrage in time or speculation as value adding economic activities on the one hand and agiotage as surcharging without value creation on the other hand permits us to classify insider trading as mere agiotage and to distinguish it from the other value adding activities in the stock exchange, i.e. as arbitrage and speculation over time.

The scholastic theorists of business ethics or scholars of the theology of business morals like Duns Scotus and particularly the Spanish natural right thinkers of early modern times already knew this distinction. Duns Scotus decided that profit is only ethically admissible if the trader or speculator has rendered some productive service to the community: „Whoever provides neither the bringing nor the storage nor the amelioration of the trading goods, nor supplies the inexperienced buyer with a guarantee of quality (through his knowledge of the merchandise), but only buys now in order to resell without fulfilling even one single of these preconditions should be exterminated from the community and exiled from it."[29] Lugo[30] and Molina[31]

29 JOHANNES DUNS SCOTUS: *Quaestiones in Lib. IV. Sententiarum*, vol. 9, Lyon (Laurentius Durand) 1639, reprint Hildesheim (Olms) 1968, dist. 15, q. 2, n. 23: „Qui nec transferunt nec conservant nec eorum industria melioratur res venalis nec certificatur aliquis alius simplex de valore rei emendae, sed modo emit, ut statim sine omnibus istis condicionibus vendat, iste esset exterminandus a republica et exulandus." Johannes Duns Scotus was born at Maxton (Scotland) in about 1265/66 and died at Cologne in 1308.

30 JUAN DE LUGO: *De iustitia et iure*, Lyon 1670, Disp. 28, sect. 10, n. 132. J. de Lugo was born at Madrid in 1583 and died at Rome in 1660.

31 LUIS DE MOLINA: *De iustitia et iure*, Madrid 1602, Tr. 2, disp. 410, n. 11.

explained that profits from arbitrage and speculation are ethically legitimate if they add real value to the economy, but that agiotage as mere surcharging overcharges others and therefore violates the principle of justice of giving to each his or her own.[32]

b) Insider Trading and the Fiduciary Relationship

Insider speculation as mere agiotage, like reselling the same good without ameliorating it and without rendering a productive contribution to the community by the reselling, violates the nature of the matter of speculative trading. This holds true even in circumstances in which the insider trading is useful to a third party. Take the case of a firm that plans a take-over. The management or one of the shareholders can tip an insider trader to buy stock of the company to be taken over in the near future. The insider will earn an extra profit from this tip, the tipping company can stretch the buying out of the stock over a longer time period and probably acquire the stock at a lower price. Thus, the tippee or insider trader is informed by the tipper, the firm, in the firm's own interest and is induced to buy stock at the insider's profit. The insider trader renders some service to the economy, namely to the firm that plans the take-over. This service, however, could also be achieved when the acquiring firm buys the stock itself or an agent buys it on its behalf under a contract of acting on behalf of the firm. The firm planning a take-over need not use the means of tipping an insider trader and, thereby, using an ethically questionable means for an end that can be reached by ethically and legally admissible means. The existence of cases where insider trading is in the interest of a third party, the tipping manager or shareholder, does not refute the thesis that insider trading is mere agiotage and not productive speculation. The tipping company has the knowledge on which the insider trading is effected and could spread it or, if this damaged its business, can withhold it[33] and act for itself by buying out the stock over time itself.

32 Cf. NELL-BREUNING (1928), p. 107f.

33 The new German legislation on insider trading, the *Gesetz über den Wertpapierhandel und zur Änderung börsenrechtlicher und wertpapierrechtlicher Vorschriften (Zweites Finanzmarktförderungsgesetz)* (Law on the Trading of Securities and on the Alterations of Existing Stock Exchange and Securities Regulations [Second Law on the Improvement of the Financial Market]) of July 26, 1994, became effective in its main parts on August 1st, 1994, and will be effective completely by January 1st, 1995. § 21 of the law obliges all companies

The example of insider trading by an insider buying stock for his private account in the interest of a third party demonstrates that insider trading cannot be judged unethical on the grounds only that it breaks a fiduciary duty.[34] In many cases, it does so and is then unethical on the grounds that it is an offence against the fiduciary duties. In quite a few cases, it is, however, the very person that constituted the fiduciary relationship who proliferates the insider information to another who trades in his private interest. The arguments in favour of insider trading claiming that insider trading improves the allocative function of the market by distributing information about stock are based on the fact that insider trading is not only in the interest of the insider trader or agent but can be in the interest of the principal, too.[35]

Again, neither the advantage of the inside trader nor the advantage of the principal nor some small allocative effect of the insider trading on the price formation in the stock market can be a justification for insider trading when its unethical character is due to the violation of the nature of the matter of speculation in the stock market, when it does not serve to reduce uncertainty. Since the insider information is already there, insider trading does not reduce uncertainty. Since all shareholders have the equal right to information about their company, the management may not pass information about takeovers to selected third parties for their enrichment.[36] Even the single shareholder may not pass insider knowledge to selected persons, since by doing so he or she violates the right of the other shareholders to this knowledge. The principle of equal right of the shareholder requires that either all shareholders know about the insider information and can pass it on or that none of them passes it on. When all shareholders pass it on, it will cease to be insider information.

The German and American legislation on insider trading, therefore, prohibits the shareholders to pass on their insider information, just as it pro-

---

that are traded at that stock exchange to publish acquisitions or sales of stock of other companies exceding or falling short of 5 per cent, 10 per cent, 25 per cent, 50 per cent or 75 per cent of the other company's stock. The Federal Supervisory Board (*Bundesaufsichtsamt*) may, however, exempt the company from this duty if its fulfillment can cause considerable damage to it (§ 25, n° 4).

34 MOORE (1990) argues that insider trading is unethical because it breaks a fiduciary relationship. This is certainly very often the case but does not cover all cases of insider trading.

35 The main proponent of this thesis is MANNE (1966).

36 The aspect of equal justice to all shareholders is emphasized in HOPT (1991).

hibits the management of the firm to do so.[37] It does not take the fiduciary relationship but the principle of equal right, i.e. the shareholders' equal right to information, and the conditions of productive speculation in the stock market to be the reason for the legal prohibition of insider trading.

c) Insider Trading as Perverse Incentive

The conditions under which speculation in the stock market is productive and conducive to the common good by bearing uncertainty are not only violated by the detrimental effects of insider trading when it occurs; rather, the detrimental effects are intensified through perverse incentives that are furthered by legally allowing insider trading. The intermediaries in the financial markets have strong incentives to invest in the search for insider trading opportunities, if insider trading is allowed. Instead of searching for the correct anticipation of the future in speculation, they will look for insider information about a future that is not really future but already present. They will be negligent in doing proper speculation and distract their attention to insider investment opportunities.

Since the insider investment opportunities are augmented by random price fluctuations and high amplitudes of these fluctuations, the incentives of insider trading further induce the financial intermediaries to support price fluctuations instead of suppressing them. Additional „perverse" incentives to increase, instead of decrease, uncertainty for the other market participants are thus created by the legal admittance of insider trading.[38] The regulation of insider trading deviates the efforts of the financial intermediaries and speculators from investing in the reduction of uncertainty to investing in the search for insider information, i.e. for knowledge that is already there, and in strategies of increasing outside uncertainty by increasing the price fluctuations in the stock market. The „perverse incentives" of insider trading direct resources to the search for unproductive instead of productive knowledge. Knowledge that is already there but is held back from the market for the private exploitation in agiotage is unproductive knowledge.[39]

---

37 The German law prohibits *all* shareholders, not only the shareholders of great holdings, to proliferate insider information, cf. *Finanzmarktförderungsgesetz* § 13 no. 1,2. For the American legislation cf. WOJTEK (1978), pp. 56ff.

38 Thus also MOORE (1990), p. 179, HOPT (1991).

39 For the distinction between productive and unproductive knowledge see SCHÄFER/OTT (1986), pp. 300ff.

d) Insider Trading and Short-Termism

The insider knowledge in the stockmarket is unproductive since it is neither used for arbitrage, equilibrating price differences between different places, nor for speculation, equilibrating price differences between different time periods. Insider trading is effected in the same market place, and it aims at short run capital gains without bridging longer time periods. Already the short-termism of insider trading hints at the fact that it is neither the bearing of uncertainty nor real capital investment. Both, the bearing of uncertainty and capital investment, require longer time periods of investment.

Insider trading cannot, however, be banned by law because of its short-termism only. When a speculator has come to the conclusion by correct and responsible reasoning that it is economically right to end an investment after a very short term of investment due to changes of the economic conditions, this can be and is very often the efficient solution. Short terms of investment are, therefore, not per se an indicator of insider trading and no sufficient reason for an exclusion of it.[40] Here the intention, i.e. whether the investor intends from the beginning either insider trading or serious long run investment or useful speculation in bearing uncertainty, is decisive.

e) Insider Trading and the Duty to Ad hoc-Publicity

Insider information is unproductive information since its general availability is hindered only by intentionally holding it back from the market. The use of the insider information does not have an advantageous effect on the economy since it is not arbitraging between places or speculating between time periods. McGee bases his argument for the legalization of insider trading on the fact that in arbitrage business transactions the arbitrageur is not obliged to inform the potential buyer that the price of the good the arbitrageur is trying to sell is higher in an other place or, in the case of speculative trade, that the price is likely to change in the future. McGee quotes Thomas Aquinas[41] who denied the duty of the seller to inform the buyer about such price differences between places or periods. McGee overlooks the underlying premise in Aquinas' argument, namely that arbitrage is economically and socially useful since it equilibrates price differences between different markets. Arbitrage will only happen if there are incentives for it in the possibility of making profit by bridging the price differences be-

40 DE GEORGE (1990) bases his critique of insider trading on its short-termism and argues for a taxation of short run capital gains with a rate of 100 per cent.

41 MCGEE (1988), p. 37, about AQUINAS, *Summa theologiae* II-II, q. 77, art. 3 (4).

tween markets. Where these incentives do not exist, no arbitrage takes place. Where the buyer would have the duty to inform the seller of grain in place A that there is a higher price for grain in place B, the seller would likely not sell him the merchandise but sell it himself in market B. The seller would, thereby, appropriate to himself the benefit of the arbitrageur's investive efforts without compensating him. For the encouragement of useful trade it is necessary to admit arbitrage in trade. That is the reason why Thomas Aquinas and the natural right theory allow it.

Where trading is only agiotage or making surplus but not arbitrage or speculation, the buyer or seller is not entitled to hold back his information and to derive profit from his knowledge about future price changes. Since the insider has not invested in productive but in unproductive knowledge, he or she is not entitled to a profit derived from the lead in knowledge which has been unjustly acquired over the competitor or is of unproductive character.

f) Detrimental Effects of Insider Trading on Allocation, Distribution, and Stability

Insider trading reallocates resources from speculation to pseudo-speculation, from spreading knowledge to withholding it. There might be a minor effect of spreading knowledge to the stock exchange by the stock purchases of insider traders and some beneficial effect in the temporal extension of stock purchases in case of take-overs supported by insider traders. These beneficial allocative effects are, however, far outweighed by the misallocation of resources in the search for unproductive insider information, by the perverse incentives of insider trading to increase price fluctuations and to destabilize the stock market, and by the problematic distribution pattern resulting from insider trading gains.

The perverse incentives of insider trading lead to questionable insider investments and profits. The problematic insider capital gains, their short-termism and so on, result in a socially destabilizing and economically and ethically questionable distribution of income. The concern of the public about the income distribution derived from insider gains[42] cannot be simply dismissed as envy.[43] Not so much the resulting distribution as the repercussions of it on the incentive structure and the allocation of productive effort

42 The concern with the effects of financial speculation on the income distribution and distributive justice is a topic since Aristotle. Cf. SEN (1993), p. 211.

43 Thus MCGEE (1988), p. 42.

in the financial markets should be the concern. Since allocation and distribution cannot be separated, huge profits from insider trading direct resources to their use in insider trading. All three economic criteria, allocation, distribution, and stability, require the suppression of insider trading. The arguments from allocative efficiency, from distributional justice, and from economic stability of the capital market coincide in the judgment derived from the nature of the matter, from the nature of the capital market, that the participants in the capital market have the duty to engage in productive investment and uncertainty bearing and not in the pseudo-speculation of insider trading.[44]

The effect that the prohibition of insider trading favours professional speculation at the expense of amateur speculation should not, therefore, be criticized, as by Schneider[45], but heralded. If the prohibition of insider trading reduces the gambling element present in stock market speculation in favour of professional speculation, it decreases that part of the capital market that deals with uncertainty and reduces it to its unavoidable size. The prohibition of insider trading eliminates those factors in the stock exchange that create unnecessary and avoidable uncertainty. The stock exchange should not be a place of gambling speculation but an institution of service to the community, of serving as the mediator for capital, and as bearer of uncertainty.[46]

Sixty-five years ago, Nell-Breuning asked the question of whether the stock exchange needs speculation in shares or whether it could work without it.[47] The analysis of insider trading demonstrates that the stock market can work without pseudo-speculation but that speculation plays an indispensable role in bearing irreducible uncertainty. In summarizing the problem of insider trading, one can conclude that the nature and function of speculation in the stock exchange requires the strict suppression of the pseudo-speculation of insider trading, of bearing bogus uncertainty. The principle of equal justice in the legitimization of norms demands the equal right of

---

44 GRUNEWALD (1990), p. 133, comes to the similar conclusion that insider trading must be prohibited in the interest of the proper working (*Funktionsfähigkeit*) of the capital market.

45 SCHNEIDER (1993).

46 Cf. NELL-BREUNING's emphasis (1928), p. 23, on the „Dienstauffassung der Börse", on the awareness that the stock exchange renders a service to the economy.

47 NELL-BREUNING (1928a), p. 54.

access to information for all shareholders and speculators and therefore rules out that management or single shareholders give insider tips to third parties. Finally, the principles of economic and legal safety and stability require that insider trading be prohibited because of its perverse incentives effects. The price fluctuations in the stock market must not be augmented by forms of speculation that are not justified by the function of the capital market to bear and transform risk and uncertainty.

4. Ethical Obligations of Investors and Issuing Companies in the Capital Market

Does the investor have ethical obligations in the capital market other than abstaining from insider trading?[48] The dominant concept of shareholder value maximization seems to allow for no further obligation for the investor than the one to maximize the value of one's shares and, thereby, to maximize allocative efficiency in the economy.

From the concept of ethical economy, this restriction of the investor's criteria to wealth maximization is insufficient and must be complemented by the criterion of justice. The investor must also consider aspects of justice in his or her investment decisions. Investment decisions should pay attention to justice along the criteria of „In which projects do we invest?“ and „In which places do we invest?“. Messner explains that investment in stock or companies that pursue morally questionable production goals are unethical. He mentions as examples investment in firms producing pornography or in colonial firms that exploit the labour of the natives.[49]

Another ethical question for investment is whether the investor should be free to invest wherever in the world he or she wants to. It must be said in advance that world capital markets should be as free as possible. From the ethical point of view, the investor is, however, obliged to ask him or herself whether the investment should be done in his or her home country or abroad. Situations of a severe capital drain from one country to another, e.g. from the elites of developing countries to the centers of the industrial world, pose the question of whether the investors are obliged, for reasons of jus-

48 For the business ethics of shareholders see also CORBETTA (1994).

49 MESSNER (1955), p. 426, and MESSNER (1984), p. 1073ff.

tice, to invest part of their capital in their own country.[50] This obligation cannot and should not be a legal one, enforced by the state. Such a law would have too many detrimental effects on economic efficiency; rather, this obligation should be an ethical one.

Although the direct influence of the minor shareholder on the corporate policy of the firm he or she holds shares in is very limited, shareholders are obliged to give consideration to the question in which projects and in which regions and countries they invest. Messner also sees an obligation to invest one's capital under the condition of bearing a reasonable risk, whereas the hoarding of money and keeping it idle does not fulfill the obligation to invest.[51]

In Germany, the ethical obligation of property is part of the constitution. Article 14 § 2 of the German Constitution (*Grundgesetz*) states: „Property obliges. Its use should serve at the same time the common good."[52] The „Sozialpflichtigkeit des Eigentums", the social obligations of property, as defined in this article is usually applied to questions of eminent domain and to restrictions of the use of private property by government and local authorities in the public interest.[53] As a „should-obligation" and not a „must-law", however, the article formulates the obligation that the investor, particularly the investor of large capital, „should" consider criteria of justice and the common good in his investment decisions.

The same ethical obligations of investment hold true for the management of the issuing companies in their decisions on business strategy and policy. In addition to these ethical obligations for the strategy and operations of the management of firms that issue shares, the issuing companies are particularly obliged to properly inform their shareholders and the public on the stock market. The issuing firms must forward to the investors all relevant information of themselves since it is in the nature of the stock market that the management of the firms has better access to the information about

---

50 There can rather be deduced an investment obligation for the rich countries to invest in the developing countries to fight this capital drain and to decrease the large differences in capital assets in the world economy. Rohatyn emphasizes the need for a workable capital market in the developing countries as precondition for foreign investment. Cf. ROHATYN (1994).

51 MESSNER (1955), p. 424.

52 *„Eigentum verpflichtet. Sein Gebrauch soll zugleich dem Wohle der Allgemeinheit dienen."*

53 Cf. HESSELBERGER (1991), pp. 136ff.

the state of its business than the public and the shareholders, particularly the holders of minor amounts of shares. Since the payment of dividends is the main signal about the state of the firm's operations to the public, the firm is obliged to practice a reasonable dividend policy which neither excessively withholds dividends for equity financing nor pays dividends in amounts that are not justified by the firm's performance. The firm may not mislead the public by paying excessive dividends, giving a better picture of the firm than corresponds to the real situation.[54]

III. The Ethical Economy of the Market for Corporate Control

The peculiarity that characterizes the bidding for qualified percentages in total shares justifies it to distinguish the trading of shares for the control of corporation from the normal trading of shares. Although the trading for acquiring control over a corporation is effected in the same market as normal trading, i.e. in the stock market, it is obvious that this trading follows a different pattern. The qualified percentages of the total shares that are necessary to reach control over the appointment of the board of directors can be bought only at higher prices than „uncritical" percentages of shares. For example, acquiring 51 per cent of the total shares will cost unproportionally more than acquiring 49 per cent. Paradoxically, the total firm might cost more than the total sum of its assets. The entrepreneurial function of disposition and management is paid for with an extra price. Nell-Breuning already observed this difference between „normal shares" and holdings and explained it by the fact that there does not exist a market for corporations as such.[55] There exists only a market for holdings in corporation being a special part of the capital market.

The market for corporate holdings and corporate control is particularly sensitive in respect to an ethic of the capital market. It is not just capital shares and the mere capital ownership relationship that are traded in this market. Rather, capital ownership is transcended to the exertion of control over corporations by holdings and holding majorities. It is not capital that is

54 For the problem of dividend policy cf. GAY (1987), pp. 896-899.

55 NELL-BREUNING (1928), p. 82.

traded but capital carrying actual control over the corporation that is supplied and bidden for. The control of the corporation implies more power than share ownership and, therefore, more responsibility and awareness of the ethical dimension of one's actions. In the market for corporate control, the right intention, the *intentio recta*, is even more important than in the market for shares since the degree of freedom of discretion and the power of the decisions on corporate control are higher in the market for holdings and corporate control. The intention with which the participants act in this market even defines what they are doing, whether they are stripping assets or trying to improve the management of a company making losses.

The *intentio recta* or the ethically justifiable motivation of doing business defines the character of a strategy in mergers and acquisitions, and the kind of action in the „friendly" or „hostile" takeover of one company by another. A merger and *leveraged buyout* are not unethical in themselves. They become unethical if they aim at only one goal: to buy a company, to raid its assets, i.e. to separate and cannibalize its capital, then to sell these parts again, all for the sole purpose of gaining profit for the buyer, without wasting one thought on the company's dedication and contribution to the economy. Take-over-bids and mergers, in case they serve only profiteering by selling out the company or parts of it or only satisfy a power-hungry board, violate the substantial purpose of the economy, because they completely separate the buyer's profit interest from the interests of the company to be bought and thus deny the company's purpose or teleology as a producing social unit.

The example of the *leveraged buyout* is especially interesting in terms of an ethical economy because it is not always clear in the beginning whether a merger financed by a leveraged buyout serves the economy's purpose or not. A threat of takeover can awaken a company, put pressure on the management, enhance performance and thus serve the interests of staff and stockholders. Such a takeover can lead to an efficient reallocation of resources. Therefore, leveraged buyouts cannot be condemned in all cases.[56] Leveraged buyouts, though, might as well be regarded as mere games (of chance) or only satisfy the narcissism of the buyers, the „raiders", who want to gain profits without becoming active in the company themselves. If the company's assets are split up and auctioned without giving consideration to the possibly existing but not yet fully exhausted or hitherto underestimated

56 N.-J. Weickart notes the positive influence of company takeovers on competition. See WEICKART (1989), pp. 128-139.

synergy effects, mere profit harvesting takes place. This is only justified when the company purchased has definitely proven to be unable to use its assets to make profitable business and conduct business contributing to the purpose of the economy, the satisfaction of consumer demand. The intention of the party planning to take over a company cannot be neglected, since in cases of mergers it is the *intentional* deeds only which define which economical and ethical facts are at hand and whether the intended merger is a truly synergetical merger or a mere *asset stripping*.

A merger done for the sole purpose of wrecking the purchased company is not a merger but *asset stripping*. On the other hand, a takeover with the intention to achieve synergies between the two companies strengthens the productivity of both companies and the allocative efficiency of the economy. Only this procedure is worth of being called „merger“ in the sense of a synergetic alliance.

Proper conduct of a merger and its *intentio recta*, the right intention objectively aimed at proper economic conduct - in our case the intention of the party planning the merger or takeover - decide on the kind of action that is at hand and thus whether an act is ethical or unethical.

The example of mergers shows that the economy is not only a formal market context of trading and exchange, on which subjective demands and subjectively defined supplies meet and are coordinated. Rather the economy serves an objective purpose which must be realized by the subjective will of the individuals, i.e. according to the will of the people in the economy. The economy does not chiefly serve the profit maximizing purpose of the individuals but its purpose is utilizing the subjective striving of the individuals for the realization of the objective purpose of the economy: the unbiased satisfaction of subjective demands by an efficiently produced and distributed supply which is organized by entrepreneurs following their subjective plans.

Bearing in mind that proper conduct is necessary for the economy, the term „profit maximizing“ must be relativized, since it contains a conversion of means and ends. Positive (not maximum) profit is a necessary condition for business, yet maximum profit is not the ultimate goal for an enterprise. Profit, i.e. market success, is the measure for the objective success of an enterprise. Still, profit cannot be the sole and foremost purpose of business. Profit should also not be „maximized“, because maximizing the residual profit is not the objective teleology of a firm. Profit as surplus is the measure for the objective success of an enterprise and functions as a control force for the whole company, including the board of directors or the boss.

Or, as one industrialist put it: „Profit is like health: You need it, and the more the better. But it's not the only reason for our existence."[57]

IV. The Ethical Economy of the Financial Markets as a Positive Theory of Market Coordination

The financial markets present considerable ethical challenges to the market participants, particularly to the financial intermediaries like banks and brokers. These challenges are caused by three characteristics of these markets: 1. by the fungible, abstract, impersonal, and mass character of the good traded, i.e. means of finance, 2. by the centrality of fiduciary relationships in banking and brokerage, and 3. by the intangible character of the financial industry that causes fears in the general public of being victim to secret operations of the financial industry.

First, since money is traded, the most fungible, abstract, and unpersonal of goods, the face-to-face control between producer and customer and the judgment of the quality of the good supplied are much more difficult than with tangible material goods. The financial industry faces, therefore, two challenges: It must fight on the suppliers' side the temptation to be caught by the very character of its business, its abstract and intangible quality, and to fall victim to fictionalization and delimitization of its business. Banks and financial intermediaries are ethically obliged to make sure that the sevices they offer are not fictional or include fictional elements. All determinations of money value in which degrees of discernment are given carry the danger with them that fictional values are set in. Financial titles and services can be fictional. Objectivity must be the state of mind of those working in the financial markets.

Secondly, banks and financial intermediaries act as trustees of their depositors and investors. Trust is ethically sensitive since it cannot, by its nature, be substituted completely by control. It contains an irreducible element of self-binding on the side of the trustee. Self-binding is the ethical relationship with oneself. Banks and financial intermediaries are, therefore, particularly subjected to the demands of the ethics of trustee relationships.

---

57 See PETERS/WATERMAN (1982).

Thirdly, in the capital and credit market, not tangible material goods are traded but financial titles and rights derived from them. The intangibility and „immateriality“ of the financial means excludes the simple empirical check of the quality of the goods traded. The public is, therefore, prone to feel subjected to the power of banks and financial institutions since the control of their „products“ by evidence is difficult. Often this results in irrational fears of the secret power of banks or even in „conspiracy theories“ about the behaviour of the „big banks and high finance“ (*Hochfinanz*). Transparency is one of the main means to fight these fears, an appropriate and followed ethical code of action for financial services the other means.

The financial markets require large resources of ethical motivation and coordination by ethics. On the other hand, the abstract and impersonal character of their business does not facilitate the building up of a personal and community ethics and does not enforce ethical behaviour by face-to-face-control between supplier and customers. Banks and financial intermediaries must, therefore, take special care that the ethical rules of action are known and adhered to among their co-workers.

Applications of game theory to theories of social coordination[58] and ethical economy[59] demonstrated that ethics as a means to coordinate human actions faces problems of prisoners' dilemma situations. These are described as situations in which all members of a group have an interest that all of them follow the ethical and legal rules but in which every single group member has an incentive to break the rule for him- or herself. Further extensions of this theory demonstrate that the readiness to follow or to break the rule is dependent on the expectations about the others' behaviour. When the individual is assured that the others follow the rules he or she will follow it too. When there is no assurance about the others' adherence to the rule the individual will break it like the others.[60]

This positive theory of ethical economy can be applied to the insider trading problem as an empirical, nonnormative analysis of social coordination by ethics. The free ethical adherence to the rule to refrain from insider trading will depend on the expectations about the average behaviour of the other financial intermediaries and investors. When the single broker assumes that most others practice insider trading he or she will have only few incentives to follow the ethical rule of refraining from it. The professional

58 See SEN (1967).

59 See KOSLOWSKI (1988), pp 20-41.

60 See KOSLOWSKI (1991).

ethics and widely agreed rules and customs of conduct in the profession will facilitate the assurance for the individual that the others follow the rule too. They can, however, not guarantee it. Professional codes of conduct and professional and trade associations are able to improve the standard of rule obedience but they cannot guarantee it. In situations, where there is little face-to-face control and where abstract contract relationships are prevalent, coordination by ethical rules breaks down and must be complemented by rules of law.

In the case of insider trading this happened in the USA as early as in the 1930ies. In Germany, the participants of the stock exchange believed until recently that the insider trading problem could be solved by the professional ethics of the stock exchange and by voluntary self-restriction of its participants. Only after a series of cases of insider trading and after being obliged to do so by the European Community, the Federal Republic of Germany decided upon the Second Law on the Improvement of the Financial Market (*Zweites Finanzmarktförderungsgesetz*).

The reason for this delay is partly due to the smaller role the stock exchange has traditionally played in Germany. The American and British stock markets are central for the pension funds that act as very important investors in stock. The pensions are organized in a completely different way in Germany where the state organizes the social insurance system (*Sozialversicherungssystem*) and collects the means for the pensions by social insurance contributions paid by the working population and levied like a tax by the state from them. Thus, the enormous funds for the pensions do not reach the stock exchange whereas in Britain the pension funds are some of the main investors in the stock market and the stock market, therefore, not only important for the private investor but of central importance to the institutional investors.[61]

Obviously, the concern about insider trading must have been greater in countries where the stock exchange plays a more important role in coordinating investments and where investment in stock is used to finance pensions. Germany's lag in insider trading legislation is partly explained by the fact that German pensions are not dependent on stock dividends. The case of insider trading legislation demonstrates that business ethics cannot substitute economic legislation but that both, ethics and law, are complementary.

---

61 DAHRENDORF (1994), p. 639, emphasizes the difference in the organisation of pension institutions between Britain and Germany.

Ethical codes are the proemium and persuasion to the law, not the substitute for legislation.

V. The Interdependence of the Credit and Capital Market

Universal banks mediate between savings and investment within their own organisations, in stock markets, however, investors find their investment opportunities themselves in the market for shares of corporate capital. Banks take the investment risk of their deposit customers and decide for them where to invest their deposits. Banks form an inner capital market comparable to the inner labour market of industrial firms.[62] The internalization of the capital market within banks has the advantage that banks are highly professional investors who might be more able to direct investment than the amateur speculator in the stock exchange. On the other hand, shifting the external capital market to the internal capital market causes that banks grow more powerful institutions. When greater parts of the capital market are shifted into the internal market of banks collusion between banks and industry increases. The comparison between systems where the internal capital market of banks plays a greater role than the external capital market of the stock exchange shows a greater degree of the banks' control over industry and more powerful banks. But the process of deliberation and collusion between banks and industry might also favour high growth rates in periods of scarce capital as the historic examples of the German and of the Japanese economy with their characteristically close bank-industry relationships indicate.[63]

The stronger emphasis on the internal capital market of banks with a concomitant support of the financing of industrial development by a state practicing industrial policy describes the corporatist model of banking and industrialization characteristic of the German and the Japanese way from 1870 up to the Second World War. The emphasis on the external capital market of freely interacting investors and issuing companies marks the

62 Cf. for the theory of the internal market of firms WILLIAMSON (1977) and WILLIAMSON (1981).

63 Cf. WILLIAMS (1994), pp. 73ff.

American and British way of a more market oriented society and a political system based on democratic competition. The stock exchange is an individualistic democratic institution which mediates between investors and companies without the interference of banks or government. The internal market of banks, on the other hand, corresponds to the corporatist model of society. The stock exchange can be a countervailing power against the power of the banks and the state.[64] In this sense, the appropriate division of labour between the credit market and the capital market is also the appropriate separation of economic powers comparable to the system of the separation of constitutional powers.

Corporatist economic systems in nations with strong banks and small stock exchanges face the problem that banks can then influence stock prices by their buying power and by directing the demand for shares by changes in the rate of interest for leveraged purchases of shares.[65] On the other hand, the „democratic“ amateur speculation in the stock exchange might cause severe crises in the stock exchange as well.[66]

In a system of universal banking like the German one, banks are not only mediators within their inner capital markets but they are also acting in the (external) capital market as investors, consultants, and supervisory board members. In their function as participants in the credit and in the capital market, banks must handle their multi-purpose business with care.[67] Their

64 It is revealing that NELL-BREUNING (1928), p. 9 and (1928a), p. 52, emphasized the democratic and power dividing character of the stock exchange in the Weimarer Republic.

65 Cf. NELL-BREUNING (1928a), p. 53, and WEBER (1898), vol. 2, p. 78. Weber emphasizes mainly the banks' potential for manipulating prices in the futures market by changing the rate of interest for credits for leveraged purchases of futures.

66 Both NELL-BREUNING (1928), p. 105 and WEBER (1898), vol. 2, p. 72, point to the fact that not only high finance but as often amateur speculation causes crashes at the stock exchange.

67 Big banks that are market leader in the credit market, in the capital market and in the market for corporate control can become insiders by their position as member of the supervisory board and as main creditor of a firm. DENNERT (1991), p. 184, note 3, even sees the danger of another type of insider trading here: „Due to the close links to the firms, the main creditor will in general obtain new firm-specific information earlier than the other creditors. Premature cancellation of credit has the same effects as the other creditors as insider trading on stock markets on the other shareholders.“ The equation between both

professional ethics should remind them of the advantages of the division of labour between banks and industrial enterprises and prevent them from following the temptation to become industrial entrepreneurs, of becoming „superentrepreneurs“[68]. On the other hand, the same holds true for the industrial corporations. They in turn must refuse the temptation to become banks instead or in addition to their industrial operations, the temptation to become „superfinanciers“. Many bankruptcies or heavy losses in industry in recent years in Germany have been caused by the financial and speculative operations of industrial firms, financial operations that had been outside the proper task and competence of these firms as industrial producers. Such severe losses that have been caused by financial operations happened at *Volkswagen*, at *Siemens* and at *Metallgesellschaft*.

Banks tend - of course in their own interest - to warn industrial firms not to understand themselves as banks or financial enterprises. They warn them to open an internal financial market inside their corporate structure. There is not an ethical rule that prohibits transcending the boundaries of the division of labour and of one's profession. There exists, however, the ethical rule to be very careful when one transgresses the limits of one's profession.

Banks must monitor the behaviour of industrial firms in order to avoid capital destruction in the credit market. This monitoring function gives them legitimate power that is necessary since the avoidance of capital destruction is the central task of banks. Executing this power ethically requires, as with any power invested in anyone, that those in charge of the power have the intention to act ethically, the *intentio recta* and have wisdom, the ability to do justice to the nature of the objective of their enterprise and to those affected by it, to do justice to the totality of the aspects of the decision situation. The demands on the ethics and wisdom of banks might be even higher than those on the ethics and wisdom of industrial firms since one bank must monitor many industrial firms at the same time whereas one industrial firm need not monitor and cannot check the actions of many banks.

The bank as the collector of savings and the mediator between savings and investments is by its nature engaged in many industrial firms and has access to detailed information about their operations. The customer industrial firm, however, has no right to the information about the inner opera-

---

seems questionable but constitutes a challenge for further research. Cf. for the problem also FRANKE (1991).

68 See RÖLLER (1990), p. 9.

tions of its bank and, furthermore, has no right to those of *many* banks at all. One way of overcoming this asymmetry between banking corporations and industrial corporations might be that the industries elect proxies that represent an industry in the supervisory board of the main banks. These industry proxies in the supervisory boards of banks might be a way for the industries to monitor the behaviour of their banks and to assure the industry in question that not only the banks monitor them but that they in turn can monitor the behaviour of the banks too.

The asymmetry between banks and industrial firms is unavoidable and, at the same time, the reason for complaints frequently heard on the side of industrial corporations about the banks. In the end, banks can only cope with this sensitive asymmetry by being fair to their industrial customers and by doing justice to the matter of the credit market, the provision of means of finance for sound investments, by supporting the formation and by preventing the destruction of capital.

References

ALTENDORFER, CH. (1992): *Insidergeschäfte. Rechtsgrundlagen und Sanktionen* (Insider Trading. Legal Foundations and Sanctions), Wien (Bank-Verlag/Orac).

ANDREAS, K. (1992): „Denkansätze für eine Ethik im Bankwesen" (Starting Points for an Ethics in the Banking System), in: P. KOSLOWSKI (Ed.): *Neuere Entwicklungen in der Wirtschaftsethik und Wirtschaftsphilosophie* (Recent Developments in Economic Ethics and Economic Philosophy), Berlin, Heidelberg, New York, Tokyo (Springer) (= Studies in Economic Ethics and Philosophy vol. 2), pp. 177-193.

ANGER, D. (1981): *Insiderregeln im Wertpapiergeschäft ausgewählter Länder* (Insider Laws in the Stock Exchange of Selected Countries), Diss. Erlangen-Nürnberg.

BRADY, F. N. (1993): „Impartiality and Particularity in Business Ethics", in: P. KOSLOWSKI, Y. SHIONOYA (Eds.): *The Good and the Economical. Ethical Choices in Economics and Management*, Berlin, Heidelberg, New York, Tokyo (Springer) (= Studies in Economic Ethics and Philosophy vol. 4), pp. 175-194.

BRAUER, TH. (1925): *Produktionsfaktor Arbeit. Erwägungen zur modernen Arbeitslehre* (Factor of Production "Labour". Reflections on the Modern Theory of Labour), Jena (Gustav Fischer).

BREUER, R.-E. (1990): „Die Deutsche Terminbörse als Vorreiter einer Börsenlandschaft der 90er Jahre?" (The German Futures Exchange as Avantgarde for a Forward Market of the Future?), *Zeitschrift für Bankrecht und Bankwirtschaft*, 2, Nr. 3, pp. 101ff.

CORBETTA, G. (1994): „Shareholders", in: B. HARVEY (Ed.): *Business Ethics. A European Approach*, Hemel Hempstead (Prentice Hall), pp. 88-102.

DAHRENDORF, R. (1994): „Europäisches Tagebuch (European Diary) (XII)", *Merkur*, 48, Nr. 7, pp. 639-640.

DEGEORGE, RICHARD T. (1989): „Ethics and the Financial Community: An Overview", in: O. F. WILLIAMS, F. K. REILLY, J. W. HOUCK (Eds.): *Ethics and the Investment Industry*, Savage (Rowman & Littlefield), pp. 197-216.

DEGEORGE, RICHARD T. (1990): *Business Ethics*, New York (Macmillian Publishing Company).

DENNERT, J. (1991): „Insider Trading", *Kyklos*, 44, Nr. 2, pp. 181-202.

DESSAUER, F. (1926): „Dienst- und Verdienstwirtschaft / Ein Wort zur Wirtschaftsnot der Gegenwart" (An Economy of Service or of Enrichment. A Word on the Economic Predicament of the Present), *Hochland*, 23,2, pp. 513-520.

DÍEZ-ALEGRÍA, J. (1951): „El problema del fundamento ontológico de la obligación en la obra De iustitia de Luis de Molina" (The Problem of the Ontological Fundament of Obligation in the Work „On Justice" of Luis de Molina), *Pensamiento*, 7, pp. 147-167.

DINGELDEY, TH. (1983): *Insider-Handel und Strafrecht* (Insider Trading and Criminal Law), Köln u.a. (Heymanns).

ECONOMIC ADVISORY BOARD (1981): *The British and German Banking System: A Comparative Study*, London.

ENGEL, G. (1991): „Zur Problematik eines gesetzlichen Verbots von Insider-Geschäften" (The Problem of a Legal Prohibition of Insider Trading), *Jahrbuch für Sozialwissenschaft*, 42, pp. 388-407.

FRANKE, G. (1991): „Inside Information in Bank Lending and the European Insider Directive", in: K. J. HOPT, E. WYMEERSCH (Eds.): *European Insider Dealing*, London et al. (Butterworth).

FREUD, S.: *Die Traumdeutung* (1900) (The Interpretation of Dreams), Frankfurt a. M. (S. Fischer) 1982, Studienausgabe vol 2.

FRIEDMAN, B. M. (1987): Article „Capital, credit and money markets", in: *The New Palgrave. A Dictionary of Economics*, London (Macmillan), New York (Stockton), Tokyo (Maruzen), Vol. 1, pp. 320-327.

GAILLARD, E. (Ed.) (1992): *Insider Trading. The Laws of Europe, the United States and Japan*, Deventer, Boston (Kluwer Law and Taxation).

GAY, DAVID E. R. (1987): Article „Dividend Policy", in: *The New Palgrave. A Dictionary of Economics*, London (Macmillan), New York (Stockton), Tokyo (Maruzen), Vol. 1, pp. 896-899.

Gesetz über den Wertpapierhandel und zur Änderung börsenrechtlicher und wertpapierrechtlicher Vorschriften (Zweites Finanzmarktförderungsgesetz) vom 26. Juli 1994 (Law on the Trading of Securities and on the Alterations of Existing Stock Exchange and Securities Regulations [Second Law on the Improvement of the Financial Market]) of July 26, 1994.

GRUNEWALD, B. (1990): „Neue Regeln zum Insiderhandel" (New Rules Concerning Insider Trading), *Zeitschrift für Bankrecht und Bankwirtschaft*, 2, Nr. 3, pp. 128-133.

HENDRIE, A. (Ed.) (1981): *Banking Structures and sources of finance in the European Community*, London (The Financial Times Business Publishing).

HESSELBERGER, D. (1991): *Das Grundgesetz. Kommentar für die politische Bildung* (The Constitution. Commentary for Political Education), Neuwied (Luchterhand) ^{8}1991, pp. 136ff.

HOPT, K. J. (1991): „Europäisches und deutsches Insiderrecht" (European and German Insider Law), *Zeitschrift für Unternehmens- und Gesellschaftsrecht*, 20, pp. 17-73.

HOPT, K. J., WILL, M. R. (1973): *Europäisches Insiderrecht. Einführende Untersuchung - Ausgewählte Materialien* (European Insider Law. Introduction - Selected Materials), Stuttgart (Enke).

JACOB, A.-F. (Ed.) (1990): *Bankenmacht und Ethik* (Power of Banks and Ethics), Stuttgart (Poeschel).

JACOB, A.-F. (Ed.) (1992): *Eine Standesethik für den internationalen Finanzmanager?* (An Ethics of the Profession for the International Financial Manager?), Stuttgart (Poeschel).

JAROSLAW, B. (1913): *Ideal und Geschäft* (Ideal and Business), Jena (G. Fischer).

JOHANNES DUNS SCOTUS (1968): *Quaestiones in Lib. IV. Sententiarum*, vol. 9, Lyon (Laurentius Durand) 1639, reprint Hildesheim (Olms).

KANTOROWICZ, H. (1963): *Der Begriff des Rechts*, Göttingen (Vandenhoeck & Ruprecht). Original: *The Definition of Law*, Cambridge (Cambridge University Press) 1958.

KING, M., ROELL, A. (1988): „Insider trading", *Economic Policy. A European Forum*, Nr. 6, pp. 165-193.

KNIGHT, F. (1921): *Risk, Uncertainty, and Profit*, New York (Houghton Mifflin).

KOSLOWSKI, P. (1982): *Gesellschaft und Staat. Ein unvermeidlicher Dualismus* (Society and State. An Inevitable Dualism), Stuttgart (Klett-Cotta).

KOSLOWSKI, P. (1982a): *Ethik des Kapitalismus*. With a comment by James M. Buchanan, Tübingen (J.C.B. Mohr [Paul Siebeck]), 4th ed. 1991. Abridged English version in: S. PEJOVICH (Ed): *Philosophical and Economic Foundations of Capitalism*, Lexington (Lexington Books) 1983, pp. 33-64.

KOSLOWSKI, P. (1988): *Prinzipien der Ethischen Ökonomie. Grundlegung der Wirtschaftsethik* (Principles of Ethical Economy. Foundations of Business Ethics), Tübingen (J.C.B. Mohr [P. Siebeck]), Reprint 1994.

KOSLOWSKI, P. (1989): *Wirtschaft als Kultur. Wirtschaftskultur und Wirtschaftsethik in der Postmoderne* (The Economy as Culture. Economic Culture and Economic Ethics in Postmodern Times), Vienna (Edition Passagen).

KOSLOWSKI, P. (1991): *Gesellschaftliche Koordination. Eine ontologische und kulturwissenschaftliche Theorie der Marktwirtschaft* (Social Coordination. An Ontological and Cultural Theory of the Market), Tübingen (J.C.B. Mohr [Paul Siebeck]).

LANDMESSER, F. X. (1926): *Die Eigengesetzlichkeit der Kultursachgebiete (Wirtschaft und Staat)* (The Relative Autonomy of the Cultural Subsystems [Economy and State]), Köln, München, Wien (Oratoriums-Verlag).

LUGO, JUAN DE (1670): *De iustitia et iure* (On Justice, Natural Right, and Law), Lyon.

LUHMANN, N. (1994): „Kapitalismus und Utopie" (Capitalism and Utopia), *Merkur*, 48, H. 3, p. 191.

MANNE, H. G. (1966): *Insider Trading and the Stock Market*, New York (The Free Press).

MARTIN, D. W., PETERSON, J. H. (1991): „Insider Trading Revisited", *Journal of Business Ethics*, 10, pp. 57-61.

MAIHOFER, W. (1965): „Die Natur der Sache" (The Nature of the Matter), in: A. KAUFMANN (Ed.): *Die ontologische Begründung des Rechts* (The Ontological Foundation of Law), Darmstadt (Wissenschaftliche Buchgesellschaft), pp. 52-86.

MAYR, G. VON (1900): *Die Pflicht im Wirtschaftsleben* (The Duty in Economic Life), Tübingen (Laupp).

MCGEE, R. W. (1988): „Insider Trading: An Economic and Philosophical Analysis", *Mid-Atlantic Journal of Business*, 25, pp. 35-48.

MEIER, CH. (1986): *Wirtschaftsdelikte im Bankengewerbe. Eine empirische Untersuchung über Entwicklung, Erscheinungsformen, Schadensfolgen und Risikoursachen bankbezogener Wirtschaftsstraftaten* (Economic Crimes in the Banking Industry. An empirical investigation on the development, manifestation, consequences and causes of bank-related crimes), Bern, Stuttgart (Haupt).

MESSNER, J. (1984): *Das Naturrecht. Handbuch der Gesellschaftsethik, Staatsethik und Wirtschaftsethik* (The Natural Right. Handbook of the Ethics of Society, of the State, and of the Economy), Berlin (Duncker & Humblot) 71984.

MESSNER, J. (1955): *Ethik. Kompendium der Gesamtethik* (Ethics. Compendium of the Entire Theory of Ethics), Innsbruck, Wien, München (Tyrolia), VIIth book: *Wirtschaftsethik* (Economic Ethics).

MOLINA, LUIS DE (1602): *De justitia et jure* (On Justice, Natural Right and Law), Moguntiae (Madrid).

MOORE, J. (1990): „What is Really Unethical About Insider Trading", *Journal of Business Ethics*, 9, pp. 171-182.

NEIDLINGER, K. (1930): *Studien zur Geschichte der deutschen Effektenspekulation von ihren Anfängen bis zum Beginn der Eisenbahnaktenspekulation. Ein Beitrag zur Börsengeschichte* (Studies in the History of the German Speculation in Stocks and Shares from the Beginnings to the Start of the Speculation in Railway Shares. A Contribution to the History of the Stock Exchange), Jena (G. Fischer).

NELL-BREUNING, O. VON (1928): *Grundzüge der Börsenmoral* (Principles of the Ethics of the Stock Exchange), Freiburg i. Br. (Herder).

NELL-BREUNING, O. V. (1928a): „Volkswirtschaftlicher Wert und Unwert der Börsenspekulation" (Economic Value and Nonvalue of Stock Exchange Speculation), *Stimmen der Zeit*, 114, pp. 46-56.

PESCH, H. (1888): „Zinsgrund und Zinsgrenze" (The Reason for Interest and the Limit of the Interest Rate), *Zeitschrift für katholische Theologie*, 12, pp. 393-418.

PETERS, TH. J., WATERMAN JR., R. H. (1982): *In Search of Excellence. Lessons from America's Best-Run Companies*, New York (Harper & Row). German translation: *Auf der Suche nach Spitzenleistungen. Was man von den bestgeführten US-Unternehmen lernen kann*, Landsberg (Verlag Moderne Industrie) 1986.

RADBRUCH, G. (1973): *Rechtsphilosophie* (Philosophy of Law), Stuttgart (Koehler) [8]1973.

ROHATYN, F. (1994): „World Capital: The Need and the Risks", *The New York Review of Books*, vol. 41, Nr. 13, 14 July 1994, pp. 48-53.

RÖLLER, W. (1990): „Zum Selbstverständnis der Banken in einer offenen Gesellschaft" (On the Way Banks See Themselves in an Open Society), in: A.-F. JACOB: *Bankenmacht und Ethik* (Power of Banks and Ethics), pp.1-14.

RÖPKE, W. (1926): Article „Spekulation", in: *Handwörterbuch der Staatswissenschaften* (Encyclopedia of the State Sciences), 4th ed., Jena (Gustav Fischer), Vol. 7, pp. 706-710.

ROTH, W. (1986): „Macht der Banken" (Power of Banks), in: *Tutzinger Materialien* Nr. 35, Tutzing.

SCHÄFER, H.-B., OTT, C. (1986): *Lehrbuch der ökonomischen Analyse des Zivilrechts* (Handbook of the Economic Analysis of Civil Law), Berlin, New York, Tokyo (Springer), pp. 300ff.

SCHIMMLER, J. (1974): *Spekulation, spekulative Gewinne und Preisstabilität* (Speculation, Speculative Profits, and Price Stability). *Eine Theorie der Spekulation unter besonderer Berücksichtigung der Auswirkungen spekulativer Transaktionen auf die Preisstabilität*, Meisenheim a. G. (Hain).

SCHNEIDER, DIETER (1993): „Wider Insiderhandelsverbot und die Informationseffizienz des Kapitalmarkts" (Against the Prohibition of Insider Trading and the Informational Efficiency of the Capital Market), *Der Betrieb*, 46, H. 29, pp. 1429-1435.

SCHÖRNER, P. (1991): *Gesetzliches Insiderhandelsverbot. Eine ordnungspolitische Analyse* (The Legal Prohibition of Insider Trading. A Political Analysis), Wiesbaden (Gabler).

SEN, A. (1967): „Isolation, Assurance, and the Social Rate of Discount", *Quarterly Journal of Economics*, 81, pp. 112-124.

SEN, A. (1993): „Money and Value. On The Ethics and Economics of Finance", *Economics and Philosophy*, 9, pp. 203-227.

SPIEGEL-magazine (1994): „Der Pleite-König. Millarden-Versagen der Banken" (The King of Bankruptsy. Billion-Failure of the Banks), *Der Spiegel*, No. 16, 18 April 1994, pp. 22-30.

STEIN, J. (1993): *The Banking System in Germany*, Köln (Bank-Verlag) 1993. German version: *Das Bankwesen in Deutschland*, Köln (Bank-Verlag).

STEINMANN, G. (1970): *Theorie der Spekulation* (The Theory of Speculation), Tübingen (J.C.B. Mohr [P. Siebeck]).

STRIEDER, J. (1925): *Studien zur Geschichte kapitalistischer Organisationsformen. Monopole, Kartelle und Aktiengesellschaften im Mittelalter und zu Beginn der Neuzeit* (Studies in the History of Organization in Capitalistism. Monopolies, Trusts and Corporations in the Middle Ages and in the Beginning of Modern Times), München, Leipzig (Duncker & Humblot) ^{2}1925.

THOMAS AQUINAS (1951): *Summa theologiae* (1267-73), Madrid (Biblioteca de Autores Cristianos).

TUCHTFELDT, E. (1988): Article „Kapitalmarkt" (The Capital Market), in: *Handwörterbuch der Wirtschaftswissenschaft* (Encyclopedia of Economics), Stuttgart, New York (G. Fischer), Tübingen (J.C.B. Mohr [P. Siebeck]), Göttingen (Vandenhoeck & Ruprecht), vol. 4, pp. 432-439.

WEBER, MAX (1894): *Die Börse, I. Zweck und äußere Organisation* (The Stock Exchange, I. Purpose and Organisation), Göttingen (Vandenhoeck & Ruprecht) (= Göttinger Arbeiterbibliothek vol. 1, Nr. 2/3, pp. 17-48).

WEBER, MAX (1896): *Die Börse, II. Der Börsenverkehr* (The Stock Exchange, II. Trading at the Stock Exchange), Göttingen (Vandenhoeck & Ruprecht) (= Göttinger Arbeiterbibliothek vol. 2, Nr. 2/3, pp. 49-80).

WEBER, WILHELM (1959): *Wirtschaftsethik am Vorabend des Liberalismus. Höhepunkt und Abschluß der scholastischen Wirtschaftsbetrachtung durch Luis de Molina* (Business Ethics on the Eve of Liberalism. Climax and Completion of the Scholastic Theory of Economics by Luis de Molina), Münster (Aschendorff).

WEICKART, N.-J. (1989): „Firmenübernahme: Festung Deutschland" („Company takeovers: Fort Germany") in: *Manager Magazin*, 19 April, 1989, pp. 128-139.

WENGER, E. (1992): „Universalbankensystem und Depotstimmenrecht" (Universal Banking System and Proxy Voting Rights), in: H. GRÖNER (Ed.): *Der Markt für Unternehmenskontrollen* (The Market for Corporate Control), Berlin (Duncker & Humblot) (= Schriften des Vereins für Socialpolitik N.F. 214), p. 93f.

WILLIAMS, DAVID (1994): *Japan: Beyond the End of History*, London, New York (Routledge) (= The Nissan Institute/Routledge Japanese Studies Series).

WILLIAMSON, O. E. (1977): „Firms and Markets", in: S. WEINTRAUB (Ed.): *Modern Economic Thought*, Philadelphia (University of Pennsylvania Press).

WILLIAMSON, O. E. (1981): „The Modern Corporation: Origins, Evolution, Attributes", *Journal of Economic Literature*, 19, pp. 1537-1570.

WOJTEK, R. J. (1978): *Insider Trading im deutschen und amerikanischen Recht* (Insider Trading in the German and American Law), Berlin (Duncker & Humblot).

WOLFF, BIRGITTA (1990): *Banking Down Under: Differences between Australian and German Banking and some Conclusions for German Banks*, working paper, University of Witten/Herdecke, January 1990.

Chapter 11

Comment on Peter Koslowski and Bettina Löhnert: Rules of Action for Banking: the German Experience*

GÜNTER FRANKE

I am very pleased to discuss a paper on banking written by philosophers. Although the interdisciplinary approach is often praised, it is rarely put into practice. This is an excellent occasion for interdisciplinary efforts in the area of banking.

The authors first discuss the meaning of ethics in banking, then apply this concept to banking behaviour in payment transactions and in credit business. After presenting the basic structure of the German universal banking system they spend much effort on discussing the nature of bank industry relationships in Germany. Overall, the paper characterizes the German banking scene properly.

My comments will be related, first, to the main arguments of the paper and, second, I shall focus on the security business in Germany, a topic which has not been addressed by the paper.

---

* This comment addresses a paper Koslowski and Löhnert which has been presented by Koslowski at the „Ethics in Financial Institutions Conference" in Madrid. The papers of Koslowski and Löhnert published in this volume are different ones, still most remarks in the comment apply equally.

GÜNTER FRANKE

I. How to Define Ethics in Banking

The authors start off by saying that banks have economic power the use of which has to be legitimized. The use of this power is legitimate if those affected by it obtain an advantage. Then the authors argue that power should be used to attain an efficient allocation of resources. As an economist, I strongly support this definition. Efficient allocation of resources is, however, difficult to define in a world of imperfect markets characterized by transaction costs and information asymmetries. Therefore the authors go a step further and say that efficient allocation is possible only if market participants compete with each other and refrain from unethical practices. By this they mean that those who exercise power have to incorporate the overall objective of the economy which is the satisfaction of needs and the self-realisation of the greatest possible number of people. This appears to me as a rather vague definition. It is vague because we know that it is difficult to determine whether a decision improves the satisfaction of many people. Most decisions involve a trade-off such that some people benefit and others lose.

Applying such concepts in banking, it is debatable whether the managers of a bank should focus on maximizing the market value of the bank or whether they should also incorporate other objectives such as subsidising certain activities in the economy. For example, should the banks set lower quality standards for loans to finance projects which also serve environmental protection? I am very sceptical on this. There exist lots of investments in an economy which benefit some group. Why should such a group be subsidised by a bank? Subsidies can be given by the government for ethical reasons, but this is not the purpose of enterprises. Similarly, banks have often been critized for being very restrictive in funding venture capital business. If the bank considers the credit risk to be too high, then the response of the bank should not be to grant the loan anyway, but to look for other arrangements like venture capital funds which provide a better allocation of risks and, thus, are considered an attractive investment.

Starting from economic theory, it appears to me that in a world of perfect competition bank managers are forced to maximize the profitability of the bank in order to survive in the long run. If there is a lack of competition and therefore bank managers have more discretionary power, then the discussion of corporate control issues tells us that there exists a danger that bank managers use this power in their own interest. In order to constrain this agency problem, the bank's owners try to motivate and monitor the managers so as to pursue the owners' objectives. Apart from the managerial aspect, a bank having some monopoly power can misuse it. What do we mean by ethical banking given some monopoly power? Is ethical banking more than striving for economic efficiency? Does it imply giving up some profits to the benefit of the bank's customers? We have some notion of „fair banking practices“ which may give us some guidance. But we lack a precise definition. This is not surprising since we face a trade-off between several objectives as in many decision problems, with the optimal solution depending heavily on the weights which we assign to the various objectives. It is essentially the choice of these weights which matters but which is very hard to conceptualise on ethical grounds. Therefore „ethics in banking“ will always be difficult to define such that it is supported by a majority of people.

Competition is the crucial element in the functioning of a market economy. Therefore it is important to look at competition in the German banking industry. As pointed out in the paper, the German system belongs to the universal banking system. This implies that the fierce competition between commercial banks and investment banks which we observe for example in the United States of America, does not exist in Germany. Therefore competition in Germany is much weaker. This statement needs to be modified, however. It is certainly true in retail banking. There is no strong price competition. Moreover, there is no strong competition in attracting new retail customers. Empirical studies have shown that German people are very reluctant to change their banking relation even if they are not satisfied. The reason is simply that changing one's bank is a cumbersome procedure since it involves informing many people and changing many transfer orders. The banks know this, and they use this rather strong position to extract all kinds of fees and commissions from the retail consumer. An example quoted by the authors is the money transfer system. It is to some extent misused by the banks through delaying the transfer and thereby collecting interest. As there are only a few transfer systems, there exists little competition so that banks have little reason to establish a fast transfer system.

In the wholesale business the situation is different. Now the big industrial firms have well-trained people in the financial departments who make sure that the company gets a good deal. Therefore margins in the wholesale business are rather small. This is reinforced by the access of big firms to the international capital market, primarily the Euromarket. Medium sized companies in Germany still rely to a large extent on relationship banking, i. e., they have rather strong ties to one or two banks. In turn, these banks support the firms also in times of financial distress. Summarizing, banks extract high profits from retail business and from business with small and medium sized companies.

What does ethics in banking imply? The cartelized behaviour of banks in retail business may be viewed as a violation of ethics. As competition does not seem to work, an answer might be sought in banking regulation. But I am sceptical. I have no confidence in public price administration. One can only hope that customers become more aware of the costs imposed on them and therefore choose more carefully the banking services which they demand. In addition, transparency about this market might be improved so that customers become more aware of what is happening. But it is not easy to escape the charges for financial services since most customers cannot avoid the use of these services.

II. Relationships Between Banks and Industry

The authors point out correctly that there exist several ties between banks and industry beyond credit business. Banks have equity stakes in major companies, in the shareholders' meeting they represent many shareholders who entrust the banks their voting rights. Therefore it is easy for the banks to obtain mandates in the supervisory board. Obviously, this menu of banking activities creates several conflicts of interest. Still, the question is whether there exists a better system. Clearly, one would assume that banks being major creditors have an interest in low dividend payments to minimize potential losses from financial distress. But the situation does not appear to be so simple. Although the supervisory board appoints the members of the managing board, the influence of the banks in the supervisory board is quite often overestimated. Even in the supervisory boards of several big German companies with 20 or 22 members half of which are representatives of the employees, banks usually hold only one or two mandates. Thus, the influence is rather limited. Moreover, if the company shows good performance, then the credit rating of the company is good enough so that competition among banks makes the management board rather independent of the bank representatives in the supervisory board.

Apart from this, one has to ask what are the implications of banking interference in business? The well-known discussion about the potential problems of publicly held corporations which dates back to the famous book of Berle and Means in 1932, has raised the question in Europe and in North America who is monitoring managers of publicly held corporations. As pointed out correctly in the paper, small shareholders usually do not attend the shareholders' meeting since the cost benefit calculus clearly shows that it is not worthwhile going to the meeting. Thus, there is a need for someone else to represent the shareholders' interests. In North America, we sometimes see proxy fights between professional investors to gain influence on the corporation. In Germany, there exist some organizations which claim to act in the shareholders' interests and ask shareholders to entrust them their voting rights. The truth, however, is that these organizations are quite ineffective. One reason for this could be that such a representation involves another principal-agent problem for which a convincing solution does not exist. In North America institutional investors now start to take a more active role in the supervision of managements. In Germany, this role has been taken traditionally by the big banks. If they stop doing this, a vacuum of power is likely to emerge which leads to even more discretionary power for managers. Thus, a reasonable alternative to the German system is not yet available.

Interestingly, there exists a study by John Cable[1] which relates the performance of German corporations to the level of bank influence. This study has found some evidence that those corporations perform better where banks have a major influence. Similarly, in Japan the saying is that the close relationships between banks and industry improve industrial performance. Although the empirical evidence is far from being conclusive, one should be careful with the assertion that banks have a negative influence on industry.

The problem in the bank-industry relationship is not so much that banks urge the managers to take investment and financing decisions in the interest of banks which are in conflict with the interest of equity holders. The main problem which I see is that the banks are also represented by managers who do not have a personal stake in the supervised corporations and that these bank managers usually do not spend enough time on supervision. Apart from the chairman of the supervisory board, most members of the supervisory board spend up to 4 to 5 days a year in supervising a corporation. It is not hard to imagine that this time span is insufficient to really deal with the problems of a corporation. Thus, the effectiveness of the German supervi-

1 JOHN CABLE: „Capital Market Information and Industrial Performance: The Role of West German Banks", *The Economic Journal*, 95 (1985), pp. 118-132.

sory board is debated intensely. Even the chairman of the supervisory board who usually sees the managers once a month, often does not have the time to really investigate the issues of the corporation. The recent example of the Metallgesellschaft provides some evidence. Another example of heavy bank involvement in industry is the involvement of the Deutsche Bank in the Daimler-Benz Group. The Daimler-Benz Group has four divisions. At least two of those are deep in the red figures, one being in the red figures for twenty years. So far, Daimler-Benz has not been able to cut back the losses. The strong involvement of the Deutsche Bank in the Daimler-Benz Group has provided neither sufficient help nor pressure.

The banks have come under pressure for their ineffectiveness in supervision. This has led to a new tendency among German banks. Banks now tend to refrain from taking the position of the chairman of the supervisory board. If the chairman belongs to a bank and something bad is happening to the corporation, then usually the bank comes under strong attack, too. Since banks have serious doubts whether they can effectively monitor the corporation and whether this would pay off, they seem to retreat from these responsibilities. Therefore, my concern with the bank-industry relationships is not so much that banks have quite a bit of power, but my concern is that if banks retreat from their supervision activities, it will be difficult to find a reasonable substitute.

So far, banks have also controlled the takeover business. Hostile takeover attempts have been very rare in Germany. One reason is probably that it is difficult to arrange a takeover without the consent of the banks. As managers of banks and managers of industrial firms usually know each other quite well, banks appear to protect industrial managers against hostile takeover attempts. Moreover, it is difficult for banks to control hostile takeover attempts. Therefore banks seem to discourage those attempts. Hence managers are not disciplined by hostile takeover threats in Germany. I can imagine, however, that the banks' resistance to an active takeover market might weaken if banks retreat to some extent from their supervisory role.

III. Security Business

One aspect of the German banking system which has not been mentioned in the paper but which appears crucial to me is the banks' involvements in the security business. Here the concentration of power is really amazing. Banks actually are everywhere decisive in the security business. In Germany banks are:

* the depositary institutions for securities,
* mediating and managing security issues,
* mediating all security transactions,
* owners of stock exchanges,
* managers of investment funds,
* trading securities on own account,
* having access to inside information about corporations and about the order flow in the securities markets.

This multiplicity of roles of the banks in the security business leads to many conflicts of interest. Let me give some examples. First, up to now there does not exist an insider law in Germany; voluntary agreements among firms and managers not to use inside information have been rather ineffective. An insider law will be passed in the near future which constrains security trades of primary insiders, not of secondary insiders. Moreover, this law will constrain only the use of inside information on corporations, not on markets. Frontrunning is presumably one of the most important sources of banks' profits in trading on own account. This is probably also true of other countries. In the United States of America, some exchanges prohibit dual trading, in Germany there are no attempts in this direction. Therefore, the question is whether front running violates fiduciary relationships between banks and their customers. Second, banks manage security issues and, at the same time, investment funds. Banks may tell the funds which they manage to buy parts of those issues which they cannot sell off in the market. Similarly, if a bank wants to sell major parts of securities from its own portfolio, it may tell its funds to buy those or it tries to persuade its customers to buy those.

Other strange observations in the market are exemplified in the following: If you look into the annual reports of investment funds, you never find a clear statement about the fund's transactions and transaction costs. Some banks appear to earn quite a bit of money simply by large transaction volumes of their funds. These transactions are mediated by the banks so that banks can collect substantial fees from this trade. One would like to get some information on those fees. Another strange fact is that the retail customer is charged a commission on security transactions which is a percentage of the monetary trade volume. He pays one percent of the monetary trade volume regardless of whether the trade volume is five thousand Marks of hundred thousand Marks. The cost for the bank in administering this trade is almost the same. In other countries, the fee percentage declines with a higher trade volume.

These examples point to a lack of transparency and a lack of competition among banks. This raises the question whether this lack of competition in the German securities market impairs efficiency of resource allocation in the economy. Although it is difficult to give a clear answer, we know that the German stock market is underdeveloped relative to the Anglosaxon markets. Also, the opportunities for venture capital financing are rather limited. One reason for this could be the deficiencies of the organisational structure of the market. This view is supported by another observation: German households hold substantial bond portfolios and little stock portfolios. Perhaps, German households feel that they might not be treated fairly on the stock exchange. Thus, it is well possible that the overall dominance of banks in the German stock market impairs efficiency of capital allocation.

This leads to the question of appropriate remedies. We know from economic theory that transaction costs and imperfect information easily lead to multiple equilibria. One equilibrium is a first-best equilibrium which comes close to a perfect market equilibrium, but other equilibria may exist which reinforce the lack of transparency and cartel behaviour. My impression is that in the German security business the equilibrium is of the latter type. Given the lack of competition, could we think of other institutional arrangements giving a better deal to the customer? In economics, we quite often rely on reputation effects. But reputation is effective only if different banks behave differently. As long as all banks behave similarly, reputation cannot work.

Is that a sufficient argument to impose more regulation on the financial market? One could think of awarding damage claims to customers against banks in case of unfair treatment. We know, however, from the insider discussion that in many cases it is very difficult to prove the existence of such damages. One could think also of amendments to the criminal law such that certain practices violating the fiduciary relation between banks and customers are punished. To some extent, this is done in Germany by introducing new laws on financial markets. This can mitigate some problems even if there is no close supervision of banks and even if the probability of detecting fraudulent behaviour is small, but here reputation could work. If a bank is caught on fraudulent practices, this could have a strong negative reputation effect. Therefore I think that some amendments in criminal law could improve the situation.

I also believe that customers get more and more informed about bank practices. This should enable them to get better contracts with banks. For the big institutional investor we have already seen such a development, with respect to the retail investor I am rather sceptical as long as the cartel behaviour of banks continues to exist. More transparency will certainly help. In this respect, the emerging industry of evaluating the performance of investment funds will force the banks to pay more attention to the interest of their customers. But we will have to go a long way before a balance between the interests of the banks and its customers will be found. Can ethics restore that balance? As far as ethics pays off, there is no problem. If, in addition, ethical bank behaviour means that a bank does not extract some profit from dealing with its customers without being rewarded financially for this behaviour, then, again, I am sceptical, especially if managers are paid according to the bank's profits. To expect such behaviour without having established a rewarding or a sanctioning mechanism appears to be wishful thinking.

Chapter 12

Ethical Behaviour in Banking: A General Equilibrium View*

JEAN-PIERRE DANTHINE

I. The Ethical Issue at the Light of General Equilibrium Theory

In the present note, I offer some reflections on the theme of ethical behaviour in the economic sphere based on standard general equilibrium theorising and I propose a few illustrations relevant to the banking sector.

To start with, it seems fair to assert that the issue of defining an ethically appropriate behaviour is relevant exclusively in situations where there is room for a choice among alternative conducts, i.e. where there is power. This introductory statement leads me to question the place open for the ethical discussion in the perfect markets, perfect competition benchmark case of neo-classical economics. Such a question appears all the more relevant because the first theorem of welfare economics states that, under the appropriate assumptions which include the two mentioned above, the exclusive pursuit of their own self-interests by economic agents, producers or consumers, results in an efficient allocation of resources, i.e. a state of affairs that has desirable welfare properties and has been accordingly labelled a Pareto optimum. Thus, in this important reference case, economic agents have no

---

* These reflections are extensions from my comments on a paper by Koslowski and Löhnert presented at the Madrid conference and withdrawn from the present collection of essays. The structure of the present note corresponds to the structure of my original comments. The latter were meant to present the views of a financial economist, not specialised in the discussion on ethics.

power, hence no freedom of choice. And if they had, they could not alter their behaviour in a direction that would yield a more desirable social outcome. For producers of goods or services in particular, this position is the repetition of Milton Friedman's that, in a competitive economy, the social responsibility of producers is limited to the pursuit of their own self-interest.

Besides technical conditions, the assumptions underlying the above mentioned theorem include the absence of market power, hence of freedom of choice, but also the absence of externalities, i.e. of situations where the decisions of an economic agent would have direct effects on the situation of another. In the following discussion I will accordingly distinguish four possible situations: with and without full - „perfect"- competition, with and without other sources of market failures.

In the perspective outlined above, it thus seems that the definition of ethical conduct in economic affairs converges toward the identification of market failures (with emphasis on those arising from imperfect competition) along lines familiar to all economists, or, more precisely, of those market failures that have not been corrected by government intervention. In the absence of market failures of any sort or when they have been appropriately corrected by government intervention, there is no ethical issue to be addressed. In a sense this also says that the best way to encourage ethical economic behaviour is in fact to promote competition in a situation where it has been insured that price signals are a good reflection of relative scarcities.

There is however one type of choice that is left open even in the abstract and hypothetical world of perfect competition. It is the choice to enter or exit a particular industry. In the powerless world of perfect competition, discretionary power remains as to the type of activities to engage into. Of course, general equilibrium theory is compatible, and indeed implicitly assumes, the existence of a legal framework commonly accepted by and enforced upon all agents. In this context, an interesting question is whether all legal activities may be considered to be ethical as well or whether the choice of one's domain of economic activity is a decision with an ethical dimension even when strictly confined to the realm of legal activities.

This being said, it is clear that the static perfectly competitive world is an abstraction and that real life economic situations typically entail some degree of economic power. In this case it might be argued - and indeed has been argued during the Madrid conference - that the legitimate use of economic power requires using it in the direction of the social good („doing justice to economic considerations"; „contributing to the overall objective of the economy defined as the satisfaction of needs and the self-realisation of the individual"; „have producers incorporate the overall objective of the economy, the satisfaction of needs and the self-realisation of the greatest possible number of people, into their own intentions".) While sounding reasonable in a discussion on ethics, I believe this position is in fact quite extreme when viewed through the lenses of standard economic theory.

This is because it implies that, whenever competition is insufficient, the exploitation of market power by those who detain it must be declared unethical, precisely because it moves the allocation of resources away from its status of a Pareto optimum and thus it does not conform to the social good.

First, this implies a deep and pervasive conflict between managers' social role and their responsibility towards firm owners or shareholders who, one presumes, normally want the managers to take advantage of their firm's market position! In addition, one may wonder how this position is to be made operational. Recall that the logic of the absence of ethical issue under perfect competition is that in a perfectly competitive world, producers have a very limited amount of discretionary power. Should they not perform at the level of their competitors they will register losses and be ultimately forced to exit the industry. But while, on paper, economists have no problem deciding when competition is perfect, and when it is not; in practice there are often no clear-cut lines along which to decide whether a manager could ethically do his best to fulfil the objectives of his shareholders or whether he should refrain from doing so to better serve the social good. One might only find out when it is too late, i.e., when the firm has been pushed out of the market, that his environment was too competitive for the manager taking the freedom to do anything else than pure profit maximising.

Another difficulty arises from the dynamic nature of the economic game, not captured in the general equilibrium perspective adopted thus far. Economic growth and social progress arise from the attempt of individual economic agents to create temporary situations of competitive advantages for themselves, i.e., situations where they will be enjoying some degree of economic power. The benefits linked with the use of this power are precisely the reward for the efforts and sacrifices that were the prerequisites for creating this niches. In other words, economic power is often the result of previous actions aimed at creating its possibility, actions which are sources of social and economic progress. Asserting that taking advantage of this power is unethical is akin to negating this fundamental process of growth and development.

The first theorem of welfare tells us of several other sources of market failures. Thus even in a perfectly competitive world, there is a possibility that not all actions of producers benefit the social good. In a world of distorted prices, it may be socially desirable for a manager to take actions, say, to produce a smaller quantity of pollutants than his competitors. If competition is too severe, it is conceivable that doing so will price his firm's products out of the market. The emphasis on power implies that in this situation the producer has no ethical duties. Again this may be disputed because the producer has at least one choice which is not to engage in the corresponding trade.

When competition is less intense, producers have some room to pursue other objectives. This combination of economic power and of other market failures probably yields the richer context for ethical considerations. Here, internalising Society's objectives is particularly relevant: the producer is in position to promote the social good, to some extent at the expense of the firm owners' financial interests, but possibly with their approval: contributing to ecological and social objectives, to increased equity, to the transmission of expertise, the promotion of women, of part-time work, etc., is a pursuit that has social rewards and may not be in conflict with stockholders' preferences in a context where the firm's survival is not at stake.

II. Ethical Considerations in Credit Decisions

The granting of credit has been said to be an economic decision particularly loaded with ethical implications. First there is a question of (social) efficiency: are pure profitability (vs. common good) considerations sufficient in the credit decision? Second there is an issue of equity: bank have to treat applicants in a just way.

First let us observe that there is no obvious, easily corrected, market failure here. If competition is sufficient, it will force bankers to be good at the difficult decision of whom to grant credit to and under which terms, although asymmetries of information will imply they will be sometimes too strict, at other times too benevolent. In other words, there seems to be no fundamental conflict between the interests of the bank shareholders and the interests of society at large. This suggests again that competition will promote ethical behaviour. Similarly, under the same competitive assumption, there will be little room for taking particularly „just“ or specifically „unjust“ credit decisions.

If, however, banks have a significant amount of market power, the conflict mentioned above is fully operative. The shareholders' interest is for the manager to exploit the bank' s market power. As a result one might expect too little credit to be granted at too high a price and economic efficiency might suffer. But it is also possible that the leeway provided managers will be used by them to pursue the common good[1] when allocating credit: considerations of equity may be given some weight, the employment effect of granting or not granting a credit may be taken into account, etc. In this case, I would think it ethically appropriate for managers to inform shareholders of their pursuit of such non-financial objectives and one may hope that such a policy would then meet the preferences of a majority of shareholders.

III. The German Banking System as a Special Case

The German banking system is dominated by large, universal banks, often playing the role of *Hausbank*. Universal German banks have large stakes, they are well represented on the supervisory boards of industrial companies and the practice of small depositors transferring their voting rights to the banks give the latter even more voting power, and thus responsibility.

There are two important consequences of this situation. First, banks have accumulated influences to a point where there is a possibility of conflicts of interests and more generally of misuse of power. Second, this possibility notwithstanding, the German form of organisation might be particularly favourable to economic efficiency; thus it might be „doing justice to its purpose.“ And one may argue that if the second point is granted, the problems raised by the first are of a second order of importance.

The latter view has received some credit in regards of the often alleged superiority, in terms of performance, of the German financial system. Re-

1 In general to take other considerations into account than purely risk-adjusted profitability. This could be their own personal objectives as well, a possibility which gives rise to other ethical issues common to all principal-agent relationship and thus not specific to banks.

cent evidence however suggests considerable caution before accepting this conclusion as a fact.

One alleged reason for favouring a system where banks have significant shareholdings and are heavily represented on the boards of their debtors is that such a situation would reduce information asymmetries that would otherwise lead to inefficient lending decisions. But a recent study by Edwards and Fischer (1993) has noted that during the period 1971-85 German enterprises without supervisory boards have made more use of bank borrowing than did enterprises with supervisory boards. This observation does not fit well with the presumed informational advantage of the German system.

It is also argued that the practice of transferring voting rights together with the involvement of banks on supervisory boards could constitute a superior way of reducing the transaction costs of constraining managerial decision making in accordance with shareholders' preferences. However a study by Gerum et al. (1988) found that for 86% of the sampled corporations the supervisory board met only twice a year - the legal minimum number of meetings -, an observation which casts doubt on the view that supervisory board monitors the management board closely.

In a study on the ownership and control of German corporations, Franks and Mayer (1994) analyse all three cases of hostile take-overs of non-financial companies recorded in Germany since World War 2[2]. They observe that „the proxy votes and voting right restrictions confer considerable power on banks in the takeover process, and therefore confirm the existence of significant impediments to takeovers“ and that, in these episodes at least, „there is little evidence that the bank placed great emphasis on shareholder interests“. They also note that „proxies may create an agency problem whereby the company provides the bank with business so as to create incentives to support incumbent managementî.

All in all, Edwards and Fischer (1993) conclude that there is no evidence of the superiority of the German banking system over the Anglo-Saxon model. If one accepts this conclusion, which it must be noted does not amount to a statement of inferiority of one model over another, the problems raised by the possibility of misuse of power and of unethical behaviour resulting from the presence of conflicts of interests deserve a fuller discussion.

---

2 These are the bid by Continental for Pirelli, the merger of Hoesch with Krupp and the share purchase and acquisition of Feldmühle Nobel by the Flick Brothers, Veba and Stora.

Of considerable significance, it seems to me, is the fact that the large equity stakes in industrial companies held by banks and their influence on the management of the corresponding firms, while creating opportunities in transmitting expertise and in controlling management on behalf of shareholders, also create conflicts of interests because of the banks' multiple role as debtors and shareholders, as brokers and investors managing their own portfolios, as supervisors and exclusive or preferential providers of services. The Anglo-Saxon solution has been to a large extent to forgo the opportunities so as to eliminate the conflicts of interests. The German solution is to take advantage of the opportunities. The issue raised by the conflicts of interests does not disappear however. It must be addressed precisely because it raises important ethical issues.

References

EDWARDS, J. and K. FISCHER (1993): *Banks, Finance and Investment in Germany*, Cambridge, UK: CEPR & Cambridge University Press.

FRANKS, J. and C. MAYER (1994): „The Ownership and Control of German Corporations", *mimeo*, London Business School and University of Oxford.

GERUM, E., H. STEINMANN and W. FEES (1988): *Der Mitbestimmte Aufsichtrat - Eine Empirische Untersuchung*, Stuttgart: Poeschel Verlag.

Chapter 13

The Structure of the German Banking System and its Ethical Implications

BETTINA LÖHNERT

The institutional peculiarities of the German banking system and some consequences for the business ethics of banking shall be investigated in this paper. It analyses the problem of the power potential of banks in the universal banking system and the close bank-industry relationship linked to it.

I. The Stucture of the German Banking System

The predominant feature of the German banking system is its universality. In contrast to many other industrialized nations, like the USA or Japan, there is generally no separation between commercial and investment banks. Most German banks, though they may differ in size, ownership, legal form, business structure or administrative organisation, have one thing in common: they conduct all types of banking business under one roof. There is no institutional separation between lending and deposit-taking on the one hand and security business on the other side.

There are three types of commercial banks in Germany (numbers refer to the end of the year 1991):

- the private commercial banks (i.e. the "big three": *Deutsche Bank*, *Dredner Bank* and *Commerzbank*, regional and other commercial banks, the private bankers and the branches of foreign banks). These banks have a share of 30 per cent in the business volume of all commercial banks in Germany.
- the public savings banks and their central institutions (*Zentralbanken*) with a share of about 50 per cent of the market.
- the credit cooperatives (*Volks- und Raiffeisenbanken*) and their central banks have a share of about 20 per cent.

Besides the *Universalbanken*, a variety of spezialised banks such as mortgage banks, building associations, Installment Credit Institutions, the Postbank etc. offer their services. [1]

II. Legal Framework[2]

The business of banking in Germany is a heavily regulated market. Whereas the bank-client relationship is governed mostly by civil and public law, it is the banking act (*Kreditwesengesetz;KWG*) which determines primarily the legal framework of banking.

According to this law, the Federal Banking Supervisory Office (*Bundesaufsichtsamt für das Kreditwesen, BAK*) tries to ensure that banks are functioning properly and that depositors are protected against loss.

The Federal Banking Supervisory Office (BAK) gives its permission before any firm can engage in the business of banking and it can also evoke this licence again. To be able to fulfill the task of "containing abuses in the banking sector which endanger the security of the funds entrusted to banks, or which impede the orderly conduct of banking business, or which could lead to considerable disadvantages of the economy as a whole" (*KWG* Art. 6(2)) the BAK has the authority to request all kinds of information from banks. It can order audits and intervene in the conduct of business: banks have to inform the BAK of very large loans (over 1 million DM), and there is a limit to the size of loans (not more than 18 times of the banks liable capital). Loans that are granted to borrowers that are either personally or in

1 Cf. STEIN (1993).

2 See *The British and German Banking System: A Comparative Study* (1981), pp. 388ff.; HENDRIE (1981), p. 1; STEIN (1993), pp. 9f.

any other way closely associated with the lending bank (so-called *Organkredit*) have to be reported. Also banks have to report their annual financial statements.

The Supervisory Office cooperates with the *Bundesbank*, which besides its supervisory functions acts as Germany's central bank.

Furthermore, banks in Germany are subject to the stock exchange law (*Börsengesetz*), securities deposit law (*Depotgesetz*) and the cheque and bills of exchange laws (*Scheck- und Wechselgesetze*).

III. Historic Background

The universal banking system evolved in the middle of the nineteenth century. The beginning industrialization caused a capital scarcity for which the traditional private banks could not compensate. Therefore new ways of financing had to be found. One possibility was the introduction of a company to the stock exchange, i.e. financing it by issuing shares.

This was especially true for companies in the mining or steel industry with capital intensive methods of production that needed the support of powerful banks to finance their conversion into stock companies. To be able to provide this kind of service some private bankers founded joint stock banks. Among them were the *Deutsche Bank, Dresdner Bank* and *Commerzbank* that are, until today, Germany's biggest credit institutions.

Their main object then was to help consolidate the young German companies or to convert them into stock corporations.

Consequently banks often bought shares of these companies themselves and, in order to control their investment, they sent bank executives to the Supervisory Boards (*Aufsichtsrat*) of these companies. The typical close links between industry and banks in Germany took their beginning during this early period. Due to their participation in the management of the firms, the joint stock bankers felt a special kind of responsibility for their clients. This became evident during the Great Depression of the 1930's, when banks turned defaulted credits of these companies into equity.

Also during the reconstruction period after World War II the system of universal banking provided efficient ways of managing the existing scarcity of capital.[3]

On the other hand, the great influence of banks on industry through financing, equity holding and Supervisory Board membership also led to controversial discussion and critique. For the evaluation of this critical discussion, it is necessary to look into the structure and effects of these close bank-industry relationships.

IV. The Nature of Bank-Industry Relationships in Germany

Due to the system of universal banking in Germany, companies can conduct all sorts of banking transactions with one bank. Consequently many corporations deal exclusively with one bank, their so-called *Hausbank.*

Since German companies finance most of their outside capital through banks, and not directly by the capital market, the credit business is of vital importance. It must be noted that the market for capital in Germany is not as developed as in the USA and Switzerland, a fact that increases the dependence of firms on banks. For the bank the granting of credits bears a certain amount of uncertainty once they put the money at the disposal of the corporation. To avoid the risk of violation of the contract, banks have to use some sort of monitoring. The credit institutions can only do this, if first they have access to information about possible contract violations and secondly they have the possiblity of actually sanctioning these violations. As can be seen in the graph below, the German *Universalbank* can apply three basic monitoring procedures and corresponding sanctioning measures:

- monitoring via *credit contract*, i.e. making sure that the debtor is fulfilling the conditions of the contract (e.g. interest rate, securities etc.). The credit contract usually intitles the bank to certain rights to information. The debtor is according to § 18 of the banking act obliged to disclosure (*Offenbarungspflicht des Schuldners*). If the bank is also the *Hausbank* of the company it additionally has some exclusive sources of information e.g. insight in the debtors account.

3 See WOLFF (1990), p. 14, and JÄHRIG/SCHUCK ([5]1989), pp. 1-4.

To sanction the contract violations the banks can either sue or terminate the contract. In total this does not represent a very powerful monitoring device. The internal informations of the debtor are hard to control and the corresponding sanctioning devices are costly and inefficient.

- monitoring via *shareholders' meeting* (*Hauptversammlung der Aktiengesellschaft*). The bank can be represented in the meeting both due to its own equity and as an agent for the small shareholders (§153 *Aktiengesetz: Depotstimmrecht*) According to § 131 (I) of the shareholders' law (*Aktiengesetz, AktG)*, every shareholder is entitled to rights of disclosure from the board of directors. This right to information is of minor importance since the facts presented at the shareholders' meeting are hard to prove and the board of directors can also refuse to deliver certain information (§131 (II) AktG).

The sanctioning device of the shareholders' meeting is the refusal to approve the board of directors (Vorstand) (§ 119 Nr. 3 AktG) which can be an important reason for the supervisory board to dismiss the *Vorstand* (§ 84 III AktG).

- monitoring via *supervisory board mandates* (elected by shareholders' meeting and/or appointed by the board of directors). According to § 90 AktG the supervisory board has comprehensive rights to information about the company's actions which must be provided by the board of directors, i.e. to information about the company politics, its profitability and so on. In addition, the supervisory board has the possibility to look into the books and writings of the company (§111) and they may consult outside experts and informants (§109). These sources of information are very helpful for banks.

Since it is the legal duty of the supervisory board to control the *Vorstand* (§ 111) it has comprehensive sanctional powers. Besides refusing to re-appoint the board of directors it can also dismiss them. Thus, the supervisory board has considerable influence on the top-management of its company. If banks want to take advantage of this powerful sanctioning device they first have to be represented in the supervisory board and secondly they must be able to get the approval of the supervisory board as a whole. Usually, banks are in the minority in the supervisory board. Therefore, they have to calculate the interests of the other members of the supervisory body. One must remember here that in Germany up to 50 per cent of the supervisory boards mandates must be given to employee representatives (*Arbeitnehmervertreter*), mostly delegates of the trade unions (*Gewerkschaften*), appointed by vote of the employees. If the party of the equity owners does not want to be out-voted by the employees they have to vote with the banks. The supervisory board is also liable for the actions of the board of directors (§116 in connection with §93). Therefore the supervisory board is obliged to sanction the *Vorstand* if the banks detect any contract violations. This is even more so since in recent years the supervisory board in Germany has developed from a mere supervisory body to one of advisory status and function.[4] If banks are represented in the supervisory board they will most likely be able to execute sanctions.

Due to the access to exclusive information and the rather powerful sanctioning potential, the supervisory mandate is the key factor of influence. The other three relevant elements of the bank-industry relationship, the status as creditor, as shareholder and the proxy voting rights, lead in the end to the supervisory board mandates and represent additional specific means of possible influence. This accumulation of influence potential is the particular trait of the German *Universalbank* system.

4 See MÜHLHAUPT (1990), p. 454.

FIGURE 1

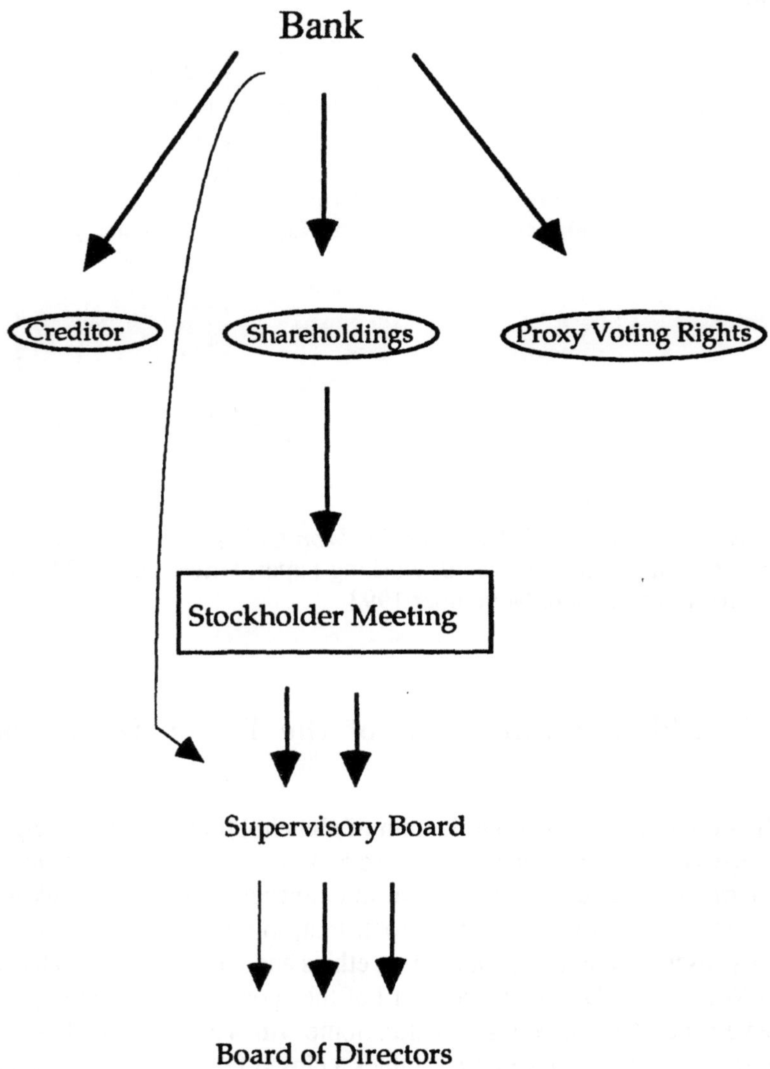

Source: KONRAD SCHACHTNER: *Monitoring durch Banken*, working paper, University of Munich, November 1993.

Through these instruments, German banks, in comparison to banks in other industrialised nations, have the greatest potential to influence the behavior of their corporate clients. It is important to note that banks have these possible means of influence, but do not necessarily use it to its full extent.

	USA	Japan	Germany
Banking System	dual banking system	dual banking system	universial banking system
Industry Relations	short-term "deal-based-banking"	long-term "relationship-banking"	longterm "relationship-banking"
Monitoring Devices	- shareholdings - board of directors mandates	- shareholdings (keiretsu) - close housebank relationship	- shareholdings - proxy voting rights - supervisory board mandates
sanctioning power	small	large	large

FIGURE 2. Source: K. SCHACHTNER: *Monitoring durch Banken: Gläubigerrechte und Depotstimmrecht,* working paper, University of Munich, Institute for Organisation, November 1993

V. Ethical Implications of the Power Discussion

It is obvious that the combination of shareholdings, proxy voting rights and supervisory board mandates create a concentration of discretionary power for German banks that is not known in countries with a dual banking system, and it is not surprising, therefore, that, in Germany, this topic is frequently discussed in the debates about ethics and banking. Especially during the 1960ies and 1970ies, the keyword of the "power of the banks" gave rise to heated and often emotional debates. Some critics even talked about a "web of influence and property that resembles a closed feudal system beyond public control in an otherwise open society"[5]. Banks usually belittled their power by arguing that strict government regulation, competition and consumer power provided the necessary counterbalance. Since power is, however, very hard to quantify the debate on the power of banks is almost impossible to appraise fairly.

It is not the aim of this paper to give an assessment of the power potential of German banks - this has been done sufficiently elsewhere[6] - but to take a look at the ethical dimension of this discussion by using the criteria of doing justice to the purpose of banks, the mediation and coordination of money in the economy. It must be examined whether the characteristics of the universial banking system are in line with this objective.

1. Shareholdings

German banks own a substantial amount of the equity of other companies. This is especially true for the very big banks. The *Deutsche Bank* for instance, in 1994, owned shares worth more than one billion DM in 77 domestic corporations.[7]

Because of these extensive possession of equity, banks are often accused of dominating industry and interfering in the management of the affected companies according to the banks' interests. They are accused of fostering a development towards monopoly-like concentration. Furthermore it is suspected that banks might encounter conflicts of interest because they are at the same time shareholders and creditors to companies.

Banks defend their equity holdings as being a means of investment and risk diversification that serves to secure their deposits. They claim that they do not intend to conduct the management of other companies. Banks argue that owning shares makes economic sense, since they help to avoid (hostile) take-overs and strengthen the business relationship between banks and companies. Furthermore they explain that many of their shareholdings are the result of the transformation of defaulted credits into equity and not the result of their insatiable hunger for power.

---

5 Thus ROTH (1986), p. 2, from the point of view of the German Social Democrat Party (SPD).

6 See BÜSCHGEN (1975), pp. 362-374; HEIN/FLÖTER (1975), pp. 342-361; MÜHLHAUPT (1990), pp. 451-458.

7 COMMERZBANK (1994).

Although the reasons banks give for owning large amounts of equity have some justification they cannot rule out the concern about the potential for misuse it represents. An effective measure to counter the suspicion that the big banks could make monopolistic use of their power as shareholder and an effective proof that they want to practice self-constraint in the management of the firms in which they hold shares is the creation of transparency: Until recently banks were required to disclosure when they owned more than 10 per cent of a given company's equity. This margin has just been lowered to 5 per cent.[8]

2. Proxy Voting Rights (Depotstimmrecht)

Bank customers often deposit the shares they own at their bank (*Depot*). If they possess only a few shares of a given company they might not want to execute their property rights personally and attend the shareholders' meeting. The reasons for this abstinence is usually the simple fact that the personal presence at the meeting would cost the shareholder an unreasonable amount of time and money (e.g. for obtaining of information, travel expenses etc.) whereas the advantage and the impact of his or her vote in the meeting would be rather small.

Banks offer their customers the service to execute the proxy voting rights as their agent, the so-called *Depotstimmrecht*. The bank regularly (every 15 months) needs their customers' written approval and it has to inform the client about the intended voting decisions at the meeting and the client may also amend certain changes to the voting suggestions. Since complete representation of the capital in shares is the objective of the shareholders' meeting the transmission of the proxy voting right from the shareholder to the credit institution seems to be reasonable. This procedure sustains the property rights of the shareholder that would be lost if he just refrained from participating at the shareholders' meeting without entrusting his vote to the bank.

If we look at the *Depotstimmrecht* from this perspective it seems to be economically efficient and, in ethical terms, it does justice to the shareholders' property rights and to the function of the banking sector. On the other hand, the shareholders leave their property rights to the banks for free, and

8 This measure is part of the new „Finanzmarktförderungsgesetz". See LORZ (1994), p. 9.

the banks have the possibility to use these proxy voting rights to their own advantage. Furthermore, this rule can create certain conflicts of interest between the bank, the shareholders represented and the board of directors of the corporation. The shareholders' aims (e.g. high dividends) differ from those of the *Vorstand* (e.g. high salaries). The credit institutions which should give attention to the interests of the small shareholders, have interests of their own (e.g. low dividends to increase the liability capital for already granted credits or to guaranty the continuation of the business relationship with that corporation). Especially when the bank has given a substantial loan to that corporation one can suspect that the directors and the bank have similar interests in small dividends, since for the bank the advantages gained through the loan are probably more important than their own interest as shareholders and the one of those they represent as proxies to recieve large dividends[9].

If banks misuse the proxy voting rights their customers have entrusted on them and use it to their own advantage they violate the fudiciary relationship to their clients. Banks must give attention to the interests of the shareholders they represent if they want to do justice to this function. Since they are in a more powerful position than the small shareholders they have to restrict themselves and not to take advantage of the trust the small shareholders put in them.

On the other hand, the banks are not the only ones who have to assume responsibility here. According to the principle of *caveat emptor*[10], the customers as free and responsible persons should be more conscious of their rights and own power.

But how can they do that? As we already saw the isolated effort of small shareholders is not very effective. Consequently they would have to organize. But attempts to organize the interests of small shareholders on a private level usally fail, due to the financial and organisational effort required by such an endeavour. These organisations can only prevail if they are supported by large corporations and banks. That this sort of shareholder representation does not fulfill its proper purpose is inevitable.[11]

---

9 See SCHACHTNER (1993), p. 3.

10 Confer for this principle KOSLOWSKI (1988), p. 240.

11 See: EKKEHARD WENGER: "Universalbankensystem und Depotstimmrecht", in: HELMUT GRÖNER (ed.): *Der Markt für Unternehmenskontrollen*, Berlin (Duncker & Humbolt) 1992 (=Schriften des Vereins für Socialpolitik N.F. 214), p. 93f. Wenger mentions the "Deutsche Schutzgemeinschaft für Wertpapierbesitz" (DSW- organisation for the protection of shareholder inter-

If one delegated the task of representing shareholders' proxy voting rights to a governmental agency one could not eliminate the commonly known problems of the principal-agent relationship. The question who should control the agents, in this case the government officials, is far from clear. Some German "bank-critics", therefore, suggest to drop representative proxy voting altogether and thus allow the formation of well-informed minorities. It is hoped that these groups would put more pressure on the management and would thus achieve a more efficient and shareholder-friendly corporate policy. [12] This proposal remains highly controversial and far reaching since it requires a change of German corporate law (*Konzernrecht*).

Therefore it seems to be the better way to provide the shareholders with the right to more comprehensive information from their banks and the possibility to give their voting rights to a bank-independent shareholder organisation if they wished. To circumvent the above mentioned drawbacks of privat or public organisations a combination seems to be the best solution: the organisations should be basically privately managed by and for shareholders while the necessary fonds should be provided by a public foundations.[13]

3. Supervisory Board Mandates

The presence of bank representatives in the supervisory board of companies is frequently subject to criticism. It is argued that the information banks have access to can be used for the aims and interests of the banks and to the disadvantage of the shareholders of the companies affected, to the detriment of competing companies or banks or even of the economy as a whole.[14] Especially the fact that banks are simultaneously shareholders and creditors evokes the suspicion that they might use this inside information to their advantage. Banks answer to this objection that the information they obtain and the sanctions they can execute through their supervisory board mandates are a legitimate monitoring device and serve the purpose of securing their credits. Furthermore they stress that it is often the explicit wish of

---

ests) that seems to be rather an organisation of bankers than of shareholders.

12 *Ibid.*, p. 96ff.

13 See: GÜNTHER ENGEL: "Bankenmacht", in: GEORGES ENDERLe ét. al: *Lexikon der Wirtschaftsethik*, Freiburg i..B. (Herder) 1993, p.114

14 See MÜHLHAUPT (1990), p. 454.

a company's management to have bank representatives at this body because they appreciate the experience and expertise of bankers.[15]

The supervisory board mandate is a powerful monitoring device. There is no clear-cut line where the legitimate monitoring intention of the financial institution turns into illegitimate influence on the management decicions. Banks have to be aware of that aspect of their power potential and use it in a responsible way. The ethics of banking might even demand that banks use their monitoring rights more powerfully. One reason why banks have failed in fulfilling this task is the fact that often one banker has too many supervisory board mandates and looses sight of their details. Consequently, the limitation by law of the number of mandates one bank executive is allowed to hold is frequently demanded.

References

ANDREAS, K. (1992): „Denkansätze für eine Ethik im Bankwesen" (Starting Points for an Ethics in the Banking System), in: P. KOSLOWSKI (Ed.): *Neuere Entwicklungen in der Wirtschaftsethik und Wirtschaftsphilosophie* (Recent Developments in Economic Ethics and Economic Philosophy), Berlin, Heidelberg, New York, Tokyo (Springer) (= Studies in Economic Ethics and Philosophy vol. 2), pp. 177-193.

BÜSCHGEN, H. E. (1975): „Zur Diskussion um das Bankensystem in der Bundesrepublik Deutschland" (On the Discussion on the Banking System in the Federal Republic of Germany), *WSI-Mitteilungen* 18, pp. 362-374.

COMMERZBANK (1994): *Wer gehört zu wem* (Who belongs to whom), Frankfurt.

15 This often-cited expertise has lost some credability since the recent case of the „Metallgesellschaft". The US-subsidiary of this German corporation conducted rather risky business with petrol futures. The characteristic of the futures market is the relatively low investment in combination with enormous gain or loss, as is well known. Apparently, the supervisory board including the bank representatives of the *Metallgesellschaft* has been aware of that adventureous business, but has not reacted what almost ruined the company.

DEGEORGE, R. T. (1990): *Business Ethics*, New York (Macmillian Publishing Company).

ECONOMIC ADVISORY BOARD (1981): *The British and German Banking System: A Comparative Study*, London, pp. 388ff.

HEIN, M., FLÖTER, H. (1975): „Macht der Banken - Folgerungen aus der bisherigen Diskussion" (Power of Banks - Consequences from the Previous Discussion), *WSI-Mitteilungen*, 28, pp. 342-361.

HENDRIE, A. (Ed.) (1981): *Banking Structures and sources of finance in the European Community*, London (The Financial Times Business Publishing).

JÄHRIG, A., SCHUCK, H. (1989): *Handbuch des Kreditgeschäfts* (Handbook of Credit), Wiesbaden (Gabler) [5]1989.

KOSLOWSKI, P. (1988): *Prinzipien der Ethischen Ökonomie* (Principles of Ethical Economy), Tübingen (J.C.B. Mohr [P. Siebeck]), Reprint 1994.

KOSLOWSKI, P. (1989): *Wirtschaft als Kultur. Wirtschaftskultur und Wirtschaftsethik in der Postmoderne* (The Economy as Culture. Economic Culture and Economic Ethics in Postmodern Times), Vienna (Edition Passagen).

LORZ, ST. (1994): „Verstrickt im Netz der Banken" (Entangled in the Net of the Banks), *Rheinischer Merkur*, 6. Mai 1994, p. 9.

MÜHLHAUPT, L. (1990): „Macht der Banken" (Power of Banks), in: H. SCHIERENBECK (Ed.): *Bank- und Versicherungslexikon* (Encyclopedia of banking and assurances), München (Oldenbourg), p. 454.

ROTH, W. (1986): „Macht der Banken" (Power of Banks), in: *Tutzinger Materialen* Nr. 35, Tutzing .

SCHACHTNER, K. (1993): *Monitoring durch Banken: Gläubigerrechte und Depotstimmrecht* (Monitoring of Banks: Creditor Rights and Proxy Voting Rights), working paper, University of Munich, Institute for Organisation, November 1993.

SCHILLING, FLORIAN (1994): "Der Aufsichtsrat ist für die Katz" (The Supervisory Board is Useless), *Frankfurter Allgemeine Zeitung*, Nr. 199, 27 August 1994, p. 11.

STEIN, J. (1993): *The Banking System in Germany*, Köln (Bank-Verlag).

WENGER, E. (1992): „Universalbankensystem und Depotstimmenrecht" (Universal Banking System and Proxy Voting Rights), in: H. GRÖNER (Ed.): *Der Markt für Unternehmenskontrollen* (The Market for Controls of Firms), Berlin (Duncker & Humblot) (= Schriften des Vereins für Socialpolitik N.F. 214)

WOLFF, B. (1990): *Banking Down Under: Differences between Australian and German Banking and some Conclusions for German Banks*, working paper, University of Witten/Herdecke, January 1990.

List of Authors

ANTONIO ARGANDOÑA, Professor of Economics, IESE-International Graduate School of Management, University of Navarra, Barcelona.

FEDERICO BASAÑEZ, Associate Professor of Economics, University of Seville.

LUIS CORTÉS, Associate Professor of Management, University of Seville.

K. ALEC CHRYSTAL, NatWest Professor of Personal Finance, City University Business School, London.

JEAN-PIERRE DANTHINE, Professor, Department of Econometrics and Political Economy, University of Lausanne.

NEKANE ECHEVARRÍA, Hong Kong and Shanghai Banking Corporation, and Doctorate student, University of Navarra, Pamplona,

GÜNTER FRANKE, Professor of Business Administration, University of Konstanz.

JESÚS DE GARAY, Professor of Business Ethics, Centro Universitario Mapfre de Estudios del Seguro, Madrid.

PETER KOSLOWSKI, Director, Forschungsinstitut für Philosophie Hannover - The Hannover Institute of Philosophical Research, and Professor of Philosophy and Political Economy, University of Witten/Herdecke.

LUIS A. LERENA, Professor of International Economics, Complutense University of Madrid, and Director, Centro de Estudios Bancarios, Fundación BBV.

BETTINA LÖHNERT, Research Assistant, Forschungsinstitut für Philosophie Hannover - The Hannover Institute of Philosophical Research.

A. CRAIG MCKINLAY, Professor of Finance, Wharton Business School, University of Pennsylvania.

JOSÉ MARÍA ORTIZ, Professor of Economic and Business Ethics, University of Navarra, Pamplona.

RAFAEL TERMES, Professor of Finance, IESE-International Graduate School of Management, University of Navarra, Madrid.

PATRICIA H. WERHANE, Professor of Business Ethics, Darden Graduate School of Business Administration, University of Virginia.

MIX
Papier aus verantwortungsvollen Quellen
Paper from responsible sources
FSC® C105338

If you have any concerns about our products,
you can contact us on
ProductSafety@springernature.com

In case Publisher is established outside the EU,
the EU authorized representative is:
Springer Nature Customer Service Center GmbH
Europaplatz 3, 69115 Heidelberg, Germany

Printed by Libri Plureos GmbH
in Hamburg, Germany